A Chart of the Sea Coasts of EUROPE, AFRICA, and AMERICA From the North Parts of Scotland, to Cape Bona Esperanca, and from Hudsons Straits to ye Maggellan Straits, According to Mr Wrights Projection, Vulgarly Called Mercators Chart. By John Thornton Hydrographer at the Signe of the Platt in ye Minories. London.

THE
DEVIL MAY
CARE

THE
DEVIL MAY
CARE

FIFTY INTREPID AMERICANS

AND THEIR QUEST

FOR THE UNKNOWN

EDITED BY

Tony Horwitz

OXFORD
UNIVERSITY PRESS

2003

OXFORD
UNIVERSITY PRESS

Oxford   New York
Auckland   Bangkok   Buenos Aires   Cape Town   Chennai
Dar es Salaam   Delhi   Hong Kong   Istanbul   Karachi   Kolkata
Kuala Lumpur   Madrid   Melbourne   Mexico City   Mumbai
Nairobi   São Paulo   Shanghai   Taipei   Tokyo   Toronto

Published by Oxford University Press, Inc.
198 Madison Avenue, New York, New York, 10016
http://www.oup-usa.org

Library of Congress Cataloging-in-Publication Data
The devil may care : fifty intrepid Americans and their quest for the
unknown / edited by Tony Horwitz.
p. cm.
Biographies selected from the American national biography.
Includes bibliographical references and index.
ISBN 0-19-516922-0 (alk. paper)
1. Adventure and adventurers—United States—Biography. 2.
Explorers—United States—Biography. 3. United States—Biography.
I. Horwitz, Tony, 1958- II. American national biography. III. Title.
CT9970.D49 2003
917.304—dc21   2003013175

Designed by Nora Wertz

Printing number: 9 8 7 6 5 4 3 2

Printed in the United States of America
on acid-free paper

CONTENTS

v

Hearts on Fire

In the New Hampshire spring of 1773, John Ledyard launched a career as one of the great solo adventurers of the eighteenth century. Ledyard had been sent to Dartmouth College to train as a missionary to Native Americans. Instead, the Iroquois converted him. On the banks of the just-thawed Connecticut River, Ledyard felled a white pine and hollowed it out, Indian-style, climbed in his canoe with a volume of Ovid, and paddled 140 miles downriver to his family's home in Hartford. "Farewell, dear Dartmouth," Ledyard wrote in a departing letter.

Soon after, Ledyard caught a trading vessel to Africa's Barbary Coast and jumped ship at Gibraltar. Later, reaching the coast of England, he walked to London and won passage with Captain James Cook on a voyage of discovery to the South Seas, Hawaii, and the American coast from Oregon to Alaska. Though a lowly marine, Ledyard so impressed the captain that Cook dispatched him on a lone scouting trip, by foot and kayak, across one of the Aleutian Islands. This experience, and his awe at the wealth and wonder of America's western fringe, led the young adventurer to conceive a grand dream. He would become the first man to walk across the American continent.

But even that wasn't bold enough. After deserting the British Navy rather than fight his fellow Americans in the Revolutionary War, Ledyard expanded his original scheme. He decided to walk across Russia, sail from Siberia to America, and then hike across the continent from west to east. "My heart is on fire," Ledyard wrote to Thomas Jefferson, who shared his countryman's passion for the unexplored parts of America.

Ledyard embarked from Stockholm in the winter of 1786 with two large dogs, an Indian pipe, and a hatchet. He trekked across Lapland to Russia and traveled over the Urals deep into Siberia, covering six thousand miles in just over a year. Ledyard got as far as the tundra-bound wilds of Yakutsk, five hundred miles from Asia's northeast shore, before the Russians arrested him as a suspected spy and dragged the American back to the Polish frontier.

Undaunted, Ledyard immediately set off on another adventure in search of the source of the Niger River. Reaching Cairo in 1788, he toured the slave market dressed as a Turk to learn about caravan routes to the African interior from Arab traders. Before he could depart, Ledyard became ill, apparently doctored himself with crude drugs, and died from a hemorrhage at the age of thirty-seven.

"Mad, romantic, dreaming Ledyard," as one contemporary described him, was a striking American character at the dawn of the American nation. A restless idealist and rugged individualist, Ledyard saw himself as "an unprotected wanderer" who relied on his wits and the kindness of strangers, whether Tartar, Arab, or Aleut. "I travel under the common flag of humanity," he wrote, "commissioned by myself to serve the world at large."

Unfortunately, the world at large has forgotten John Ledyard. Apart from a Dartmouth canoe club and a society of college dropouts named in his honor, Ledyard is virtually unknown today. Strictly speaking, he's not historically "significant"; Meriwether Lewis and William Clark achieved the continental crossing Ledyard only dreamed of—albeit fifteen years later, from east to west, with an expeditionary force backed by the U.S. government. But Ledyard's daring exploits deserve attention: as a reminder of what adventure meant before jet planes and "Rough Guides", and also, quite simply, as a wonderful yarn worth retelling. It is in this spirit that I undertook the very different adventure that became this book.

* * *

Last autumn, a fat envelope arrived at my home in Virginia. It contained an index for the *American National Biography,* a compendium of which I'd never heard. A cover letter explained that the Biography includes profiles of 18,000 men and women who have contributed to the shaping of

America. Would I be interested, the letter asked, in choosing fifty explorers, adventurers, and intrepid travelers for inclusion in "a yet-to-be named book"?

Like most people, I'm wary of encyclopedia salesmen. And the proffered task—culling fifty names from a pool of 18,000—sounded as folly-ridden as Ledyard's walk around the world. The *Biography* has twenty-four volumes; the index alone runs to eighty pages of eye chart–sized print, with names bunched by "occupations and realms of renown." I was about to stuff the index into my potbelly stove when a heading on the front page drew me back.

ADVENTURERS, See also Explorers; Filibusters; Privateers; Spies; Swindlers; Trappers; Travelers

I squinted at the names listed beneath this label, and didn't recognize any of them. Nor did I know any of those under the next rubric: ADVENTURESSES. And what did "filibusters"—a term I associated with Southern legislators reading phone books on the floor of the Senate—have in common with privateers, trappers, spies, and swindlers? I turned the page, and then another: ALLEGED HERETICS, BLOCKADE RUNNERS, CAPTIVES OF AMERICAN INDIANS. By the time I reached the index's last page—UTOPIAN COMMUNITY LEADERS, VICTIMS OF SHIPWRECK, VOLCANOLOGISTS—I'd booked passage for a journey I had never intended to take.

Like all good adventures, this one led down unforeseen byways: into the history of balloons and parachutes, for instance, and the strange tale of nineteenth-century filibusters (who, I learned, promoted the extension of the Plantation South into Latin America). At times, I became lost—or, as the great pathfinder Daniel Boone once put it, "bewildered." The *Biography* includes thousands of people who might qualify as travelers, explorers, or adventurers. Each time I tried to limit my reading, I'd bump into another alluring category—SANSKRITISTS, SEEDSMEN, STAGECOACH ROBBERS—that drew me back into the maze. By the time I'd found my way out, I had wandered from the tenth century to the twentieth, from the Arctic to the Antarctic, from ALIENISTS to ZIONISTS. Many of the territories and job titles I encountered—Norembega, the Sultan of Ternate, the President of the Republic of Lower California—have long since vanished from atlases and textbooks.

I also traveled well-known thoroughfares, enjoying a refresher course on figures familiar to me from boyhood, such as Juan Ponce de Leon and Davy Crockett. Then again, none of my elementary schoolteachers ever told me, as the *Biography* did, that the aging conquistador hoped the "fountain of youth" would prove a source of "sexual renewal." Nor did I know that Crockett was so legendary in his own lifetime that a contemporary claimed he could "save the world by unfreezing the sun and the earth from their axes and ride his pet alligator up Niagara Falls."

But the greatest virtue of the *Biography* is the introduction it offers to characters few of us have ever encountered. As a result, most of the fifty figures that made my final cut are, like John Ledyard, little-known today. Instead of Daniel Boone, I've selected Simon Kenton, a Kentucky pioneer who survived just as many backwoods perils, including two escapes from immolation at the stake. I've passed over Sacagawea in favor of another extraordinary translator and guide, an Iowa tribeswoman named Marie Dorion. And rather than reprise Buffalo Bill, I've chosen Buffalo Jones, a forgotten frontiersman who literally tamed the Wild West—with a lasso rather than a six-shooter.

Lest this anthology seem too obscure, I've included a few household names—though only of figures whose full stories startled me, as I suspect they will many readers. John Smith, of Jamestown fame, began his career as a crusader against the Turks, coined the name "New England," and had as great an impact on that region as he did on Virginia. I also learned that Duncan Hines—a name previously known to me only as a brand of cake mix—was a gastronomic road warrior who logged more than two million miles in quest of plain American cooking he could recommend to motorists.

It may seem that little connects travelers such as Smith and Hines— men separated by three centuries, their missions, and their modes of transport. As my compass, I've used a very broad definition of adventure. "To risk oneself," reads one of the Oxford Dictionary's citations. "To dare to undertake." Risk is a constant in this collection. And all the risk takers in it were pioneers in their fields, whether as Arctic explorers, surfers, soldiers of fortune, or black aviators who confronted Nazi racism by challenging the German air marshal, Hermann Goering, to a duel above the English Channel.

Another thread: each of these life stories leapt off the page for me, sometimes in the first sentence. "Princess, adventurer, and wartime humanitarian" reads the introduction to a woman with a name befitting her extravagant career: Agnes Elisabeth Winona Leclercq Joy Salm-Salm. The entry for Belle Livingstone begins: "Showgirl, adventuress, and Prohibition Era saloonkeeper, [she] was a foundling, purportedly discovered under a clump of sunflowers in Emporia, Kansas." Also irresistible is Sir Alexander Cuming, the "visionary and erratic second baronet of Cutler," in Scotland, whose voyage to the Carolinas sprang from a dream of Lady Cuming. The baronet became a Cherokee emperor, bank swindler, and longtime resident of a London debtors' prison.

As Cuming's story suggests, personal virtue isn't a prerequisite for inclusion in this book. Nor is my roster intended as an exercise in national uplift. The epic tale of adventure and exploration in America merits an "R" rating for rampant carnage, rape, racial bondage, and environmental ruin. Just three years after "discovering" America, Christopher Columbus seized 550 Caribbean islanders to sell in Spain. Hernando de Soto probed the Mississippi Valley with attack dogs and iron collars to subdue hostile Indians. Pathfinders crossing the Appalachians and Rockies often did so with slaves in tow, and spread venereal disease and other ills that ravaged the native population. The pioneers that followed them hunted and trapped and logged vast stretches of the American wilderness to near destruction.

All this has become a familiar theme in contemporary scholarship, and a corrective to the storybook treatment of frontier "heroes" such as George Custer that prevailed until about 1970. The *Biography* reflects this revisionism, but it doesn't turn American history into one long morality play. Rather, its entries are balanced and unsanitized reports on individual lives. What struck me, after reading hundreds of these profiles in succession, is how often the conflicting impulses of the American character are twinned within the same character. Time and again, I met people who were venal and altruistic, visionary and small-minded, violent and tender.

John Sutter, best known for the gold strike at his sawmill in California, founded a paternalistic settlement near Sacramento and displayed great compassion toward starved, transcontinental travelers. Yet Sutter was also a deadbeat who skipped out on his creditors, as well as on his wife and children in Europe. Then there's Albert Pike, a Byronic Boston poet who became a duelist, Confederate guerrilla leader, and Ozarks recluse. So sympathetic to Native Americans that he sued the federal government on tribes' behalf, winning multimillion-dollar settlements, Pike also championed groups such as the anti-immigration Know-Nothings and the early Ku Klux Klan. It isn't necessary to admire every aspect of Sutter's and Pike's careers to recognize that they led extraordinary lives.

Viewing America through the lives of its most intrepid men and women is also a reminder of the chronic restlessness that has always set the New World apart from the Old. Many of those who headed for the frontier were serial refugees, having left their homelands abroad before abandoning the settled parts of America. A large number of them just kept going: to Latin America, Alaska, Asia, Australia, never settling down anywhere for long. Hungarian-born Agoston Haraszthy de Mokcsa fled Europe to pioneer a Wisconsin settlement in 1840, captained a wagon train to California nine years later, spent the next decade shuttling from San Diego to San Francisco to Sonoma (where he *did* put down roots: grape vines), then started all over again in the 1860s when he colonized Nicaragua, only to die after falling into an alligator-infested arroyo.

Haraszthy's dramatic and unfortunate end is typical of many of these adventurers. Others in this anthology fell victim to jungle fever, firing squads, typhoons, posses, balloon crashes, and gorings. Two were decapitated to prove their demise, and one had his corpse put on public display. A surprising number made fortunes only to die penniless. Chaotic domestic life—illegitimacy, repeated divorce or spousal death, even bigamy—is another common trait. The fur trapper and Western scout, James Bridger, wed three different Indian women and became known to the Crow as "Blanket Chief" for his alleged sexual prowess. Frances Wright founded a Utopian settlement in Tennessee to educate and liberate slaves, but had to abandon it amidst charges of free love and miscegenation. In many cases, family troubles proved an impetus for adventure. Anne Royall became a travel writer to support herself after relatives of her deceased, plantation-owning husband overturned his will, claiming his widow had forged it.

While each of these life stories can be read individually, I've arranged and introduced them chronologically, by date of birth, to give a sense of the narrative sweep of adventure in America. The popular abridgment of America's exploration and settlement, as enshrined in textbooks and national holidays—Columbus Day, Thanksgiving, Independence Day—portrays steady progress from east to west, and the founding of a nation on British principles. But this destiny was by no means manifest. Long before the creation of the United States on America's eastern seaboard, adventurers from non-Anglo nations probed from every direction, establishing now-extinct domains: New Spain, New France, New Netherland, New Sweden, and Russian America. The tiny sample of adventurers in this book includes the son of a Haitian slave, a priest of Siberian and Aleut parentage, and men and women from a dozen other countries. Nor is it easy to separate the exploration of the present-day U.S. from that of its neighbors. Many adventurers ranged across the Americas, and national allegiances and borders remained fluid until well into the nineteenth century.

Hindsight also inclines us to see the conquest of the American "wilderness" and its inhabitants as pre-ordained, despite the fact that there were periods in colonial history when the white population of New England and Virginia dramatically decreased due to Indian wars, disease, and other hardships. We tend, as well, to view exploration and settlement as a crude, one-way process in which Europeans imposed their will and culture on "primitive" natives. The actual story, vividly demonstrated in these biographies, is far more complex. Frontiersmen often married Indians, came to admire tribes they'd set out to dispossess, and, in some cases, "went native" rather than return to white society.

A chronological look at travel and exploration over the course of five centuries also illustrates the evolution of adventure itself. After 1492, it wasn't easy to find an entire continent unknown to Europeans. Yet for roughly three hundred years following Columbus, "first contact" with native peoples remained a dominant part of "discovery." As the American frontier gradually closed in the late nineteenth century, adventurers could still seek lands and peoples untouched by the West: on polar expeditions, or in treks to the mountains and jungles of Africa, Asia, and South America. Others began exploring the limits of their own endurance, and that of their machines. Scattered through this collection are people who can best be described as thrill seekers, including an early aeronaut, a daredevil known as the "Jumping Man," and an Irish-born New Yorker who brawled his way around America—and into the U.S. Congress.

Travel derives from the French word *travail*, meaning 'toil'. Only in recent centuries has it come to be regarded as a recreational pursuit. Initially, pleasure travel was a very privileged pastime. In eighteenth-century England, wealthy young men known as "dilettanti" or "macaronis" sought leisure and refinement in "grand tours" of the European continent. Americans, more isolated and egalitarian, and possessed of a vast territory of their own to explore, were relative latecomers to global tourism. We have, of course, made up for lost time; wide-bodied jets and luxury cruise ships now carry Americans to Pacific atolls and Arctic glaciers. The last story in this volume, about a twentieth-century traveler named Richard Halliburton, brings the story of human adventure full circle. Halliburton found expression for his daring and wanderlust in death-defying stunts, as well as in replays of fabled exploits, including Ulysses's seminal travels in the Odyssey.

It is tempting to lament this trend. In an era when every sea has been charted and every mountain climbed, many adventurers resort to manufactured challenges or reenact epic voyages of yore. Others prefer the interior journey; with no worlds left to explore, modern travelers seek self-discovery. But if something has been lost, much has also been gained. Women feature more prominently over the past century as independent adventurers. People of modest means or limited mobility can venture forth as never before. Vast regions that were once inaccessible to all but mountaineering parties, camel caravans, and dog-sled teams can now be visited by far less taxing means.

All of which raises the question: Is true exploration and adventure still feasible today, short of rocketing into space? And why travel at all? Even when we embark for distant lands, we've already been there before we arrive: through travel brochures, television documentaries, and IMAX films. It's difficult to experience traditional aspects of adventure—chance, risk, surprise, solitude, escape—in a world where travelers study the same guidebooks, preview their destinations on Web sites, and, when abroad, discover the franchise outlets and satellite TV stations they know from home. "The first thing we see as we travel round the world," Claude Levi-Strauss famously remarked, "is our own filth, thrown into the face of mankind."

This despairing observation is true, to a point, but it's also become an excuse for lazy travelogues, and for staying at home. Airport terminals and hotel rooms and coffee shops may look alike the world over—though often they don't—and there's little doubt that American culture has penetrated almost every nook of the globe. But the people who live there still possess a culture of their own. And that culture—at least in my experience of traveling to fifty countries—is always very foreign to America's, even in societies that seem superficially similar to ours.

I've been married to an Australian for two decades, and have spent long stretches living and working in Sydney, a city that exhibits a familiar skin of American brands and Hollywood programming. Yet I'm invariably struck by how alien Australia feels—not just in its inverted seasons and exotic fauna, but its ribald wit and rhyming slang, its frequent mockery of church and state, and its social distance from America. On my last visit, just after Australia Day, the *Sydney Morning Herald* asked leading citizens to define "un-Australian." The answers included: overt displays of patriotism (such as "singing the national anthem above a mumble"), enormous CEO salaries, putting tofu on the barbecue, and using the term "un-Australian." The premier of New South Wales pointed to the kookaburra as Australia's defining symbol: "a unique species of bird that sits in a tree and laughs at us."

Needless to say, it's hard to imagine Americans responding to a July Fourth survey on national identity in quite the same way.

"If you have lived about," Henry James observed, "you have lost that sense of the absoluteness and the sanctity of the habits of your fellow patriots which once made you so happy in the midst of them." Perhaps at no stage in our history has insight about the world—and our place within it—seemed more essential than it does now.

If travel remains a broadening experience, so too is armchair adventure. There's nothing like a few frigid pages on Ernest Shackleton to put one's own coddled life in perspective. And whenever I'm inclined to feel sorry for myself because I can't make Internet contact, or am delayed an hour during the day-long flight to Sydney—a whole day!—I try to think of Captain James Cook, who sailed eighteen months to reach Australia and almost sank his small wooden ship while navigating the coral and currents of the Great Barrier Reef. "Were it not for the pleasure which naturaly results to a Man from being the first discoverer, even was it nothing more than sand and Shoals," he wrote in his journal, "this service would be insupportable."

John Ledyard, who sailed with Cook on the captain's final voyage, seems never to have voiced such doubts. The pleasure and fame of "being the first discoverer" overrode all else in his character. Even on his deathbed in Cairo, there may have been some consolation. "If he fails and is never heard of—which I think most probable," one of Ledyard's acquaintances confided in a letter about the adventurer, "and if he composes himself in his last moments with this reflection, that his project was great, and the undertaking what few men were capable of—it will, to his mind, smooth the passage."

THE
DEVIL MAY
CARE

ALVAR NÚÑEZ CABEZA DE VACA

[c. 1490–c. 1559]

Spanish explorers of America suffer from a bad press as blood-soaked conquistadors. Cabeza de Vaca represents a dramatic exception. Shipwrecked off Texas in 1528, he and three other castaways, including an African-born slave, survived several years of wandering the southwest by acting as magical healers to Native Americans. Later imprisoned and sentenced to banishment in Algeria for opposing the enslavement of Indians in Brazil, Cabeza de Vaca left an unusually vivid and sympathetic record of his encounters with the people of the New World.

Alvar Núñez Cabeza de Vaca, soldier, explorer, and writer, was born in Jérez de la Frontera, Spain, the son of Francisco de Vera, a member of the municipal council, and Teresa Cabeza de Vaca, a noblewoman. Little is known about Núñez's early life. He chose to use his matrilineal surname to emphasize his relationship to Martín Alhaja, who was ennobled in 1212 with the name Cabeza de Vaca (Head of Cow) after directing the king's armies by marking their route with a cow's skull. Núñez's paternal grandfather, Pedro de Vera, was a conquistador and early Spanish governor in the Canary Islands. Núñez trained for a military career and by the time he left for the New World already had experience in battle.

In 1527 Núñez was appointed second in command for Pánfilo de Narváez's expedition to la Florida (the lands north of the Gulf of Mexico from the Florida peninsula to Mexico). From the very start Núñez and Narváez disagreed with one another concerning the best way to proceed. After landing on the Florida peninsula somewhere south of Tampa Bay, Narváez, against Núñez's advice, chose to send the ships north in search of a safe harbor while the main body of the expedition marched overland. Those on land never saw the fleet again. Instead, the expeditionaries,

Tom Lea's Cabeza de Vaca Performing the First Recorded Surgery on the North American Continent–1535 *draws inspiration from de Vaca's writing: "I was the most daring and reckless of all in undertaking cures. We never treated anyone that did not afterwards say he was well, and they had such confidence in our skill as to believe that none of them would die as long as we were among them."*

some four hundred in all, walked to Apalache (near modern-day Tallahassee), and then to the Bahía de Caballos (Bay of Horses, perhaps Apalachicola Bay), so called because the party ate its horses to keep going. From April to September 1528, hoping to sail along the Gulf of Mexico to Spanish settlements in New Spain (modern-day Mexico), they built five makeshift boats, using their stirrups and armaments to forge nails and tools and their shirts to make sails. The 242 surviving men traveled along the Gulf Coast until the flotilla was broken up in a storm off the Texas coast.

On or near Galveston Island, at a place the Spaniards named the Isla de Malhado (Island of Bad Luck), Núñez landed, but his boat was washed out to sea. Few other Spaniards survived the storm, and those who did were scattered throughout several Native American villages in the region and held as slaves. Núñez worked the next six years as a trader between various coastal and inland tribes until September 1534, when, along with three others—Andrés Dorantes, Alonso del Castillo Maldonado, two of the Spanish leaders of the Narváez expedition, and Esteban, an African-born slave brought on the Narváez expedition by Dorantes—Núñez escaped and began a two-year trek across what is now the southwestern United States and northern Mexico.

At first, the four men suffered from starvation and exposure, at times unable to find either corn or the fruit of the prickly pear cactus, staples of the region's diet. As time went on, however, the four began to serve as faith healers among the Native Americans. Originally Núñez and the others were forced to participate in a Native-American shamanistic healing ritual. According to Núñez's account, though, he and the others called upon God, and in their minds they turned the event into a Christian laying on of hands ceremony. The sick man recovered, and as a result news of the four men's healing powers spread. An entourage formed, growing larger in each village they passed through, where people would bring the men food in exchange for their healing services. Finally reaching Spanish settlements in early 1536, Núñez returned to northern Mexico to convince the Native Americans there to stop hiding from slave traders and return to their homes. He did so by persuading them that if they would convert to Christianity, they would be safe.

In 1537 Núñez sailed back to Spain, where he hoped to be commissioned as the commander of his own expedition to la Florida, but Hernando de Soto had already been named the *adelantado* (military and civil governor) of these lands. At first, Núñez remained silent about what he had found in the region, which made many people believe there were great riches there, inspiring them to accompany de Soto. In time, on 18 March 1540, Núñez was named *adelantado* of the Río de Plata region of South America; he arrived at Santa Catalina Island off the coast of Brazil in early 1541. From the mainland near there, Núñez led an expedition overland, finally arriving at Asunción, Paraguay, on 11 March 1542. The next summer, he led an expedition up the Paraguay River. By early 1544, however, dissension had grown among Núñez's men, at least in part because of his liberal treatment of the native population, outlawing their enslavement. In April the colonists revolted, imprisoned Núñez for several months, then sent him back to Spain where he remained imprisoned from 1545 to 1551. In 1551 he was tried for malfeasance, found guilty, and exiled to Oran, Algeria, but in 1556 his sentence was reversed. After being awarded a government pension, Núñez lived in Valladolid until his death.

Sometime between 1536 and 1541 Núñez wrote his *Relación* (1542), an account of his time in la Florida. Renamed *Naufragios* (*Shipwrecks*) when it was published in 1555 (along with an account of his years in South America, the *Comentarios*, by an author known simply as Pedro Hernández), Núñez's work is both an exciting adventure tale and an excellent ethnographic study. His sympathetic treatment of Native Americans makes his descriptions of them useful to modern scholars. In addition, *Naufragios* includes some of the earliest written references to the buffalo and the opossum. In many ways Núñez's importance lies as much in his role as a writer of ethnography, natural history, and literature as in his role as an explorer.

E.T.S.

JOHN SMITH

[1580–21 JUNE 1631]

The legendary encounter with Pocahontas was but one episode in Smith's auda-cious career on several continents. Determined as a child to "get beyond the Sea," Smith fled England at age fourteen and became a latter-day knight, doing battle against Muslims of the Ottoman Empire. Taken prisoner in Transylvania, he escaped and returned home via Turkey, Russia, and Morocco. He then shipped out for Jamestown, where he survived his famed capture by Powhatan Indians, as well as the explosion of a powder bag in his canoe. Undaunted, Smith set off to explore the little-known coast to the north, which he named New England. His promotion of this territory as a fishing and farming colony strongly influ-enced the Puritan settlement of Massachusetts.

John Smith, colonial governor, promoter, and historian, was born in Willoughby by Alford in Lincolnshire, the son of George Smith, a yeo-man, and Alice Rickard. His earliest schooling may have been under Francis Marbury, father of Anne Hutchinson, who was schoolmaster in Alford. Toward the end of his life Smith published an autobiography, one of the first examples of the modern genre, which he titled *The True Travels, Adventures, and Observations of Captaine John Smith* (1630). Although the order and dating of events in his early life recounted there do not cor-respond to dates that can be established independently, the shape of his early career seems clear. His first patron was Lord Willoughby of Eresby, his father's landlord. He was apprenticed in 1595 to Thomas Sendall, a mer-chant in King's Lynn, having already formed a resolution to "get beyond the Sea." After his father's death the next year (Smith wrote that his father had died when he was thirteen), he left his apprenticeship because Sendall refused to send him abroad.

Smith traveled to France, where he "first began to learne the life of a Souldier." He wrote that he went to Europe initially as escort to young

Smith's extremely detailed map of the area known as Virginia is unique in its careful documentation of the numerous tribes and kin groups inhabiting the Chesapeake Bay watershed at the time of European contact.

Peregrine Bertie, son of Lord Willoughby, and that he decided to stay in France. But, as Bertie did not receive a license to travel until 1599, and Smith, by his own account, served as a soldier with an English company in France and the Low Countries for "three or foure yeeres," it is unclear how the Bertie commission fits into the story. On leaving the Continent he went to Scotland, futilely seeking the life of a courtier. He then returned to his English home and studied to prepare himself for the life of a knight.

Soon, "desirous to see more of the world," he decided to "trie his fortune against the Turkes, both lamenting and repenting to have seene so many Christians slaughter one another." In late 1600, after adventures in the Mediterranean and in Italy, he signed on with Austrian forces fighting the Turkish Empire. He was promoted to the rank of captain before being captured in Transylvania. He escaped from captivity in Turkey and traveled via Russia through Europe to Morocco before returning to England in the winter of 1604–1605.

Smith was selected by the newly formed Virginia Company of London in 1606 to be one of the governing council in Virginia, the only person chosen because of his experience. He sailed with the contingent that settled Jamestown in May 1607. He spent much of the first year exploring, one venture ending with his capture in December 1607. His captors were clients of Powhatan, who was in the process of creating an "empire" of client tribes around the Chesapeake. As a captive for about three weeks, Smith was shown to several villages and finally met Powhatan himself. He was subjected to what was probably an adoption ceremony, in which Powhatan's daughter, Pocahontas, played a crucial role; Smith thought she had rescued him from death. Powhatan informed Smith that he was now a *werowance,* or subchief, under him.

Smith devoted the summer of 1608 to exploration of the Chesapeake Bay. He had an excellent eye for important detail and a highly developed ability to understand relationships; from his experience exploring and trading for corn he produced an important report on the Virginia Algonquian Indians. His ethnographical account has gained in stature as modern archaeological research has confirmed elements of it. From his notes he also supervised the engraving of the highly accurate map included in his book describing the land and its people, A *Map of Virginia* (1612). Part Two of A *Map of Virginia,* focusing primarily on the colony and its development, was published separately as *The Proceedings of the English Colonie in Virginia* (1612). Smith carefully supervised publication of these and his subsequent books; an earlier work had been badly edited and published in garbled form in London as A *True Relation of Such Occurrences and Accidents of Note As Hath Hapned in Virginia* (1608) while he was still in America. Smith, like others involved in new enterprises, understood the importance of print technology and was determined to use it effectively.

While Smith explored, the colony's leadership was mowed down by disease and crippled by poor planning. On his return in September 1608 he was elected president of the council, effectively governor of Virginia. Smith, having observed Indian practice, dispersed the colonists to live off the land in small groups away from the river. He forced all colonists, even the gentlemen and "tufftafety humorists," into productive activity, digging wells and building sound fortifications. The death rate from disease dropped dramatically during his administration.

Smith was particularly proud of the respectful, wary relationship he established with the "great emperor" Powhatan; he argued that only an experienced military man could gain the respect of such a leader and approach him on terms of equality. All colonial leaders, Smith among them, believed that the English must always dominate in their relationships with Indians; the only possible alternative was Indian domination of the settlers. Thus he followed a policy of intimidation which, he argued, increased Powhatan's respect for him. He contrasted his success with the spectacle of Captain Christopher Newport's humiliating failures in Indian relations. Newport, the admiral of Virginia Company supply fleets, was always in command when he was in the colony. Smith claimed that he had to repair damaged American respect for the English after Newport left.

The Virginia Company sent out a new administration under their renewed charter of 1609. Since the proposed leaders were shipwrecked on Bermuda and prevented from arriving in Virginia, Smith initially refused to give up command. He decided to return to England in October 1609 after he was severely burned by the accidental explosion of his powder bag as he traveled in a canoe. Back in England he became a critic of the Virginia Company for failing to put strong leaders in control and then trusting them to govern wisely. He argued that the settlers' attention had been diverted from the primary necessity of building strong colonial foundations to premature and fruitless searches for precious minerals and other commodities offering quick and easy returns. He was also harshly critical of the quality of the gentlemen the company had chosen for command. The Virginia Company was uninterested in what he had to say, and it may have been opposition from leading members that caused him to publish his *Map of Virginia* in Oxford rather than in London.

Smith now turned his attention to the land north of Virginia. Norembega, as it was called, had been seen as barren and inhospitable since the failure of the western merchants' Virginia settlement at Sagadahoc in Maine in 1607. In 1614 Smith, backed by west-country merchants, made a brief voyage to New England and published a tract promoting that region, *A Description of New England* (1616), which included a map decorated with an inset portrait of Smith. The backdrop for this promotion was popular knowledge of the high death rate in Virginia and of that region's enervating heat. Smith coined the name New England, a brilliant propaganda ploy implicitly arguing that colonists in the north, unlike those in Virginia, could live a recognizably English life in a familiar setting. The primacy of New England as a focus of English colonization, supported by statistical information about the fishing industry, was reaffirmed in his *New Englands Trials* (1620; 2d ed., 1622). Despite his promotional activity and the plans he outlined, he was unable to get the backing to found a new colony in the north with himself in command.

Smith spent the last fifteen years of his life writing to promote a coherent theory of empire and analyzing the colonial record. Although he is best known as the man of action who stepped in to force the disoriented Jamestown colonists to save themselves, his contribution as historian and theorist was extremely important. In 1624, he published his large *Generall Historie of Virginia, New-England, and the Summer Isles,* just at the time that the royal government was pursuing the quo warranto proceedings that resulted in the revocation of the Virginia Company's charter. Like all promoters, Smith borrowed heavily from the work of other writers in compiling his history, but he differed from others in that he had firsthand experience of the difficulties of creating a colonial society. He reshaped every work he used to fit his own argument on the meaning of the colonial experience. Moreover he was the only participant-writer who treated all of English America as a coherent venture.

Against the backdrop of the Virginia Company's failure, and building on his previous work, Smith enunciated a new vision of colonization in his *Generall Historie* and in his final and most philosophical book, *Advertisements for the Unexperienced Planters of New England, or Anywhere* (1631). He argued that the English effort had suffered from inadequate leadership and unrealistic, poorly conceived goals. Because aims had not been intelligently delineated, the wrong kinds of people had been sent; those who had gone to America had spent their time foolishly. Smith was the first experienced theorist to argue that North America had riches to offer Europe, but that these would come only when people were prepared to emigrate and to produce commodities through their own hard work. Riches would come from humble commodities such as fish and agricultural products, not from easily obtained and high-value goods. Land should be offered to all comers with secure tenures, which alone would lure the right kind of settlers. Only a society built on such foundations would be truly English; had the hopes of early promoters been realized, they would have produced perversions of England. Smith was contemptuous of tobacco, already emerging as the chief commodity of Virginia and argued that it was not an appropriate crop on which to build a society.

Smith placed his hopes on New England. In fact, though they did not acknowledge it, the Puritans of Plymouth Colony and Massachusetts Bay designed their colonies on the lines Smith indicated, a fact he pointed out in his *Advertisements*. But, as he wrote, they were not willing to offer him a place in their plans.

Between the *Generall Historie* and the *Advertisements*, Smith published several other books. He produced two books on seamanship, *An Accidence or the Path-way to Experience: Necessary for All Young Seamen* (1626) and *A Sea Grammar* (1627), primarily glossaries of terms taken from other books. His autobiography, as well as telling the story of his early life, brought the history of the colonies up to date from the end of the *Generall Historie*. John Smith is buried in London, his place of death unknown.

Most of what we know about John Smith's life comes from his own writing. His accounts of his young manhood and his exploits in Virginia were judged by nineteenth-century scholars to be too extraordinary and internally inconsistent to be true. This assessment was shared by Henry Adams, who employed newly developed techniques of textual criticism. Partly because his own role was magnified as he retold his stories in successive works, Smith was put down as a braggart whose accounts were not to be trusted. In the latter half of the twentieth century, however, scholars established the authenticity of his work, demonstrating that the people and events of which he wrote, adjusting for Smith's rendition of names in unfamiliar languages, can be identified. His account of adventures in the wars against the Turks has made him an important source for that poorly documented period in Eastern European history just as ethnohistorical and archaeological work in American history has enhanced the scholarly estimation of his achievements.

K.O.K.

Having faced off against both the largest terrestrial carnivore and galleys brimming with buccaneers, de Vries next challenged himself by establishing the first Dutch colonies in North America.

DAVID
PIETERSEN
DE VRIES

[1593–c. 1655]

Tracing the exploits of this roving Dutchman offers a crash course in early modern geography. De Vries sailed "the wild ocean waste" to every quarter of the seventeenth-century map, from Suriname to Ceylon, from Tortuga to the Arctic. Along the way he battled scurvy, polar bears, and Berber pirates. De Vries also took part in a largely forgotten chapter of American colonization: the settlement of present-day Delaware and New Jersey by the Dutch and the Swedes. His peripatetic career serves as a reminder of tiny Holland's sprawling maritime empire, and of the way in which America's early history belongs to a much broader drama: the scramble by competing European nations for colonies and trading posts around the globe.

D avid Pietersen de Vries, merchant adventurer and colonizer, was born in La Rochelle, France, the son of Pieter Jakobszoon de Vries, a ship captain, and a Dutch mother (name unknown). His father was from Hoorn, a northern Dutch province, and his mother was from Amsterdam. They moved to La Rochelle in 1584 and back to Hoorn when David was four. He attended Latin school, obtained a knowledge of geography and astronomy, and learned French, Dutch, and English as a result of his family's contact with the international Calvinist community.

In 1608 de Vries accompanied his father to rescue the English Separatists of Scrooby, who settled in Leiden. (Some were later part of the group that founded the Plymouth colony.) In Leiden, he worked for a printer of English religious books. He served as first mate and supercargo on his father's Baltic voyages. In 1615 he married Seitgen Huygh of Hoorn. Shortly after the birth of their only child, a daughter, in 1616, de Vries sailed on an Arctic trading venture for the Noordsche Compagnie. On this trip he killed a polar bear, contracted scurvy, and traded with Dutch whalers and Russian fur trappers before returning with a valuable cargo in a badly damaged ship.

De Vries is principally known for six eventful voyages to the Mediterranean, Asia, and America from 1618 to 1644. During the first, to Genoa in 1618, Turkish galleys attacked his ship but were successfully repulsed. In 1620 he sailed for Newfoundland. On his return he carried a cargo of fish to Spain, where eight Berber pirate ships attacked. De Vries won the battle and built his reputation as a brave fighter. When the Strait of Gibraltar closed to Dutch ships in 1621, de Vries offered to help the duc de Guise fight the pirates. When Guise planned an attack against La Rochelle, however, de Vries resigned, sold his ship, and returned home in 1623. De Vries entered a partnership in 1624 to sail to Canada for furs, but the newly chartered Dutch West India Company stopped the venture. In 1625 the king of France seized his ship in La Rochelle for military use. His American voyage temporarily frustrated, he sailed in 1627 as fleet captain to the Dutch East Indies, where he was appointed chief merchant and a councilor. By 1628 he managed the posts along the Coromandel Coast and on Ceylon. He began his return voyage to Holland in December 1629, arriving six months later. In terms of official duties and power, his three years of service in the East Indies marked the high point of his career.

In 1630 de Vries and eight directors of the Dutch West India Company associated to plant a colony named Swanendael on the South (Delaware) River of New Netherland. These patroons sent thirty-two men in 1631 to the outpost near present-day Lewes, Delaware, to hunt and process whales. In May 1632, de Vries sailed for America, just after hearing of the Indians' destruction of Swanendael. He arrived at the ruins in December. Delaware Indians explained the events leading to the massacre, and de Vries exchanged presents and made peace with Indian leaders. Nevertheless, he was deeply suspicious of the Delawares as he explored the area in early 1633. He sailed to Virginia for corn, returned to Swanendael for whale oil, and then stopped at New Amsterdam, where he quarreled with the director general, Wouter Van Twiller, who tried to search his ship. By the time he returned home, he was keenly aware of English competition in North America and disgusted with the West India Company's leadership in New Netherland. De Vries sailed in 1634 to establish a patroonship in Suriname, carrying colonists there and establishing a governmental structure for them. After satisfying himself that the colonists could carry on without him, he delivered English refugees from Tortuga to Virginia in May 1635 while on the way to New Amsterdam. In September he returned to Virginia, where he wintered. After learning of the Suriname colony's demise, he decided to give New Netherland another chance and sailed there from Virginia in 1636. He registered a claim to Staten Island before returning in August to Holland, where he sought unsuccessfully the directorship of New Netherland. He returned in 1638 and soon settled "his people" (the colonists under his authority) on a Staten Island patroonship in partnership with Frederick de Vries of Amsterdam. Meanwhile, Director General Willem Kieft sent him on a diplomatic mission to the English in the Connecticut River valley, territory claimed by both nations, to assess the situation. His partner failed to supply more people for Staten Island, so, in 1640, de Vries founded a third patroonship, Vriessendael, near present-day Edgewater, New Jersey.

For the remainder of his years in New Netherland, de Vries lived at Vriessendael as a prominent citizen, consistent critic of the colony's leadership, and sympathetic observer of Delaware Indian culture. He claimed to know their language well, and he gained a reputation among them as a trustworthy "good chief." In 1643 de Vries mediated between the Dutch and natives fighting Kieft's War. His small patroonships on Staten Island and at Vriessendael were destroyed nonetheless. He left New Netherland for the last time in October 1643 on a Rotterdam ship. With de Vries assisting as pilot, it stopped at the New Sweden colony and continued to Virginia, where he remained through the winter, spending some of his time there as a guest of Governor William Berkeley. In 1644, he returned safely to Hoorn, an event he said later in concluding his memoir "for which our God must be eternally praised, that he should have brought me again to my Fatherland, after such long and tedious voyages, and through so many perils of savage heathens."

Little is known of de Vries after his return to Hoorn. A portrait dated 1653 identifies him as an artillery master. He published his memoirs in 1655 as *Short Historical and Journal Notes of Various Voyages Performed in the Four Quarters of the Globe.* The date and circumstances of his death are unknown. De Vries exemplifies the entrepreneurial spirit and Calvinist zeal of Holland's "golden age." His unusually wide-ranging experiences and his position among the merchant elite brought him into contact with people and events of great historical interest. He described his book as "not embellished with ornaments of words—as is not to be expected of a person who has passed the most of his life upon the wild ocean waste." Yet there is much of value in his writing, especially his ethnographic descriptions of Native Americans and his firsthand accounts of the Dutch, English, and Indian competition for America.

J.H.W.

FRANCESCO GIUSEPPE BRESSANI

[6 MAY 1612–9 SEPTEMBER 1672]

Religion, rather than the search for riches, propelled many of America's earliest adventurers across the Atlantic. Bressani typified the stoic breed of Jesuit "black robes" that brought Christianity to "New France" and today's northern United States. Tortured and maimed by Mohawks, and saved from burning at the stake by an elderly tribeswoman, Bressani transformed his ordeal into a badge of faith and a tool for his missionary work.

Francesco Giuseppe Bressani, priest, Jesuit missionary, and astronomer, was born in Rome, Italy. His parents' names are unknown, and very little is known about his early life. Bressani entered the Society of Jesus as a novice on 15 August 1626. Over the next few years he requested repeatedly to be sent to Canada as a missionary. After studying in Rome and later in Claremont, France, he became an accomplished teacher of philosophy, literature, mathematics, and astronomy. In 1642 Bressani got his wish and was sent to Quebec, the seat of the Jesuit mission in New France. Finally, on 27 April 1644, having become sufficiently fluent in Huron to undertake missionary duties, he set off for Sainte-Marie in the Huron country, near the present Midland, Ontario, accompanied by six Christian Hurons and a French boy. Three days later, just east of the mouth of the Richelieu River, the group was captured by twenty-seven Mohawk warriors. Thus began Father Bressani's ordeal.

The war party returned home up the Richelieu River–Lake Champlain route, and on 15 May, reached a Mohawk fishing village of 400 people on the upper Hudson River near its junction with the Sacandaga. Here Bressani underwent preliminary torture until his tormentors learned

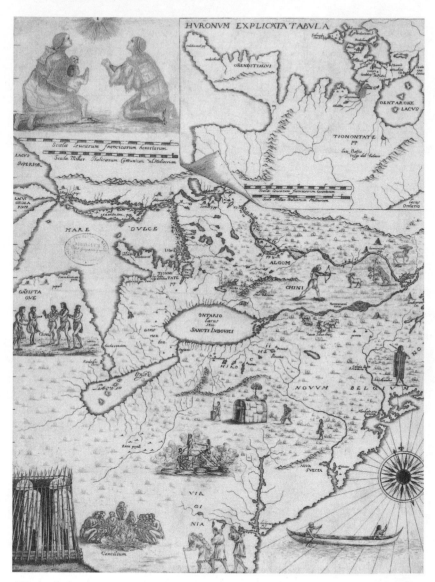

This detail of Bressani's 1657 map of New France displays Native American activities that he may have observed while serving as a missionary in the New World, trying to give the Indians a "better conception… of the truths of our faith."

from a Huron captive that he was "an important personage and a captain of the French." He was then told that he would eventually die by fire. The following day, 26 May, Bressani was taken to the Mohawk country, reaching his first village, probably Ossernenon near the present Fultonville in New York, four days later. In this village and the second one, probably Kanagaro, located a few miles upstream from Ossernenon, his tortures were intensified. In order to keep his sanity, Bressani prayed, observed phases of the moon, and tried to keep track of time. Several times he asked to be spared from death by fire and executed in some other manner. Once, briefly, he contemplated suicide by drowning. On 19 June, thoroughly degraded and physically broken, he was told he would now be burned to death. Instead, however, just as had happened to Father Isaac Jogues in 1642, Bressani was ransomed by an old Mohawk woman for "a few beads" as a replacement for her grandfather who had died at Huron hands many years earlier. Totally unfit for work and so horrible in appearance that the Mohawk woman's daughters were afraid to look at him, she permitted the Dutch to ransom him for fifteen or twenty doppias (in value about 150 to 200 French *livres* or about thirty to forty pounds of beaver pelts).

On 19 August 1644 Bressani left the Mohawk for New Amsterdam, where he was treated by a doctor while staying with the Reverend Johannes Megapolensis. He wrote to Megapolensis later and thanked him for his kindnesses. Ever the missionary, he also asked him to consider becoming a Catholic. Finally well enough, Bressani was sent to France and reached La Rochelle on November 15. From there he went to Rome for an audience with Pope Innocent X, who gave Bressani a dispensation to conduct mass without the use of the fingers on his right hand, which had been partially removed by Mohawk torture.

By July 1645 he was back in Canada, and at the Huron mission by the early autumn. He had finally achieved his lifelong goal, to serve as a missionary. According to his colleagues, the ordeal he had suffered had made him a better preacher. He often displayed his mutilated body, especially his hands, to give the Huron a "better conception . . . of the truths of our faith": that, as a Christian, he would endure torture for his faith and still not be afraid of encountering more by returning to Canada.

On 30 January 1646 at Sainte-Marie, 25 May 1649 at Trois-Rivières, and 18 November 1649 at Quebec, Bressani used his scientific knowledge and skill to time lunar eclipses. His results were to be compared with observations made in Europe in order to calculate longitudinal distances. Considering the poor quality of the instruments at his disposal and the difficulties he must have had with his hands, his observations were phenomenally accurate. In fact, they were not equaled for the next hundred years. His calculation for the difference in time between Quebec and Sainte-Marie was exact at thirty-five minutes (8° 45' longitude), while his timing of the eclipse on 18 November at Quebec, which was also timed by Fathers Riccioli and Grimaldi at Bologna, Italy, had an error of only five minutes and thirty seconds (1° 22' 30" longitude). As late as 1755, the British cartographer and geographer Thomas Jefferys still cited Bressani as the authority for the coordinates of Quebec at latitude 46° 55' and longitude 52° 13' west of Ferro. These figures carry errors of only 7' and 29', respectively.

In 1649, while Bressani was at Quebec, the Huron country faced its final onslaught from the Iroquois League. In June of the following year, Bressani, accompanied by about thirty-five Frenchmen and an equal number of Huron warriors, set off with supplies for their beleaguered colleagues. Halfway to Huronia, the group was ambushed by ten Iroquois warriors, and Bressani received three arrow wounds to the head. Shortly after this encounter, they met the survivors of the Huron disaster and all returned to Quebec.

With the Huron mission destroyed, some of the Jesuits, including Bressani, embarked on 2 November 1650 for France on the *Chasseur*. Eventually he returned to Italy, where he published *Breve relatione d'alcune missioni de'PP. della Compagnia di Giesù nella Nuova Francia* (1653), his account of the Huron mission and its martyrs. The book was to be illustrated with a map, which was not ready at press time. The only map fitting the book's description of it is the *Novae Franciae Accurata Delineatio*, engraved by the Italian master Giovanni Federico Pesca in 1657. With its accurate vignettes of native life and the earliest depiction of the martyrdom of Fathers Brébeuf and Lalemant, it is considered the most beautiful map of seventeenth-century New France.

Bressani spent the remainder of his life in Italy as a priest. By repute he was an effective preacher, continuing the practice of showing his mutilated hands to disbelievers as evidence for the strength of faith against adversity. He died in Florence.

C.H.

A romanticized nineteenth-century artist's rendition of Duston's bloody escape from the Indian family who had held her prisoner.

HANNAH DUSTON

[3 DECEMBER 1657–1736]

Despite popular images of the first Thanksgiving, Indians fiercely resisted white settlement of New England for roughly a century, and often took captives to replace family members lost in war. Duston, a frontier farm wife, had just given birth to her twelfth child when Abenaki raiders seized her in 1697. She pulled off an astounding and bloody escape that made her a New England heroine—and a very controversial figure to later generations.

Hannah Duston, Massachusetts settler and Indian captive, was born in Haverhill, Massachusetts, the daughter of Michael Emerson and Hannah Webster. Her father was an English shoemaker who immigrated to Massachusetts and married the daughter of an original settler of Ipswich. Hannah was one of fifteen children. Nothing is known of her life before her marriage. In December 1677 she married Thomas Duston (also written as Dustin, Dustan, and Durstan), a bricklayer and farmer originally from Dover, New Hampshire. They lived in a cottage two miles from Haverhill and had thirteen children. Thomas became a respected citizen and was appointed a constable for Haverhill.

Hannah Duston's fame came as a result of events that occurred in 1697, shortly after she gave birth to her twelfth child. The widow Mary Neff had come to live with the Dustons to help Hannah regain her health. King William's War had increased fear of Indian attack in this frontier area, and Thomas Duston had been appointed captain of the local garrison. On 15 March 1697 Thomas was working in his fields when he saw a group of Indians approaching his home. He managed to escape with seven of his children, but Hannah Duston, Mary Neff, and the newborn infant were not warned in time to escape. The band of Indians captured Duston and Neff and killed the infant by smashing its head against a tree. Duston and Neff were then marched toward Canada. The distance they traveled is uncertain, but they probably marched about one hundred miles to the Merrimack River in New Hampshire. Duston and Neff, along with a boy named Samuel Lennardson, who had been taken prisoner eight months earlier in Worcester, were given as prisoners to an Indian family of two men, three women, and seven children. The Indians were converts to Roman Catholicism and prayed daily. According to Duston's account the three were told that they would be made to run the gauntlet when they arrived in Canada, and so she decided to try to escape. Lennardson got one of their captors to explain to him how to kill and scalp a person, and on the night of 30 March 1697, the three English settlers put the information to use. Lennardson killed one Indian, and Duston killed nine. Only one Indian woman and one child managed to escape. The dead Indians were scalped so that there would be proof of what Duston and Lennardson had done. The three traveled by river and foot back to Haverhill, and a few days later took the story and scalps to Boston. Here Hannah Duston recounted her adventure to the General Court and to many citizens of Boston, including Samuel Sewall and Cotton Mather. Her husband, Thomas, requested that the General Court reward his wife for her deed, believing that he also deserved reimbursement for the loss of his home. The General Court, in keeping with its policy of providing bounty for Indian scalps, gave him £25 on behalf of Hannah and gave Neff and Lennardson £12, 10 shillings each for their bravery. Hannah Duston's deeds were publicized throughout the colonies, and she received many accolades and gifts, including one from the governor of Maryland. Duston spent the rest of her life in Haverhill. She had one more child in 1698. After Thomas died in 1732, Hannah lived with her son Jonathan. She died probably in 1736, the year her will was proved at Ipswich.

Hannah Duston became a legend in the New England area, and regional histories in the eighteenth and nineteenth centuries always recorded accounts of her capture and escape. At first her story was recorded as a moral tale following the lead of Cotton Mather, who exonerated Duston for killing the Indians since they were Catholic and because she feared for her own life. Americans of the nineteenth century found it harder to justify her killing Indian children, but many accepted the interpretation of John Greenleaf Whittier in "The Mother's Revenge"; he excused her action in light of the murder of her own child. Nathaniel Hawthorne, however, in "The Duston Family," published in 1836, condemned Duston for killing the Indians, presenting her as an example of the destruction of the innocent American wilderness by the brutal Puritan settlers. Other nineteenth-century New Englanders, however, continued to celebrate her heroism, and in 1874 and 1879 monuments were erected commemorating her deed. Little attention was paid to her for the next one hundred years. In 1980 Laurel Thatcher Ulrich reprised Duston's tale for a new generation of women's historians. Ulrich used Duston as a symbol around which to analyze societal reaction to female heroism and violence. Ulrich argued that for the Puritans Duston was a symbol of feminine strength and assertiveness but at the same time representative of the destructive power that Puritans believed was behind the feminine mask. Ulrich further observed that nineteenth-century condemnation of Duston rested in part on aversion to her violent acts, which were contrary to expectations of female behavior. Hannah Duston's heroic and bloody history continues to draw attention. However, she has become less admirable in the eyes of the public and is now viewed as evidence of the ambiguity surrounding English settlement in North America.

A.S.M.

SIR ALEXANDER CUMING

[*c.* 1690/1692–AUGUST 1775]

While early New England was Puritan in character, the Carolinas attracted more motley and flamboyant adventurers. Perhaps none proved so colorful as Cuming, a Scottish baronet who became a self-appointed emissary to the Cherokee, and was crowned as their "emperor." Cuming's wild schemes, which included the founding of a huge Jewish colony in Indian country, also resulted in bank fraud and financial ruin.

S ir Alexander Cuming, leader of a Cherokee delegation from America to England, was born in Culter, Aberdeenshire, Scotland, the son of Sir Alexander Cuming, M.P., the first baronet of Culter, Aberdeenshire, and Elizabeth Swinton. The visionary if erratic second baronet of Culter had a varied career. Called to the Scottish bar in 1714, he also held captain's rank in the Russian army. He left the law when he received a pension of £300, bestowed by the government at Christmas 1718 for services either done by his family or to be performed by him. Cuming lost the pension three years later, either because he was thought unable to provide the expected services or, according to Cuming, because Sir Robert Walpole, just named first lord of the treasury and chancellor of the exchequer, had been angered by the elder Cuming's opposition in Parliament.

On 30 June 1720, Cuming was elected to the Royal Society, remaining as a member until 9 June 1757, when he was removed for failing to pay the annual fee. He married Amy Whitehall, the daughter of Lancelot Whitehall, a customs commissioner in Scotland. The couple had two children.

Cuming is best known for an unusual journey taken on his own responsibility to the Cherokee Indians in 1730, resulting in Cuming naming a Cherokee "emperor," himself receiving a crown, and then escorting the first Cherokee delegation to England, where a treaty important to British interests was concluded. The journey to North America is said to have

28

Detail of an engraving of Cherokee Indians who were brought to London in 1730 by Sir Alexander Cuming. A treaty they signed during their visit acknowledged British sovereignty and gave the English the exclusive right to trade with the Cherokee.

originated in a dream of Lady Cuming. On 13 September 1729, he set sail for Charleston. He arrived on 5 December in a colony that had over-thrown its proprietors ten years earlier and that had just become a royal colony. Cuming attempted to establish a bank by issuing promissory notes to Carolinians in exchange for their deposits.

While in Carolina, Cuming learned about the unsettled relations with the Indian nations, including the Cherokees. On 13 March 1730, he set out for Cherokee country, inquiring about, inspecting, and collecting chunks of iron ore and other minerals, useful herbs, and other "natural curiosities." The Cherokees were a numerous people living in sixty or so towns stretched east-west from the upper reaches of the Savannah River to the Tennessee River Valley, 300 miles from Charleston. When Cuming arrived at the Cherokee town of Nequassee, having been assisted by resident Carolina traders, he received a warm welcome, made more so by his bold actions and appearance. Making clear that he acted unofficially, Cuming called on Cherokee leaders of other towns to meet with him. The Cherokees concurred in his "nomination" of Moytoy of Tellico as emperor and brought forth from Tennessee their crown, which they bestowed on Cuming along with five eagle tails and four scalps, which were to be "laid at the feet" of the English king.

Cuming returned to Charleston, completing the several-hundred-mile trip on 13 April. He quickly embarked on the *Fox* for England with seven Cherokees, including the future leader Attakullakulla, known to the English as Little Carpenter, and trader/interpreter Eleazar Wiggan, who had first settled among the Cherokees in 1711 and was affectionately known as "The Old Rabbit." Apparently Cuming also departed from Charleston with his "bank's" assets. Concerned depositors broke into his bank, found it empty, and immediately dispatched letters to London accusing Cuming of defrauding the depositors, charges he never answered. The *Fox* anchored at Dover on 5 June.

The Cherokee delegates sparked great interest in England and were shown the sights and entertained at the expense of the Crown. They were presented to the king at Windsor on 18 June and four days later laid the eagle tails and scalps at his feet, signifying their power over their enemies, while Cuming tendered his crown. All public excursions drew large and curious crowds. Cuming, however, was increasingly ignored, perhaps because even though he had created an opportunity for the British government, he was no longer needed. The Cherokee delegates were eventually put under the supervision of South Carolina's new governor, Robert Johnson. On 9 September six delegates agreed to a treaty, although they made clear their displeasure at the exclusion of their "friend" Cuming from the proceedings.

By the Treaty of 1730, in return for guns, powder, and other goods, the Cherokees acknowledged British sovereignty and agreed to trade only with the English and to allow no one but the English to reside among them.

They also promised to return any fugitive slaves and to surrender any Cherokees accused of murdering English colonists. The delegation, accompanied by Johnson, departed in October and arrived safely home, laden with numerous goods provided in the treaty.

The next decades found the English continually having to shore up their relations with the Cherokees, who with other interior tribes received overtures from the French. Increasingly annoyed by pressures on their lands, and never as tightly controlled by their leaders as Europeans assumed and hoped, tribes posed persistent problems for colonial governments. Cuming's role in British-Cherokee relations was fortuitous and fit into an unsteady relationship made more difficult by trader excesses for two years before he arrived. His nomination of a Cherokee emperor echoed an arrangement negotiated by Governor Francis Nicholson in 1721. The Cherokee delegation he brought to England was the first for that people, but twenty years earlier, a delegation of Mohawks had come to England, and in 1725 a delegation of Indians from the Illinois Country visited Louis XV in Paris. It seems likely that Cuming may have been influenced by these events.

After 1730, Cuming continued to concoct schemes, proposing at one point a plan to enrich the British treasury by settling 300,000 Jewish families in Cherokee country. Official London viewed this and schemes to address colonial taxation problems as impractical. Cuming never escaped the shadow of the failed bank scheme. As a debtor, from 1737 to 1765 he was confined in London's Fleet prison and was supported by the contributions of friends. Lady Cuming died in 1743. In 1762 Cuming interpreted for a second delegation of Cherokees in London under the auspices of Virginia. In 1766 he was appointed a pensioner in the Charterhouse, a charitable institution in London, by Archbishop Thomas Secker; Cuming died there.

D.D.M.

ANN HENNIS
TROTTER BAILEY

[1742–22 NOVEMBER 1825]

As Virginia settlers pressed inland during the eighteenth century, a rough new breed of log-cabin pioneers emerged along the Appalachians. We tend to imagine these frontier families as traditional folk: men chopping trees and shooting game, while their wives churned butter and swaddled infants. But one of the most remarkable mountaineers was "Mad Ann Bailey," who wore buckskins, boxed, drank whiskey, and took a legendary night ride through "track-less forest" to save a fort under Indian attack.

Ann Hennis Trotter Bailey, revolutionary war scout, was born in Liverpool, England. Little is known about her parents, although it is believed that her father had been a soldier under the duke of Marlborough's command. As Bailey was literate, she received an education in Liverpool, although details of it are not recorded. Orphaned as a young adult, she immigrated to America in the wake of relatives named Bell. She arrived in Staunton, Virginia, at the Bells' home in 1761. In 1765 she married Richard Trotter, a frontiersman and Indian fighter, and they had a son in 1767. Lord Dunmore, the royal governor of Virginia, recruited men in 1774 to fight the marauding Indians who were disrupting the settlers on or near the Scioto River. Richard Trotter volunteered and followed Colonel Charles Lewis to the point where the Kanawha and Ohio Rivers meet, known as Point Pleasant. He was killed in the battle there on 10 October 1774.

In order to "avenge" her husband's death, Bailey began her career as a frontier scout, "clad in buckskin pants, with petticoat, heavy brogan shoes, a man's coat and hat" armed with knife and tomahawk and a "long rifle on her shoulder" (Ellet, pp. 249, 251). Nineteenth-century interpretation of Bailey's choice of career is critical of her step beyond the traditional

Serving as a scout and spy during the American Revolution, Bailey came to be known as the Heroine of the Great Kanawha Valley in the nineteenth century.

female role. She is described as "short and stout, and of coarse and masculine appearance" while "among her masculine habits" she drank hard liquor and would exercise "her skill in boxing." She scouted for and relayed messages to the existing forts in order to protect the pioneer families in the Shenandoah Valley from hostile Indians. During the Revolution, Bailey served as a spy, keenly aware that many of the indigenous population were allied with the British. As she traversed the Shenandoah Valley from one frontier outpost to another, Bailey actively recruited patriots to join the militia.

On 3 November 1785 she married John Bailey, a member of a frontier group called the Rangers. He spent much of his time "hunting and fighting hostile Indians," and when he was assigned to the garrison at Fort Lee (also known as "Clendenin's Settlement"; now Charleston, West Virginia), they moved there. As they had no children, marriage did not detract from her own duties, and she continued riding horseback between outposts and living a rugged outdoor life.

Bailey's most famous exploit occurred in 1791. The area around Fort Lee had been the site of frequent Indian attacks on families. One particular night, when the outpost was surrounded by Indians and gunpowder supplies were crucially low, Bailey volunteered to ride to Fort Savannah (also called Fort Union) near present-day Lewisberg, West Virginia, to get the needed supplies. Passing stealthily through the Indians surrounding the fort without harm, she journied a hundred miles through a "track-less forest" and reached Fort Savannah safely. The commandant of the fort gave her two fresh horses, one to ride and the other to carry the gunpowder. Completing her mission within a period of three days, she single-handedly saved Fort Lee from certain destruction.

Much of the Indian hostility ended in the Kanawha Valley area after the Indian chief Little Turtle signed the Treaty of Greenville with General Anthony Wayne in 1795. The treaty followed Wayne's victory over the Indians at the Battle of Fallen Timbers (in the Ohio Country) in 1794, which firmly established the power of the U.S. government. Bailey continued her frontier life, however. She became well known to the people of West Virginia, who always greeted her warmly as she rode about on her horse, Liverpool. The Shawnee Indians of the area called her "The White Squaw of the Kanawha" and thought the "Great Spirit" protected her. The settlers called her "Mad Ann Bailey" because she knew no fear.

Her son, William Trotter, and his wife settled on the Kanawha River in

1814, and Bailey lived with them for three years. When William sold his property in 1817, Bailey moved with the family to a former French settlement, Gallipolis, Ohio, where she died. Bailey became a legend in Gallia County, Ohio. As the person solely responsible for saving Fort Lee by her famous ride to Lewisberg, she gained prominence as the "Heroine of the Great Kanawha Valley." In 1861, a U.S. Cavalry man, Charles Robb, wrote a poem entitled "Ann Bailey" to commemorate her famous ride.

H.L.

By 1776, the trading post that du Sable had established with a single cabin by the Chicago River had grown to a town complete with a church, a school, several commercial buildings, docks, and a mansion house with fruit orchards.

JEAN BAPTISTE
POINT DU SABLE

[c. 1745–28 AUGUST 1818]

In the late eighteenth century, the Mississippi Valley formed America's emerging "West," a wide-open territory where traders and adventurers from many nations competed for furs, land, and other resources. Du Sable, born to a Haitian slave and a French Canadian, traveled up the Mississippi and pioneered Illinois, becoming a prosperous merchant and the first non-native settler of Chicago—a contribution to the Windy City's history that went unrecognized until well into the twentieth century.

Jean Baptiste Point du Sable, explorer and merchant, was born in San Marc, Haiti, the son of a Negro slave woman (name unknown) and Dandonneau (first name unknown), scion of a prominent French-Canadian family active in the North American fur trade. Surviving historical journals record the name of Jean Baptiste Point du Sable (Point au Sable by some accounts), a Haitian of mixed-blood ancestry, as the first permanent settler of Chicago. In her 1856 memoir of frontier life in the emerging Northwest Territory, Juliette Kinzie, the wife of fur trader John Kinzie, makes note of the fact that "the first white man who settled here was a Negro." Several of the voyageurs and commercial men who regularly traversed the shores of southern Lake Michigan in the last decade of the eighteenth century kept accurate records of their encounters in journals and ledger books. One such entry describes du Sable as a "large man; a trader, and pretty wealthy."

Du Sable's pathway to economic reward in the emerging West began in Haiti many years earlier. As a mulatto, du Sable was excluded from direct political participation but enjoyed the same basic rights as freedmen and thus was allowed social intercourse with the French settlers. By the terms of the Treaty of Ryswick, Santo Domingo was ceded to France by the Spanish on 20 September 1697. The French merchants and seafarers enticed the Haitians with many intriguing stories of the opportunities to be found in Spanish Louisiana. There is no historical rendering of du Sable's activities prior to his departure from Santo Domingo. In general, though, his occupation seems to have been that of a trader. Accordingly, du Sable sailed from Haiti to pursue the dream of greater economic reward in a foreign land aboard the sloop *Susanne*. He arrived in New Orleans in 1764. Less than a year later du Sable completed a historic 600-mile journey up the Mississippi River in the company of Jacques Clamorgan, a successful explorer and merchant who went on to become one of the first judges of the Court of Common Pleas in St. Louis. Du Sable's association with a man of Clamorgan's stature indicates that he was welcomed into a higher social class than one might normally expect of a man born to a slave woman in those times. There seems to have been less social rigidity in the western frontier, thus allowing du Sable to engage in commerce with the white settlers.

Du Sable staked a claim to 800 acres of farmland in Peoria and tended this property for several years until he made the decision to relocate to northeast Illinois in the land the Potawatomi tribe called "Eschecagou" (Chicago: literal translation, 'land of the wild onions'). There du Sable founded the region's first commercial enterprise, a trading post on the marshy north bank of the Chicago River overlooking Lake Michigan. Juliette Kinzie's memoir provides some additional details of du Sable's holdings during this period. In addition to his "mansion" (measuring 22 x 40 feet), du Sable owned two barns, a horse mill, bakehouse, dairy, workshop, henhouse, and smokehouse. The inventory of farm equipment indicates that du Sable was harvesting wheat and cutting hay. To run such a busy trading operation and farming enterprise required that du Sable employ skilled labor. Undoubtedly many of his "employees" were Potawatomi Indians.

Du Sable cultivated a good relationship with the native peoples. For a time he lived among the indigenous tribe and took Catherine, the daughter of Potawatomi chief Pokagon, as his common-law wife. The marriage was formalized at Cahokia in 1788, but the union had been sanctioned by Indian tribal customs years earlier. The couple had two children.

The flourishing frontier outpost along the Chicago River was disrupted by the arrival of Charles-Michel Mouet de Langlade, a French nobleman and commercial trader, in 1778. De Langlade, whom midwestern historians consider to be the "father of Wisconsin," drove the mulatto and his family from the region in order to claim the local trade and because of his racial enmity. Du Sable abandoned his claim and moved his family farther east. He took up residence in Michigan City, Indiana, but hostilities between the American colonists and the British government resulted in du Sable's arrest in August 1779. British regulars garrisoned at Fort Michilimackinac (Mackinac Island, Michigan) descended on du Sable's cabin adjacent to the River Chemin and removed him to their military encampment at Port Huron, north of Detroit.

Du Sable and his family were detained by the British for the duration of the American Revolution, a five-year period ending in approximately 1784. A report submitted to his senior commanding officer, Colonel Arent Schuyler de Peyster, by Lieutenant Thomas Bennett describes the circumstances of du Sable's arrest and subsequent confinement. "Corporal Tascon, who commanded the party, very prudently prevented the Indians from burning his home, or doing him any injury. The Negro, since his encampment, has in every respect behaved in a manner becoming to a man in his situation and his many friends who give him a good character." Du Sable fully cooperated with his captors and signaled his willingness to take charge of the Port Huron trading post after reports filtered back to Lieutenant Governor Patrick Sinclair that du Sable's predecessor, a Frenchman named Francois Brevecour, had badly mistreated the Indians. The "Pinery," as the British outpost and commissary was known, was maintained by du Sable until 1784, when historians believe that he returned to Illinois to reclaim his vacated properties following the cessation of war. Whether he had further encounters with de Langlade is difficult to ascertain.

The Great Lakes region was fast becoming an important hub of commerce; much of the trade came from the Spanish settlements west of the Mississippi River. Thus, du Sable built and maintained a successful trading post at the mouth of the Chicago River. Historians differ on the precise year du Sable started his business. However, journal accounts maintained by Hugh Heward, a Detroit commission agent, establish the presence of du Sable in Chicago on 10 May 1790. During this period du Sable supplied his customers with pork, bread, and flour in return for durable goods and cash. He lived in peace with the Indians, and the white traders passing through the region commented favorably on his character and business acumen.

These early entries describe the region's first settler as an honest man, fond of drink but well-educated by contemporary standards. When du Sable sailed to Mackinac with his Indian companions in 1796, the British soldiers greeted him with a cannon salute as a token of esteem. It was a remarkable gesture, indicative of his reputation and good character up and down the Great Lakes.

In May 1800, Jean Baptiste du Sable disposed of his property for reasons not entirely clear. With certainty we can say that Chicago's first settler completed Chicago's first real estate transaction of any consequence when he sold the trading post to Jean la Lime, a French-Canadian trapper from St. Joseph, for the sum of 6,000 *livres*. The sale was witnessed by John Kinzie of Niles, Michigan (who in turn would purchase the estate from la Lime four years later in 1804), and was duly recorded in Detroit, the seat of government for the territory of Illinois.

We can only speculate about du Sable's motivations for wanting to leave Chicago. Perhaps his decision to vacate the region at this historic juncture had something to do with the arrival of the eastern settlers who were already pouring into this desolate marshland previously populated only by American Indians and wild animals. Fort Dearborn (named for General Henry Dearborn, secretary of war) would be erected in April 1803 to protect the interests of the white settlers from the native peoples. This frontier outpost would soon evolve into the city of Chicago.

Du Sable briefly returned to his farmland in Peoria and remained there for little more than a decade. It is believed that Catherine died in Peoria prior to June 1813, when du Sable retired to St. Charles, Missouri. In his declining years, du Sable took great precautions to ensure that he could live out the remainder of his life in comfort. He deeded his home in St. Charles to a granddaughter, Eulalie Baroda Denais, in return for her assurance that she would care for him and provide him with a proper burial in the local Catholic cemetery. Whether du Sable achieved these modest aims is less certain, but village records from St. Charles suggest that the venerable pioneer encountered serious financial setbacks late in life and was imprisoned as a debtor in September 1814. Du Sable died at his daughter's residence. No information is available concerning his financial condition at this time.

For many years afterward there was a self-conscious tendency on the part of Chicago chroniclers to deny Jean Baptiste Point du Sable credit for his role in the development of Chicago as the commercial hub of midwestern commerce. The fact that du Sable was a mulatto disturbed the nineteenth-century writers who touted the accomplishments of Chicago's original settlers in any number of civic boosterism tomes to appear during that era. His questionable lineage, his friendship with the American Indians, and his dealings with the English army during a time of war cast du Sable in an unfavorable light for many years to come. Not until 1935 and the opening of du Sable High School in Chicago was any significant honor accorded this man. In 1961 Margaret Burroughs founded the du Sable Museum of African-American History on the city's South Side, and over the years she has remained one of his most staunch admirers. Her museum remains a shrine to his memory.

R.C.L.

SAMUEL MASON

[*c.* 1750–JULY 1803]

A century before the "Wild West" entered legend as America's unruly fron-
tier, outlaws roamed the eastern half of the continent, preying on flatboats,
Kentucky pioneers, and travelers along the Natchez Trace. Mason, "bad from
his boyhood," graduated from tavernkeeper to horse thief to river pirate to
highwayman until cut down by two members of his own gang. His pica-
resque exploits in riverside haunts such as Cave-in-Rock recall scenes from
Huckleberry Finn.

S amuel Mason, outlaw and pirate, was born in Virginia of unknown
parents. Virtually nothing is known of his early life, although historian Samuel Draper noted that he was "connected by ties of consanguin-
ity with the distinguished Mason family of Virginia, and grew up bad
from his boyhood." Mason first appeared in historical records during the
American Revolution, during which he served as a captain in the Ohio
County, Virginia (now West Virginia), militia. He fought in several engagements against Native Americans in 1777 and served at Fort Henry in the
upper Ohio Valley until the autumn of 1779. Retiring from active service,
he retained his captaincy in the militia until at least May 1781 and apparently also ran a tavern in the vicinity of present-day Wheeling, West Virginia.

Prosperous enough by this time to own slaves, he had also begun a
criminal career at some time prior to the war by stealing horses in Frederick
County, Virginia. Following the Revolution, he drifted down to what is
today eastern Tennessee and occupied (in squatter fashion) some cabins
belonging to General John Sevier. There, Mason and a band of companions apparently engaged in petty thievery and otherwise made such a nuisance of themselves that Sevier summarily evicted them. By 1787, Mason
was in western Kentucky, possibly to claim a land grant that was a reward
for his wartime service. Although he had signed a petition in 1790 (along

This illustration of the den Mason chose for his gang first appeared in 1924 as artwork in The Outlaws of Cave-in-Rock *by Otto A. Rothert.*

with 114 other "respectable citizens") urging the creation of Logan County in what is today southwestern Kentucky, his veneer of respectability was apparently insufficient to sustain him in the community, and by 1794 he had removed to Henderson, Kentucky, where he dwelt among "horse thieves, rogues, and outlaws." In 1795 a disagreement between Mason and the local constable, John Dunn, led to Mason (with four others) physically attacking Dunn in ambush and leaving him for dead. While making his headquarters in Henderson County, Mason, his family, and his gang also stole slaves and were parties to at least one murder.

By 1797, Mason and his ensemble had moved once again, to Cave-in-Rock, Illinois. A large natural cave that overlooked the Ohio River in Hardin

County, Illinois, the site was long noted as a haven for criminals as well as a temporary shelter for travelers. Numerous river pirates preyed on the slow-moving flatboats that brought settlers and supplies down the river during the period, and Mason ranked among the most successful of the lot. Operating under the alias of Wilson, he opened "Wilson's Liquor Vault and House for Entertainment" in the cave to lure unsuspecting passersby. The site offered an excellent long-distance view of the river in both directions, thereby giving Mason and his associates early warning of both potential victims and militias sent to curtail Mason's activity. Some flatboats were lured to shore by the use of a man or woman (posing as a stranded settler) hailing the boats from the riverbank as they passed. While some of the captured crewmen were killed to ensure their silence, Mason always promoted himself as a robber who only killed when necessary. As a result, he frequently forced his victims to join his gang in lieu of murdering them.

Ever restless and fearing the repercussions that were likely to follow his growing notoriety, Mason moved his operation southward, establishing a base on Wolf Island in the Mississippi River (about twenty-five miles south of the mouth of the Ohio). In March 1800 he applied for and received a passport to the Spanish-held western bank of the Mississippi in New Madrid, Missouri. This passport, he hoped, not only would allow him to purchase land in Spanish-held territory but also would allow him to concentrate his operations on the eastern (American) side of the river and use the western bank as a safe haven. In the latter part of his career, Mason continued to rob riverboats on the Mississippi and also turned highwayman by expanding his operations to the Natchez Trace. Using agents in places like Natchez to inform him concerning movements of mule trains on the trace, Mason plundered trade moving through the two major thoroughfares of the Mississippi Valley.

Mason's continued notoriety led to his capture at Little Prairie, Missouri (about thirty miles south of New Madrid), in January 1803. Along with his four sons, a daughter-in-law, three grandchildren, and a man with several aliases (John Taylor, John Setton, and Wells), he was questioned at length by the Spanish commandant Don Henri Peyroux de la Coudreniere. Don Henri then sent the band under guard to his superior in New Orleans, Intendant Manuel Salcedo. After arriving downriver, the gang was questioned by Salcedo. Although unable to prove any criminal activity within Spanish territory, the intendant suspected that infractions had been committed on the American side, and arrangements were made to turn Mason over to the American authorities in Natchez. Leaving New Orleans by boat, the party traveled upriver until a broken mast forced a repair stop and provided Mason with his chance. On 26 March 1803, Mason grabbed a rifle from his captors and escaped with the rest of his band, with Captain Robert McCoy dying during the attempt from gunshot wounds. News of Mason's escape traveled quickly, and a reward of $1,000 was soon offered by the Americans for his recapture. Sometime in July 1803, Mason was killed by two members of his gang, John Setton and James May. The two men cut off Mason's head and attempted to collect the reward money in Mississippi but were recognized as members of the gang and were put on trial. During the trial, it came to light that John Setton was actually the notorious Wiley "Little" Harpe, who with his reputed brother Micajah "Big" Harpe had cut a murderous swath through Kentucky and Tennessee several years earlier. Following the trial, the two men were executed by hanging on 8 February 1804 at Old Greenville (no longer in existence), Jefferson County, Mississippi. The disposition of Mason's gang is unclear, but he was survived by his wife (name and date of marriage unknown) and four sons.

During his years of operations on the Ohio and Mississippi Rivers and the Natchez Trace, Mason was a widely known and feared individual. His gang made early journeys through these regions more perilous.

E.L.L.

Present with Cook on his third voyage, which ended in the Sandwich Islands (Hawaii), Ledyard went on to earn considerable fame of his own when he published A Journal of Captain Cook's Last Voyage to the Pacific Ocean, and In Quest of a North-West Passage *in 1783.*

JOHN LEDYARD

[NOVEMBER 1751–10 JANUARY 1789]

This Connecticut Yankee was one of the first American-born travelers to embark on truly global adventures. A college dropout and navy deserter, he wandered by ship, carriage, canoe, and sledge, ultimately reaching five continents and undertaking a solo journey around the globe. Regarded by Thomas Jefferson as a "man of genius, of some science, and of fearless courage and enterprise," Ledyard promised the future president that he would "go to Kentucky and endeavor to penetrate westwardly." Ledyard died in Egypt before carrying out this mission, which later fell to Lewis and Clark.

John Ledyard, explorer, was born in Groton, Connecticut, the son of John Ledyard, a merchant captain, and Abigail Hempstead. He was baptized in Groton on 21 November 1751 and spent the first ten years of his life in that seafaring town. His father died at sea in 1762, and Ledyard went to live with his maternal grandparents in Southold on Long Island, New York. After his mother's remarriage when he was thirteen, Ledyard went to live with his paternal grandparents in Hartford, Connecticut. In 1771 he was recruited by Dr. Eleazar Wheelock to come to the newly formed Dartmouth College and study to become a missionary to the Indians. Ledyard went to Dartmouth in April 1772 but remained there for only one year. Although he was a good student, he resisted discipline, and he became renowned at Dartmouth for his pranks. In April 1773 he hollowed out a canoe, Indian-style, and floated down the Connecticut River as far as Hartford (his memory is today preserved by the Ledyard Canoe Club at Dartmouth). Having departed from schooling, he commenced a life of high adventure.

Ledyard shipped out of New London, Connecticut, as a common seaman in late 1773. While his ship was anchored off Gibraltar, he had the temerity to desert and join a British regiment there, but he was soon reclaimed by the captain of his ship, Richard Deshon. Ledyard returned to

New London in late August 1774 and then went to New York City, whereupon he soon shipped for England. Arriving in Plymouth, he walked to London, where he arrived penniless. Learning that the famous Captain James Cook was about to leave for the third of his voyages of exploration, Ledyard went to Cook and persuaded the captain to take him on as a corporal of marines aboard Cook's ship the *Resolution*.

Cook's expedition, with Ledyard aboard, sailed from England on 12 July 1776. The explorers sailed through many parts of the South Pacific Ocean before they turned northward and reached Nootka Sound on the west coast of Vancouver Island on 28 March 1778. This landfall was apparently a turning point in Ledyard's thinking. Seeing the extreme west side of the North American continent and visualizing the riches that could be made in a fur trade, he dreamed that he might be the first American (though he was at the time in British uniform) to walk across the continent. His dream intensified a few months later when he walked across Unalaska Island to locate a Russian settlement there. Subsequent landfalls on Kamchatka and in southern China increased Ledyard's belief in his vision and possibly expanded it to include the notion of walking across Russia and Siberia to reach the Pacific Ocean.

After Captain Cook died in the Hawaiian Islands on 14 February 1779, Ledyard returned with his ship to England, reaching Deptford on 6 October 1780. He served in army barracks in England rather than serve against his fellow Americans during the remaining two years of the Revolutionary War. He then served on a British warship. When that ship went to Long Island, he deserted and returned to his mother and family. He wrote *A Journal of Captain Cook's Last Voyage to the Pacific Ocean* (1783).

Ledyard made futile efforts to interest American merchants in the fur trade that he foresaw in the Northwest and then went to Spain and later to France, where he made the acquaintance of both John Paul Jones and Thomas Jefferson. He proposed several abortive projects having to do with the Northwest and finally came up with an idea that suited his restless nature. He planned to walk across Russia and Siberia, take a ship from there to Nootka Sound, and then walk across North America to reach the American settlements on the East Coast. Thomas Jefferson approved the idea, and Ledyard set out from London to Stockholm and thence to St. Petersburg. He left the Russian capital on 1 June 1787 and reached Irkutsk on 15 August. He then took a boat down the Lena River and reached Yakutsk on 18 September. He returned to Irkutsk on 16 January 1788 and was soon arrested by the police of Czarina Catherine the Great, who brought him back to Moscow by 10 March and then to the border with Poland by 18 March 1788. Ledyard was warned not to repeat his attempt and was barred from entering Russia.

By May 1788 Ledyard was in London, where he won the support of Sir Joseph Banks, who recruited his services for the newly formed Association for Promoting the Discovery of the Interior Parts of Africa. Ledyard went from London to Paris, where he saw Jefferson for the last time, and then to Marseilles, where he took a ship to Alexandria, arriving there on 15 August 1788. Moving to Cairo, Ledyard sought to join a caravan that was to leave for Sennar. The circumstances of his death in Cairo are not certain, but it appears that he went into a violent rage over the delay of the departure of the caravan and that he suffered a broken blood vessel and died after three days. He had never married.

Ledyard was a dreamer and a visionary. Probably the first American to see what would become the American Northwest and British Columbia, he became entranced with those areas in the same manner that many other Americans would in the future. He accurately foresaw the profits that were to be made in the fur trade, and, had the merchants of New York and Philadelphia responded to his invitations, Americans might have cornered the market in furs in the Northwest. As it was, the American claims to the Northwest had to wait until the journey of Meriwether Lewis and William Clark (1804–1806) and the founding of Astoria (1811–1812). Clearly, Ledyard had a manner that could impress some of the notables of his time, Jefferson in particular. But he was ahead of his time in his projects, and his name had to yield place to the explorers who came almost twenty years after him, men such as Lewis and Clark who were better supplied and supported, as well as more careful in their journeys than the impetuous man from Groton, Connecticut.

S.W.C.

SIMON KENTON

[3 APRIL 1755–29 APRIL 1836]

Daniel Boone has been enshrined in storybooks and television shows as "the rippin'est, roarin'est, fightin'est man the frontier ever knew." But Kenton's career on the Appalachian frontier was just as remarkable. An illiterate Virginia farm boy, he became a scout, spy, Indian-fighter, and survivalist, living off forest roots and greens. Like Boone, Kenton also kept moving almost until the day he died, as an old man in an Ohio cabin.

Simon Kenton, frontiersman, was born near Hopewell village in Fauquier County, Virginia, the son of Mark Kenton, an emigrant from Ireland, and Mary Miller, of Scots-Welsh descent. His parents were farmers. Kenton was unschooled and never learned to read or write. As a youngster he avoided as much farm work as he could.

At age fifteen Kenton fell in love with Ellen Cummins, who, however, decided to marry a young farmer, William Leachman. In April 1771 Kenton, bared to the waist, greeted the newlyweds as they exited the church and challenged Leachman to a fight. Kenton was thoroughly thrashed. Several months later Kenton again provoked a fight with Leachman; managing to tie Leachman's long hair to a sapling, Kenton had the advantage and knocked his opponent unconscious. Believing he had killed Leachman and would be punished accordingly, Kenton fled to the western frontier of Virginia, along the Ohio River Valley. Living off roots and greens in the forest, he became a master of survival techniques. Kenton changed his last name to Butler to avoid detection. Eventually he earned enough money from assisting pioneer farmers to purchase a gun and powder, and he made his way to Pittsburgh. During the winter of 1771–1772 and 1773, Kenton and several companions hunted along the Cheat, the Ohio, and the Great and Little Kanawha Rivers. They were attacked by Indians along the Ohio and barely made their escape.

A master of wilderness survival, Kenton earned a reputation and the enmity of many Native Americans by leading raiding parties, even saving Daniel Boone from death at the hands of Shawnee warriors. This illustration originally appeared in The Romance and Tragedy of Pioneer Life *by Augustus L. Mason (1883).*

Kenton's first military experience was as a scout for Colonel Angus McDonald's unsuccessful campaign of June 1774 against Indians in the Muskingum Valley of Ohio. He served in the same capacity for the militia army of Virginia commanded by John Murray, earl of Dunmore, in its Indian expedition down the Ohio River in the fall of 1774. Kenton carried dispatches between Dunmore and Colonel Andrew Lewis, who commanded a wing of the army. Kenton was not present at the battle of Point Pleasant, 10 October 1774.

In spring 1775 Kenton explored north central Kentucky and made his campsite at Limestone (now Maysville), Kentucky, on the Ohio River, where he built a cabin and planted corn. He became a greeter and guide for newcomers and surveyors entering the Kentucky bluegrass country. He spent much of his time at Boonesborough and Logan's Fort. An event of 24 April 1777 brought fame to Kenton as a preeminent Indian fighter as well as a frontiersman. One hundred Shawnees led by Blackfish surprised the settlers at Boonesborough. Daniel Boone and a small party, outside the fort at the time, were set upon by warriors. Kenton rushed out of the gate and shot an Indian about to tomahawk Boone, whose leg had been broken by a gunshot. Hoisting Boone on his shoulders, he darted through a number of Indians to the safety of the fort. Variations of the story include Kenton himself tomahawking an Indian, knocking another down with the barrel of his rifle, and throwing Boone's body against two of the Indians.

From May to July 1778 Kenton served as a captain on George Rogers Clark's western expedition. From Kaskaskia, on the Mississippi River, Kenton went as a spy to the British post at Vincennes (Indiana) on the Wabash River. Kenton's report on the inadequate defenses of this post was sent to Kaskaskia by another scout, while Kenton returned to Kentucky, bearing news of Clark's capture of Kaskaskia.

Two months later Kenton accompanied Boone and a raiding party across the Ohio River. On 13 September 1778, while Kenton was attempting to get recovered horses across the river, he was captured by Shawnees. Kenton's capture was the beginning of an ordeal of many months—one of the most renowned episodes of American frontier history. Because the Indians had a score to settle with Kenton, he was sentenced to be burned at the stake—not as a local event, but as an intertribal ceremony to be held at Sandusky. Kenton gained a short reprieve by being adopted by a squaw but was subsequently tortured in various ways, including being forced to run the gauntlet nine times. He was twice saved from burning, first by the intervention of the renegade Simon Girty and then by both Chief Logan of the Mingo Indians and Pierre Druillard, an Indian trader and interpreter for the British. Eventually Kenton was turned over to the British garrison at Detroit. Escaping in June 1779, Kenton made his way to join Clark's troops at Vincennes.

Kenton is credited with many exploits, including the summer 1780 sinking of a boat in the Ohio River carrying a British cannon as an Indian raiding force led by British captain Henry Bird was returning from a devastating incursion into Kentucky. Kenton served as a scout in the expeditions against Shawnee towns led by Clark in 1780 (he fought at the 8 August Battle of Piqua) and November 1782, and by Benjamin Logan in 1786.

About 1780 Kenton, learning that his boyhood victim Leachman had lived, resumed using the name Kenton instead of Butler. Returning to Virginia in late 1783, Kenton brought his family to settle at Kenton's Station, near Limestone. His father died on the trip. From 1786 to 1794, with the rank of major, Kenton had charge of 100 Kentucky spies and scouts, known as "Kenton's boys." In this capacity, Kenton served with Kentucky militia assigned to General Anthony Wayne's army during 1793–1794. Kenton, however, was not present at the battle of Fallen Timbers on 20 August 1794.

Kenton married Martha "Patsey" Dowden in 1787. A fire at the Kenton house near Limestone in 1796 left his wife badly burned and caused her to have a miscarriage; she died a few days afterward. Kenton then married Elizabeth Jarboe, a cousin of his first wife, in 1798. In all, Kenton had twelve children: four with his first wife, seven with his second, and an illegitimate son with Ruth Calvin. At the end of 1798, the Kenton family moved across the Ohio River to a 1,000-acre farm four miles north of Springfield, Ohio.

Always searching for new lands to claim, Kenton, on his own hook, signed a treaty in 1802 with the "Wabash" Indians for lands between the Miami and Wabash Rivers—an action that had no legal standing. Kenton declined an appointment as brigadier general of the Ohio militia in 1804 because he and his son were about to leave for Missouri to visit Boone and to attend to land and business affairs there. In all, Kenton made four trips to Missouri. In 1810 Kenton joined the Methodist church, and the family moved near to Urbana, Ohio. During the War of 1812 Kenton joined Isaac Shelby's Kentucky troops; he was present but had no major role at the battle of the Thames, 5 October 1813.

Kenton invested in several frontier stores. His land speculation was enormous. Because of his illiteracy, he had to rely on other persons for his record keeping. Kenton at one time claimed some 400,000 acres in Kentucky, Ohio, Indiana, and Missouri. When he moved to Ohio he assigned 145,000 acres in Kentucky in trust to his son John. Because of unpaid taxes and court losses over disputed claims, Kenton forfeited most of his lands and in later life existed on the verge of poverty. He was imprisoned for debt in Urbana in 1810 for about a year and again, briefly, in 1812. Tricked into testifying in a land case in Kentucky in 1820, he wound up in the Mason County jail for debt, being released only after Kentucky abolished all imprisonment for debt in December 1821.

In 1820 Kenton settled in Zanesfield, Ohio, and in 1827 the state of Ohio provided him with a $20 monthly pension. In 1832 Kenton gave his Zanesfield property to his newlywed son, William, and then resided in a cabin four miles north of the town, where he died. He was buried near Zanesfield but was later reinterred at Urbana. Kenton County, Kentucky, established in 1840, is named for him. Kenton's life was a grand adventure. He seemed to be everywhere on the early trans-Appalachian frontier. As an Indian fighter and scout, he had no peer.

H.M.W.

GEORGE CROWNINSHIELD, JR.

[27 MAY 1766–26 NOVEMBER 1817]

Today, travel evokes images of luxury and ease. We travel to enjoy ourselves, to see sites, to "get away." But travel as a pastime is a relatively new concept. Its pioneers included wealthy Englishmen who formed the Society of the Dilettanti in 1743, a group devoted to opera, antiquities, fine wine, and other pleasures associated with touring Europe. Dilettantism gradually migrated across the Atlantic to men such as Crowninshield, the scion of a rich merchant family who commissioned the first American pleasure yacht, and sailed off in quest of European royalty and Napoleonic relics.

George Crowninshield, Jr., merchant and yachtsman, was born in Salem, Massachusetts, the son of George Crowninshield, a merchant, and Mary Derby. Though never married, he had one daughter, Clarissa (called Clara), whose mother was Elizabeth Rowell. The Crowninshields, among the richest Salem merchant families, gained their wealth through privateering and in the Far Eastern trade for which Salem was famed in the late eighteenth and early nineteenth centuries. After studying navigation and going to sea as a captain's clerk, Crowninshield commanded a ship to the West Indies in 1790 and, according to records, commanded the *Belisarius* to the East Indies four years later. Crowninshield's work was largely in the outfitting of ships, but he was known around Salem for his extracurricular activities, such as driving around the city in his bright yellow curricle, dressed in ostentatious style. He also chased fires, but rescuing people from ships in distress, for the purpose of which he maintained a vessel, was a passion.

In 1813 the American *Chesapeake* was defeated off Marblehead by HMS *Shannon*. Captain James Lawrence (of "don't give up the ship" fame) and a Lieutenant Ludlow were killed in the action, and their bodies were buried by the British in Halifax, Nova Scotia. Crowninshield captained the family

An oil on canvas painting of Crowninshield traditionally ascribed to Samuel Finley Breese Morse, an artist better known for inventing the telegraph.

ship that brought their bodies back for a ceremonious reburial in Salem and final interment in New York. Though the idea had not been his and the costs were shared by prominent Salemites, he was lavishly praised for the deed.

Crowninshield gained a measure of national and international fame (or notoriety) with his *Cleopatra's Barge,* the first American vessel built solely as a pleasure yacht. Launched in 1816, this barkentine was 83 feet long at the waterline, 23 feet in beam, and was built for speed. The elaborately painted and gilded vessel boasted a sumptuous interior. Its $50,000 cost of construction was probably matched by the expense of equipping and provisioning; everything about it was calculated to awe and impress.

Setting sail from Salem on 30 March 1817 with fourteen men and 300 letters of recommendation from prominent Americans, the yacht touched at the Azores and went on to Gibraltar, where Crowninshield hoped to receive the Princess of Wales aboard. That was the first of a series of disappointments: though *Cleopatra's Barge* attracted huge crowds of sensation-seekers at various ports around the Mediterranean, Crowninshield was unable to attract the royalty he had envisioned entertaining. The diary kept by his cynical cousin, "Philosopher Ben" Crowninshield, refers to the throngs of curiosity seekers as *canaille*, 'low class'. It records scenes of crowded disorder, drunkenness, seasickness, and uproar.

At Florence, George Crowninshield daily sought an introduction to the Empress Marie Louise, wife of Napoleon—then in exile on St. Helena. He had to settle for common souvenirs of the great man. At Elba he managed to acquire a piece of carpet and some tile fragments from Napoleon's rooms, as well as a pair of boots supposedly left behind by the fallen emperor because they were too small. At Rome, Bonaparte relatives managed to fob off on the gullible American a supposed adopted son of Napoleon. Not until the yacht was at sea did it become clear that the young man was merely a penniless nuisance. He and his four companions disappeared after their free passage to the United States.

By 3 October 1817 *Cleopatra's Barge* had returned to Salem, and, two months later, Crowninshield died there of a heart attack. He had been contemplating a similar cruise to northern Europe. The *Barge* went on to become the personal yacht of Kamehameha II, king of Hawaii, its intimacy with royalty coming only after the death of the man who thought that American wealth and ostentation could gain him entrée to the titled society of the Old World.

H.S.

THE

BLACK BOOK;

OR,

A CONTINUATION OF TRAVELS,

IN THE UNITED STATES.

IN TWO VOLUMES.

BY MRS. ANNE ROYALL,
Author of Sketches of History, Life, and Manners, in the United States,
and the Tennessean.

VOL. I.

WASHINGTON CITY, D. C.
PRINTED FOR THE AUTHOR
1828.

With her second foray into publishing (title page shown here), Royall began to inject more social criticism into her writing, railing against evangelism with claims that in "all countries, and in all ages, from the Druids down to brother Beecher, priests have aimed at universal power."

ANNE NEWPORT ROYALL

[11 JUNE 1769–1 OCTOBER 1854]

In our own time, the emergence of tourism as mainstream recreation—and as one of the world's largest industries—has created a new genre of travel journalism: newspaper sections and magazines filled with glossy stories about tropical resorts and package holidays. Anne Royall practiced a very different craft, using her travels through the American South to become an early muckraker. Her eccentricity and attacks on evangelical religion even led to her being prosecuted, under an archaic statute, as a "common scold."

Anne Newport Royall, travel writer and journalist, was born near Baltimore, Maryland, the daughter of William Newport and Mary (maiden name unknown). The Newports moved to the Pennsylvania frontier in 1772 and by 1775 were living near Hanna's Town, the Westmoreland County seat, after which time William Newport disappears from the records. Anne learned to read at an early age from her father and briefly attended school in a log cabin. After the death of her mother's second husband (*c.* 1782), she moved with her mother and her half brother to Middle River, Virginia. In 1787 she and her mother became domestics for William Royall of Sweet Springs Mountain, now in West Virginia.

Appreciating her intellect and wit, William Royall undertook Anne's education by introducing her to the works of Thomas Paine and Voltaire and by instructing her in the principles of Freemasonry. She married William Royall in 1797 and managed his estate until his death in December 1812. Selling the plantation the year after his death, she indulged a long-held desire to travel, spending most of the next decade in Alabama. No children had issued from the marriage.

Anne Royall turned to literature for a livelihood after relatives of William Royall succeeded in overturning his will in 1819, claiming that she had forged the will, treated her husband badly during their marriage, and cohabitated with him before marriage. She denied all but the last charge. While dodging creditors, Royall supported herself by writing about the rapidly expanding and developing nation. In preparation for what was to become *Letters from Alabama on Various Subjects* (1830), Royall gathered the letters she had written between 1817 and 1822 to her young lawyer friend, Matthew Dunbar, as she traveled through Kentucky, Tennessee, and Alabama. While still in Alabama, she began work on *The Tennessean* (1827), a historical romance describing a secret expedition of frontiersmen to Spanish-ruled New Mexico, which unsuccessfully combines the conventions of the domestic romance, dime novel, and shipwreck narrative. To support herself, Royall also petitioned the federal government for a pension as a Revolutionary War widow.

Using Washington, D.C., as her home base, Royall traveled extensively from 1824 to 1830. Recording her journeys in nine published volumes, Royall described every substantial city and town in the United States. Her dauntless personality and her husband's Masonic connections enabled her to gather an impressive list of subscribers for *Sketches of History, Life, and Manners in the United States* (1826), signed "a Traveller," which traced her trip from Alabama to New England from 1823 through 1825. In this work she discussed politics, education, religion, and social vices, depicting in detail colleges, schools, churches, hospitals, almshouses, prisons, museums, theaters, and libraries. She also interviewed prominent citizens and included population, crop, and trade statistics. A signature mark of both her travel writing and her later journalism was the "pen portrait," a brief, vivid sketch of a celebrity's appearance and character. Royall's travel works demonstrate her talents as a roving correspondent: boundless curiosity, attention to detail, and investigative skills.

Except for *Sketches of History*, which is good-humored, her travel writing also reveals a liberal political philosophy and acerbic wit that some readers found offensive. In *The Black Book* (3 vols., 1828–1829), *Mrs. Royall's Pennsylvania* (2 vols., 1829), and *Mrs. Royall's Southern Tour* (3 vols., 1830–1831), she attacked, often fervently, political corruption, the enemies of Freemasonry, and Protestant evangelicals such as Ezra Stiles Ely and

Lyman Beecher. In her *Southern Tour*, Royall dismissed tract literature and missionary societies as "vile speculations to amass money" with the explanation that their promoters collect "money . . . from the poor and ignorant, and no man of sense would pay for the gospel which is to be had without a price" (vol. 3, p. 244). Despite her diatribes against opponents and flattery of subscribers, Royall's travel works are still of historical and social value.

Royall's revelations and her animosity toward Evangelicals, whom she contemptuously labeled "Holy Rollers," "Holy Willies," and "Blackcoats," resulted in her widely publicized trial in 1829 on the obsolete charge of common scold or public nuisance. Royall was convicted for twice berating members of a neighboring evangelical congregation who tormented her with heckling and stones, "usually at night," noted Royall, " 'when the out-pouring of divine goodness' is most powerful" (*Pennsylvania*, vol. 2, app., p. 2). Deeming the traditional punishment of a public dunking too ludicrous, Judge William Cranch fined Royall $10 and ordered her to post a $100 bond as a guarantee of her future conduct. Many journalists viewed the event as an attack on freedom of speech and the press, and two reporters for the *Washington National Intelligencer* paid her fine and bond. James Gordon Bennett (1795–1872), a Washington reporter who later founded the *New York Herald,* sat with Royall throughout the trial.

The infirmities of age and the hostile reception she sometimes met with on her 1830 tour of southern states encouraged Royall to settle in Washington and to abandon travel writing for the more sedentary occupation of journalist. With the help of Sarah Stack, a younger friend who acted as her assistant and companion, Royall began publishing on 3 December 1831 a four-page weekly newspaper called *Paul Pry.* Named after an 1825 English comedy by John Poole and printed in Royall's kitchen, *Paul Pry* contained ads, humorous and poetic fillers, local news, political news, and editorials. An independent newspaper, *Paul Pry* is notable for its exposés of government graft and the Bank of the United States, its editorials pleading for civil service and public health reforms, and its attacks on Evangelicals and Anti-Masons. The last issue of *Paul Pry* appeared on 19 November

1836. It was succeeded on 2 December 1836 by the *Huntress,* in which Royall continued to expose ills and espouse causes. She denounced the beef monopoly, defended Catholic foreigners, berated legislators from blocking improvements in the western states, and argued against abolition. The *Huntress* also included a joke column and a literary page with poems and sketches reprinted from popular writers, including Dickens and Seba Smith, creator of the comic Yankee character, Major Jack Dowling. As Royall aged, she relied increasingly on others to assist with the paper, particularly John Henry Simmes, an orphan she took into her household. By 1854, Simmes was both printing and writing almost every issue. When he married in March 1854, Royall attempted to carry on without him, but publication of the paper ceased in May. In June 1854, Royall revived the paper in a pamphlet-size format, but the second series lasted for only three issues. In the final issue, which appeared on 24 July, Royall offered a prayer for the eternal "Union of these States" and noted that she had "thirty-one cents in the world" (quoted in James, p. 386). She died in Washington, D.C.

Royall's contemporaries viewed her as an eccentric—sometimes even as a figure of fun—because of her indifference to her appearance, her tart tongue, her strongly held and often unfashionable views, and her reformer's zeal. Frederick A. Packard of the *Hampden Journal* represented the views of many when he dismissed Royall as "a silly old hag" who belonged in "some asylum or work house" (18 July 1827). Yet Royall contributed significantly to social history and journalism. Her work not only contains valuable descriptions of institutions, customs, and personalities but also demonstrates the potency of the press as a watchdog of freedom against government corruption and abuse.

J.M.M.

JOHN COLTER

[c. 1775–NOVEMBER 1813]

After serving Lewis and Clark as a skilled marksman and scout, Colter chose to stay out West for another five years, trapping furs and expanding on the explorers' discoveries. During one epic trek, alone and in winter, Colter ranged across the mountains and river valleys of Wyoming and Idaho, and may have become the first white man to see the wonders of Yellowstone. Colter also survived several encounters with hostile Indians, including a legendary escape from Blackfoot warriors who stripped him naked and let him run for his life across a cactus-studded plain.

John Colter, fur trapper and explorer, was probably born in the vicinity of Staunton, Virginia, the son of farmers John Colter and Ellen Shields. The Colter family (also spelled Coalter and Coulter) that farmed near the Shenandoah Valley community of Staunton traced its lineage back to Micajah Coalter, a Scots-Irish settler who arrived in Virginia about 1700. Virtually nothing is known about John Colter's youth or early adult years. The earliest record of him dates to 15 October 1803, when Meriwether Lewis, on his way by keelboat from Pittsburgh to St. Louis, stopped at the Ohio River town of Maysville, Kentucky. There Captain Lewis enlisted Colter—then about thirty years of age—and several other men as privates in the Corps of Discovery.

Colter began his service with the Lewis and Clark expedition as a boat-man, but excellent marksmanship earned him promotion to hunter by the time the party reached the great falls of the Missouri in 1805. Colter subsequently served as a hunter, scout, and messenger during the outward journey to the Pacific and the return east. In August 1806, while descending the Missouri (in present-day South Dakota), the homeward-bound expedition met two American trappers, Joseph Dixon (or Dickson) and Forest (or Forrest) Hancock. Colter asked permission to join these

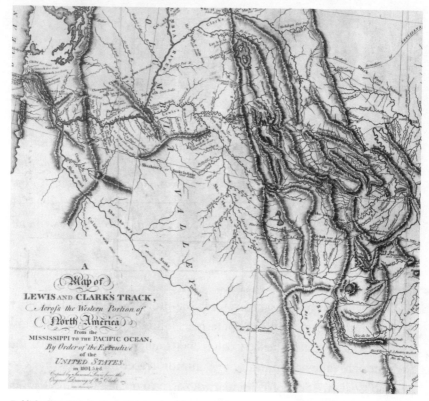

Published in 1814, the first official map of the country opened by Lewis and Clark shows the territory covered by Colter before he parted company with the Corps of Discovery in present-day South Dakota.

men, who were headed upstream. William Clark wrote in his journal that the request was granted because "we were disposed to be of service to any-one of our party who had performed their duty as well as Colter had done."

Colter and his new companions spent the winter of 1806–1807 trapping beaver in the upper Missouri drainage. Among the first American trappers to penetrate this far west, they may have included portions of the Yellowstone River drainage in their travels. For unknown reasons, the partnership dissolved the following spring, and Colter resumed his return trip toward St. Louis.

Near the mouth of the Platte in August 1807, Colter encountered the supply-laden boats of St. Louis fur trader Manuel Lisa, who convinced Colter to join his expedition. (One probable factor in Colter's decision to return upstream once again was that Lisa's group included fellow hunter George Drouillard and two other veterans of the Lewis and Clark expedition.) Colter's fame as an explorer and mountain man rests on events that occurred subsequently, during his three-year stint in the upper Missouri basin as one of Lisa's "free trappers."

Perhaps on Colter's recommendation, Lisa established his trading post, Fort Raymond (or Manuel's Fort), not on the Missouri but on the Yellowstone, at the mouth of the Big Horn River. This location (in present-day south central Montana) lay within the traditional territory of the Crow Indians, a fact that probably angered the Crows' traditional enemies, the Blackfoot Indians. From there Colter set out in November 1807—alone, "with a pack of thirty pounds weight, his gun and some ammunition" (Brackenridge, p. 91)—to visit the Crows in their villages along the upper Yellowstone and encourage them to come trade at Lisa's post. During this winter trek, Colter explored much of present-day northwestern Wyoming. He probably ranged as far west as Jackson Hole and perhaps the upper Snake River's Teton Basin (in present-day Idaho) before returning to Fort Raymond sometime in the spring of 1808.

The only direct testament to Colter's 1807–1808 route is William Clark's 1810 manuscript map. This map contains major inaccuracies (of both scale and location) for the Yellowstone River basin. Clark's cartographic effort (which served as the basis for the famous map that first appeared in Nicholas Biddle's 1814 official *History of the Expedition under the Command of Captains Lewis and Clark*) shows a dashed line marked "Colter's Route," but much of that route is contradicted by the region's actual geography. Historians agree that during his epic winter journey Colter became the first Euro-American to explore portions of present-day Yellowstone National Park. However, the area of hot springs that Colter saw and described—which became known to trappers as Colter's Hell—was located well to the east of Yellowstone, along the Shoshone (or "Stinking Water") River.

In the summer of 1808 Colter traveled west to the Three Forks headwaters of the Missouri. There he met a hunting party of Crow and Flathead

Indians. Shortly after Colter joined the group, it was attacked near the Gallatin River by a large party of Blackfoot Indians. Colter fought alongside his companions. (Meriwether Lewis's unfortunate 1806 encounter with a Blackfoot party on the Marias River notwithstanding, many historians trace the origin of the Blackfoot Indians' decades-long enmity toward American trappers to Colter's presence at the 1808 battle.)

Later that year, while trapping on the Jefferson River, Colter and John Potts, another Lewis and Clark veteran, were surprised by Blackfoot Indians. Potts was killed almost immediately. Colter, captured and stripped naked, was permitted to run for his life while being pursued by a group of armed young men. Colter's footrace across the cactus-studded plains, between five and six miles to the banks of the Jefferson (or, in one version of the episode, the Madison) River—and his subsequent escape back to Lisa's post—became one of the most durable tales in western American history, immortalized in Washington Irving's *Astoria* and Hiram Chittenden's *Fur Trade of the Far West*.

During the spring of 1810, after another year on the upper Missouri, Colter returned to the Three Forks region as a hunter and guide for Lisa's expanding Missouri Fur Company. Incessant Blackfoot attacks thinned the ranks of company employees. After narrowly escaping death once again, Colter supposedly declared, "I will leave the country day after tomorrow—and damned if I ever come into it again" (James, pp. 65–66). Within a month's time, he canoed to St. Louis. There he provided geographic information to William Clark (used in Clark's 1810 map) and to Wilson Price Hunt, leader of the 1811 Astor overland expedition to the Pacific. He also predicted the feasibility of wagon travel over the passes of the Continental Divide. He never returned to the Far West.

Almost nothing is known of Colter's physical appearance. A fellow trapper simply recalled him as of medium height and build. In 1811 he settled a small farm near the lower Missouri River hamlet of La Charette (where one of his neighbors was octogenarian Kentucky woodsman Daniel Boone). His wife, whom he married in 1811 (and about whom nothing is known but the name Sally, also shown as "Loucy"), possibly was an Indian.

Although no birth records document the fact, local tradition asserts that he had a son named Hiram. He died of jaundice in La Charette.

Colter's explorations of the upper Missouri River drainage (specifically the Three Forks and Yellowstone River country) contributed directly to the initial expansion of the American fur trade into that region. It is ironic, then, that Colter's coincidental presence among the Crows in 1808 has been seen as the initial cause for the bitter warfare between Blackfoot Indians and trappers that retarded effective American penetration of the area for a number of years.

For almost two centuries tales of Colter's exploits—especially his solitary winter trek and his desperate race to escape Blackfoot pursuers—have found an appreciative audience among Americans eager to read about dramatic adventures of the mountain men. Colter probably owes at least some of his initial popular fame to the fact that he was the first American trapper of British (that is, not French or Spanish) ancestry to explore the northern Rockies; as such he was ready-made for apotheosis by Washington Irving and other nationalistic nineteenth-century writers. However, the stories of his legendary feats are based on credible testimony about actual events, and they will doubtless continue to provide drama to the history of the Far West fur trade.

J.L.

GIACOMO
CONSTANTINO
BELTRAMI

[1779–6 JANUARY 1855]

*Early nineteenth century America became a magnet for European travelers
who were curious to understand the new nation and explain it to their coun-
trymen. The most famous such observer, Alexis de Tocqueville, focused on
the social and political attitudes of the young republic. Others condemned
Southern slavery, or Yankee philistinism; one English captain published a diary
so scathing that Americans burned him in effigy. Giacomo Beltrami, by contrast, showed little interest in the people of the New World. Instead, he relished
the rawness of nature in America—while shielding himself from thunderstorms beneath a red silk umbrella.*

Giacomo Constantino Beltrami, explorer, was born in Bergamo, Italy,
the son of Giovanni Battista Beltrami, a Venetian customs official, and
Margherita Carozzi. His early career was formed by the Napoleonic presence
in northern Italy. Enamored of the ideals of the French Revolution and an
admirer of Napoleon Bonaparte, Beltrami joined the militia of the Cisalpine
Republic in 1796 and rose to become a vice inspector of armies. In 1807 he
became chancellor of the Department of Justice of Parma and served as a
judge until 1813. As the Napoleonic empire began to crumble, Beltrami
retired from the bench and became a member of the Florentine salon of
Louise Maximilienne Caroline, the countess of Albany and the widow of
Charles Edward Stuart, better known as the "Young Pretender" or "Bonnie
Prince Charlie." Beltrami also forged important relationships with Countess
Giulia Spada de Medici and Countess Geronima Compagnoni.

Because the political climate of his homeland was at that time hostile to
his ideals, Beltrami left Italy in 1821. He traveled in France, Germany, and

An 1844 watercolor by John Casper Wild of Fort Snelling, where Beltrami arrived in 1823, determined to find the source of the Mississippi River.

England before deciding to go to North America. He sailed from Liverpool in November 1822 and arrived in Philadelphia, Pennsylvania, on 30 December 1822. While in the United States he was able to draw funds from an account with the Baring Bank in London; the account was quite possibly created through the good offices of the countess of Albany. Beltrami went to Baltimore, Maryland, and then to Washington, D.C., where he had an impromptu meeting with President James Monroe. Beltrami traveled to Pittsburgh, Pennsylvania, which served as a point of departure for his travels in the Old Northwest (presently the American Midwest).

Beltrami proceeded to St. Louis, Missouri, and took the steamboat *Virginia* to Fort St. Anthony (later Fort Snelling) at the junction of the Minnesota and Mississippi Rivers. In July 1823, Beltrami joined the exploratory party of U.S. major Stephen H. Long and headed northward from Fort St. Anthony. In the company of the American explorers, Beltrami was definitely the odd man out; he cherished thunderstorms and raging rivers while his companions simply endured them. Beltrami lamented in his letters to Countess Compagnoni that he was in the company of "people who had no idea of stopping for anything but a broken saddle" (*A Pilgrimage*, p. 318).

After an altercation with Major Long, Beltrami left the American party on 9 August 1823 and pushed southward from Pembina (on the U.S.–Canadian border) with a part-Indian interpreter and two Chippewa guides. Determined to find the source of the Mississippi River, Beltrami entered Sioux territory, whereupon his interpreter and guides deserted him. Beltrami forged on alone for several days, pulling his canoe behind him since he had not learned how to paddle. His red silk umbrella served both as a flag of civilization and as a covering for his personal effects. Beltrami met another Indian who agreed to guide him, and he continued his journey. On 28 August 1823, he came to a small, heart-shaped lake that lay between the watersheds of the Red and Mississippi Rivers. Beltrami named this Lake Julia in honor of Countess Giulia (who had died in 1820) and exulted that "these sources are the actual sources of the Mississippi" (*A Pilgrimage*, p. 413). In fact, he was mistaken. Nine years later Henry Schoolcraft found the actual source—Lake Itasca. But Beltrami was in good company: David Thompson (1798), Zebulon Pike (1806), and Lewis Cass and Henry Schoolcraft (1820) had all named incorrect sources.

Confident that he had achieved his goal, Beltrami returned to Fort Snelling and proceeded to St. Louis and then to New Orleans, where he wrote *La découverte des sources du Mississippi* . . . (1824). He traveled across Mexico and then returned to the United States, where he wrote pamphlets defending his claim. He then returned to Europe and lived in Paris (c. 1830–1834) and Germany (1834–1836) before finally returning to Italy. He lived in retirement on his estate in Filottrano and died there, several years before Italian unification was achieved.

Beltrami's romantic spirit was indicative of the European attitude toward the American wilderness. To a generation of Europeans who had been inspired by the promise of the French Revolution and the power of the Napoleonic empire, post-1815 European politics appeared both stale and regressive. Beltrami was one of a number of Europeans who came to the United States in order to experience nature firsthand. In this he was highly successful. Beltrami admired the American wilderness more than he did the young American Republic and the North American Indians. It is perhaps fortunate that he witnessed American institutions before the advent of Jacksonian democracy, which might have confirmed his doubts as to the viability of the democratic experiment in North America.

As an explorer, Beltrami has received less credit than he deserves, although the state of Minnesota has named a county, a village, and a park after him. Although Schoolcraft discovered the source of the Mississippi, Beltrami deserves recognition for having floundered through brush, stream, and unknown land in search of the source. Striving to be another Christopher Columbus, Beltrami left a series of letters (published in English in 1828) that provide insight into the influence of early-nineteenth-century romanticism on a European traveling in North America.

S.W.C.

A detail from a painting by Western artist John F. Clymer entitled Marie Dorion Escape *that seeks to convey the harsh conditions she endured after her husband's trapping party was murdered in the winter of 1814.*

MARIE DORION

[*c.* 1790–5 SEPTEMBER 1850]

Explorers have always relied on native guides for help in navigating the language, customs, and landscape of unknown territories. Often, the very survival of an expedition has hinged on a go-between's skills as interpreter and conciliator. Yet very few of these interlocutors merit more than a footnote in history books; in America, only Sacagawea endures in popular memory. One of the many native guides who deserves greater attention is Marie Dorion. A young Indian married to a fur trader, Dorion, with two young boys in tow, served as an interpreter for an expedition that followed in the footsteps of Lewis and Clark. She bore another child along the way, and also survived innumerable perils as a pioneer in Oregon.

Marie Dorion, interpreter, was born into the Iowa tribe as Marie Aioe, or Marie L'Aguivoise; both versions of her maiden surname, variations on the word "Iowa," appear in early nineteenth-century records of Oregon and Washington territories. Nothing is known of her life until she became the common-law wife of a half-Sioux, half–French Canadian fur trader, Pierre Dorion, Jr., around 1806 in the vicinity of what is now Yankton, South Dakota. Pierre Dorion, Sr., had been an interpreter and a guide with the Meriwether Lewis and William Clark expedition (1804–1806). By 1811 Marie had become the mother of two sons, who themselves became interpreters and guides later in life.

Early in 1811 Pierre Dorion was invited to become an interpreter with the overland division of the Wilson Price Hunt expedition on their journey to Fort Astoria, the Pacific Fur Company outpost being built at the mouth of the Columbia River. Despite the objections of Hunt, the expedition leader, Dorion insisted that Marie and their sons accompany him, and the party left St. Louis in March, traveling up the Missouri River by keelboat.

Disembarking at the present site of Pierre, South Dakota, the Hunt expedition continued westward by land. During the arduous journey, Marie Dorion gave birth to a third son, who lived eight days. On 15 February 1812, the travelers finally reached Fort Astoria, in what is now Oregon; since their departure from St. Louis, they had traveled 3,500 miles. Their arrival was due in large part to the interpreting skills of Marie Dorion. Later chroniclers, including Washington Irving, singled out Marie for her steadfastness and courage during the trek, which saw several members of the party drop out from exhaustion.

After spending more than a year at Fort Astoria, the Dorions joined a beaver-trapping expedition to eastern Oregon in July 1813. A campsite was established some 300 miles from Astoria at the confluence of the Boise and Snake Rivers, on what is now the Idaho-Oregon border. Marie and her children remained behind while Pierre Dorion and a trapping party went off to catch beavers. Sometime early that winter, Marie set out to join her husband, perhaps to warn him of an impending Indian attack. In January 1814, however, she learned that Pierre Dorion, along with the rest of the trappers, had been massacred by Indians; when she returned to the campsite, she discovered that everyone who had remained behind had also been killed by Indians.

Marie Dorion fled on horseback with her two children and headed northwest to the Columbia River. Again she faced hardship as bad weather forced her to camp for nearly two months in the Blue Mountains before she and the children were given shelter by friendly Walla Walla Indians. In April, resuming her journey, she reached the Columbia and encountered the surviving members of the original Hunt expedition who were returning to St. Louis. The party took her and her sons to Fort Okanogan, a Canadian-owned fur-trading station nearly 200 miles to the north. Here she settled, apparently without incident, for a number of years. A liaison with a French Canadian trapper named Venier resulted in the birth of a daughter in 1819.

Sometime in the early 1820s, Dorion began living with a French Canadian interpreter named Jean Baptiste Toupin; a son was born to the couple in 1825, followed by a daughter two years later. In 1841, the family moved westward to a farm in the Willamette Valley, near the present site of Salem, Oregon. In July of that year, Dorion and Toupin were formally married in a Roman Catholic ceremony. By this time, the story of Marie Dorion was widely known throughout North America, the consequence of its appearance in Washington Irving's book *Astoria* (1836), an account of the expedition and settlement, and in published memoirs of early settlers.

Dorion died near Salem, apparently from natural causes. The priest who officiated at her burial service noted incorrectly that her age was "about 100," an indication that the harshness of her life had taken its toll on her appearance. Acclaimed during her lifetime as a heroine of the wilderness and the equal of Sacagawea, the renowned Indian guide and interpreter on the Lewis and Clark expedition, Dorion fell into obscurity after her death; her feats and contributions were rediscovered in the twentieth century.

A.T.K.

On a mission to test the United States' commitment to liberty, a young Wright, illustrated here in 1881 by J. Gorbitz, arrived in New York in 1818 and spent the next thirty years battling against America's resistance to social change.

FRANCES WRIGHT

[6 SEPTEMBER 1795–13 DECEMBER 1852]

The early decades of the nineteenth century witnessed a florescence of utopian and social reform movements, and Wright was one of the period's most colorful radicals. She traveled across America, agitating against slavery, organized religion, capital punishment, and the degradation of women—views that incited mob violence and earned her the sobriquet "The Great Red Harlot of Infidelity."

Frances Wright, reformer and author, was born in Dundee, Scotland, the daughter of James Wright, a linen merchant, and Camilla Campbell. Wright's father was an ardent supporter of Thomas Paine, and although "Fanny" was younger than three when her parents died, she later remarked on "a somewhat singular coincidence in views between a father and daughter, separated by death when the first had not reached the age of twenty-nine, and when the latter was in infancy" (Eckhardt, pp. 5–6). After her parents' death, she and her siblings were parceled out to various relatives, and Wright went to live with her aunt and maternal grandfather in England. She and her sister Camilla were reunited in Dawlish around 1806, only to suffer the death of their brother and their grandfather three years later.

Although Wright was, by her own account, surrounded by "rare and extensive libraries" as a child, her practical education came from the streets of London, where she had seen thousands of beggars whom her grandfather, an idle socialite, said were too lazy to work. She also witnessed enclosures by wealthy lords in Dawlish who ruthlessly forced peasants from their land. Such injustices left indelible marks on Wright's psyche, leaving her to "wear ever in her heart the cause of the poor and helpless," a cause she would spend the rest of her life trying to further (Eckhardt, p. 11).

Wright and Camilla left Dawlish in 1813, moving to Scotland to live with their uncle James Mylne, a professor at the University of Glasgow whose staunch opposition to the slave trade also made a lasting impression on Wright. In Scotland she began to explore her talents as a writer, completing her first version of *Altorf,* a tragedy about the Swiss fight for self-rule, as well as a historical fantasy about a young female disciple of Epicurus, which she eventually published in 1822 as *A Few Days in Athens.*

By the time Wright turned twenty-one, her sights were firmly set on America. Eager to test the new Republic's commitment to liberty, she and her sister set sail for the New World in August 1818, a portentous trip that would begin Wright's controversial relationship with a country whose ideals were more noble in theory than in practice. Initially staying in New York, Wright fell in love with America, a country that seemed characterized by neither extreme wealth nor extreme poverty.

During Wright's two-year stay, *Altorf* was staged in New York (1819) and in Philadelphia (1820) with modest success, although its publication went largely unnoticed. Wright then set out to see the "real" America, traveling throughout the Northeast and collecting observations that would eventually become *Views of Society and Manners in America* (1821), a memoir constructed from a series of letters to a Scottish friend. Published after her return to England, the book was warmly received by Americans who liked her romantic portrait, which naively asked, "What country before was ever rid of so many evils?" (Eckhardt, p. 45).

Despite a patronizing reception in England, the text also won Wright the support of European reformers like Jeremy Bentham and the marquis de Lafayette. Wright's friendship with the latter was particularly intimate and, in 1824, she returned to the United States as part of his entourage amidst rumors that the two were lovers. Although Wright suggested that Lafayette either marry or adopt her, the general did neither, and by the time he returned to France in 1825, his young protégée's attentions were fixed elsewhere.

Wright had become consumed with the issue of slavery. In 1825, after visiting Robert Owen's utopian society in New Harmony, Indiana, she purchased 640 acres near Memphis, Tennessee, named the settlement "Nashoba," and began her grand effort to confront the country's most painful dilemma. After acquiring several slaves, Wright set out to prove that the institution was unprofitable. She argued that if slaves were given an education and a goal—the promise of freedom in approximately five years—they would not only work harder, but in the end the settlement would undersell its competitors. Although radical in its inception, Wright's proposal was tentatively endorsed by Thomas Jefferson, who thought her plan had "its aspects of promise," and hesitantly supported by James Monroe.

Ultimately, Wright's experiment was destroyed by alleged improprieties. In addition to lean harvests and overwhelming debt, her health failed, and during her brief return to Europe the *Genius of Universal Emancipation* (1827) printed excerpts from Nashoba overseer James Richardson's journal, which described the "free love" practiced at the colony. Suggestions of miscegenation angered even abolitionists, and Wright did little to refute the contents of the journal. Upon her return to the United States she printed a full account of her views in the *Memphis Advocate* and embarked on a crusade against organized religion. This final affront to morality cost the settlement its financial backing, and by 1828, all of the other free members, including Camilla, had abandoned the project. Keeping her promise to her thirty slaves, Wright nevertheless secured their freedom a year later, personally escorting them to Haiti.

First, however, Wright joined Robert Dale Owen as coeditor of the *New Harmony Gazette,* making her one of the first women to edit a widely circulated paper in the United States. Likewise, in July 1828, Wright shocked Americans by becoming one of the first women to speak publicly in front of a mixed audience. Traveling from Boston to New Orleans, Wright blasted religion, capital punishment, and the treatment of women while simultaneously promoting equality and tolerance. Despite her rhetorical brilliance, in some cases her "strengths and virtues, themselves, became primary offenses" (Kissel, p. 8), and in several cities mob violence erupted during her lectures.

Settling outside of New York City, in 1829 Wright purchased a church near the Bowery, converting it into a "Hall of Science," a building that served as a lecture hall as well as a publishing house for the *Free Enquirer* (formerly the *New Harmony Gazette*). Although a vehement supporter of women's rights (the promotion of birth control earned her the title of "The Great Red Harlot of Infidelity"), she increasingly fixed her attention on public education, calling for free state boarding schools funded by a graduated property tax. Wright's push for educational reform eventually led to her leadership of the free-thought movement in New York and her involvement in the Workingman's party, which the opposition facetiously dubbed "the Fanny Wright party."

Wright returned to Europe in 1830 with her sister. After a brief stay in Paris, Camilla died, and in 1831, Wright married William Phiquepal, a French physician with whom she had traveled to Haiti in 1829. The couple had one child, and Wright spent several years in Paris away from the limelight. Unfortunately, her efforts in America collapsed without her presence. The Hall of Science was converted into a Methodist church, public interest in education waned, and the *Free Enquirer* ceased publication in 1835. Nevertheless, when she returned to America with her husband, Wright resumed her role as lecturer, joining Democrats on the campaign trail in both 1836 and 1838. Although she valiantly argued against the Bank of the United States in 1836 and continued to support both an independent treasury and gradual emancipation, she became discouraged by the public's lack of interest in her increasingly Comtean view of social ills. She left the United States in 1839 for France and spent the next decade embroiled in financial struggles, traveling from America to Europe five times. She and her husband divorced in 1850, and Wright lost custody of her child. She died in Cincinnati.

A controversial figure, Wright dared to hold America to its promise of "liberty and justice for all." Equally hated and adored, she paved the way for later social reforms, and ultimately her life reflects the story of America's resistance to change, of "how much people love the rhetoric of equality and how little they are inclined to make equality possible" (Eckhardt, p. 4).

D.G.P.

GEORGE CATLIN

[26 JULY 1796–23 DECEMBER 1872]

The 1830s proved a devastating decade for Native Americans. Whole tribes were ravaged by epidemic disease and the westward march of white settlers. This was also a period at the cusp of the photographic era. Were it not for Catlin, a romantic artist who traveled the plains to paint Indians on their own turf—"a vast country of green fields where the men are all red"—we would have little visual image of the Mandan and many other tribes.

George Catlin, artist, was born in Wilkes-Barre, Pennsylvania, the son of Putnam Catlin, a lawyer, farmer, and minor officeholder, and Polly Sutton. Catlin grew up in northwestern Pennsylvania and Broome County, New York. He entered law school in Litchfield, Connecticut, in July 1817, and the next year he was admitted to the bar in Connecticut and Pennsylvania.

Catlin abandoned his law practice within a few years, sold his law books, and in 1821 moved to Philadelphia, determined to make his mark as an artist. He had dabbled as a painter in the past, but now art became his profession. He brought to it an unquenchable romanticism and, at most, a rudimentary talent. Catlin specialized in miniatures (those of some of his family members show him to advantage), exhibited regularly, and became a member of the Pennsylvania Academy of the Fine Arts in 1824. But portraiture was dull, and miniatures were inadequate to the scope of his ambition. Catlin was already nurturing the idea of becoming a historical painter when he moved to New York in 1827, the year after he was elected a member of the newly founded National Academy of Design.

In 1828, Catlin married Clara Gregory, the daughter of a prominent Albany family. Recognition had already come his way with a commission from the New York Common Council to paint a full-length portrait of Governor

An 1849 oil painting by William Fisk depicts Catlin who as a young man in 1830 abandoned his law practice and headed west to become the first artist to offer the world a representative picture of Indian life.

DeWitt Clinton (City Hall, New York). Modest success was in the offing, but Catlin was still restless, still in search of an animating purpose for his life and art. He found it, he recalled, when he spotted a delegation of western American Indians on a visit to Philadelphia: their appearance captivated him, and he resolved to paint Indians, "thus snatching from a hasty oblivion what could be saved for the benefit of posterity, and perpetuating it, as a fair and just monument, to the memory of a truly lofty and noble race" (*Letters and Notes*, vol. 1, p. 3). Realism was never Catlin's strong suit. He was a dreamer, wildly impractical, and a driven man beset by contrary impulses, at once exploitive and tenderhearted, negligent and loving, self-centered and altruistic. His stated goal was to win fame and fortune by creating an Indian Gallery. Confident his endeavor would command public support, in the spring of 1830 he moved to St. Louis, Missouri, to launch his career as a painter of Indians.

Catlin polished his artistic skills on visiting members of various tribes (he was good at painting faces but weak at anatomy), and then he boarded a steamboat on 26 March 1832 for the 1,800-mile trip up the Missouri River to Fort Union, in the heart of Indian country. He painted Blackfeet, Crow, and all the river tribes, concentrating on the Mandan, whose devastation by smallpox five years later confirmed the importance of his visionary enterprise. Subsequently he toured the southern plains (1834), the Mississippi River and the Great Lakes region (1835), and the sacred red pipestone quarry on the Coteau des Prairies (1836). He described his travels in letters to the newspapers, which were collected in his 1841 classic *Letters and Notes on the Manners, Customs, and Conditions of the North American Indians,* and between trips he exhibited his growing collection of Indian paintings to help cover expenses.

Catlin's Indian Gallery was a novelty. Artists before him had painted Indian dignitaries visiting in Washington, D.C., or had portrayed them in council with American officials in the field. Catlin's claim to originality turned on the nature and extent of his coverage. Besides more than 300 portraits of men and women from some fifty tribes, he displayed 200 paintings of Indians on their own turf, going about their everyday activities. His catalogs and advertising emphasized these "beautiful Landscapes of the Prairies of the 'Far West'—Views of Indian villages—Dances, Sports and Amusements" (*New York Morning Herald*, 27 Nov. 1837). He rightfully insisted that he was the first artist to offer the world a representative picture of Indian life based on personal observation. Though he described his paintings in his 1837 catalog as "rather as *fac similes* of what he has seen, than as finished works of art" (p. 36), his best portraits (*Black Hawk, Buffalo Bull, Red Bear, Mint, Mountain of Rocks, Sky-se-ro-ka, Osceola*, and *Little Wolf*, for example) show people, not romantic stereotypes, and the ethnographic value of his work has only appreciated with the passage of time.

Catlin formed his Indian Gallery without government patronage, but he turned to Congress in May 1838, confident it would reward his enterprise by purchasing his collection. Frustrated in this hope, he nevertheless became a regular supplicant, petitioning Congress with an urgency that mounted with his debts. Certain he would find a more receptive audience in Europe, he moved to England in November 1839. After touring his gallery throughout Great Britain, he took his collection in April 1845 to Paris, where he was entertained by King Louis-Philippe. But fame never translated into fortune for Catlin, and in 1848, fleeing ahead of a revolution that swept Louis-Philippe off the throne, he returned to London with his three daughters; his wife and only son had died during his stay in France. His gallery was no longer a novelty in England, and though a book recounting his experiences abroad (*Notes of Eight Years' Travels and Residence in Europe, with His North American Indian Collection* [1848]), lectures, and American emigration schemes kept his name before the British public, Catlin continued to slide toward financial ruin. His 1852 appeal to the U.S. Congress— his fifth in seven years—was thus a desperate one. "My Collection is in the hands of and at the mercy of, my creditors," he wrote Daniel Webster, "I have not the power to save it—but the Congress of My Country has, provided their action is quick" (15 April 1852, Webster papers). Congress rejected Catlin's latest plea for purchase, and his life's work was lost to his creditors.

Bereft of his Indian Gallery, Catlin entered a period of obscurity and frequent despair, punctuated by three trips to South America in the 1850s that are still shrouded in mystery (his primary motive may have been a search for precious minerals). He lived by his wits, selling compilations ("albums unique") of pencil outlines previously copied from his Indian portraits and publishing two successful children's books recounting his travels, *Life amongst the Indians* (1861) and *Last Rambles amongst the Indians of the Rocky Mountains and the Andes* (1867). He wrote a quirky self-help manual that was an unlikely popular success, *The Breath of Life; or, Mal-Respiration* (1861); a book defending his Mandan studies against charges of inaccuracy, *O-Kee-Pa: A Religious Ceremony; and Other Customs of the Mandans* (1867); and another advancing a theory of geological catastrophe in the creation of the Western Hemisphere, *The Lifted and Subsided Rocks of America* (1870). He also painted a second Indian gallery, a group of 600 "cartoons," half recapitulating his original collection, the rest showing Indians of the Northwest Coast and South America, which he exhibited in Brussels in 1870. The next year, after an absence of more than three decades, he returned to America and showed his Cartoon Collection in New York and in February 1872, at the invitation of the Smithsonian Institution, in Washington, D.C. That May he petitioned Congress to purchase his original gallery, thereby allowing him to redeem it from storage in Philadelphia, where his principal creditor resided. Congress had taken no action before Catlin died in Jersey City, New Jersey, his daughters by his side.

Amazingly, Catlin's two Indian collections have survived in Washington largely intact, the Indian Gallery owned by the National Museum of American Art and the Cartoon Collection owned by the National Gallery of Art. They attest to Catlin's peculiar genius. He had set out to show "a vast country of green fields, where the *men* are all *red*" (*Letters and Notes*, vol. 1, p. 59). In paintings sometimes naive and awkward, sometimes poignant and profound, he fashioned the prism through which Americans still view a vanished world.

B.W.D.

October 17th.

SAM PATCH.

To the Ladies and Gentlemen of Western New York, and of Upper Canada.

ALL I have to say is, that I arrived at the Falls too late to give you a specimen of my Jumping Qualities, on the 6th inst.; but on Wednesday, I thought I would venture a small Leap, which I accordingly made, of Eighty Feet, merely to convince those that remained to see me, with what safety and ease I could descend, and that I was the TRUE SAM PATCH, and to show that some things could be done as well as others; which was denied before I made the Jump.

Having been thus disappointed, the owners of Goat Island have generously granted me the use of it for nothing; so that I may have a chance, from an equally generous public, to obtain some remuneration for my long journey hither, as well as affording me an opportunity of supporting the reputation I have gained, by Æro-Nautical Feats, never before attempted, either in the Old or New World.

I shall Ladies and Gentlemen, on Saturday next, Oct. 17th, precisely at 3 o'clock, P. M. LEAP at the FALLS of NIAGARA, from a height of 120 to 130 feet, (being 40 to 50 feet higher than I leapt before,) into the eddy below. On my way down from Buffalo, on the morning of that day, in the Steamboat Niagara, I shall, for the amusement of the Ladies, doff my coat and spring from the mast head into the Niagara River.   SAM PATCH.
Buffalo, Oct. 12, 1829.   Of Passaic Falls, New-Jersey.

Due to disappointing attendance, Patch announced that he would jump into the Niagara River a second time, from an even greater height, on October 17, 1829, as this broadside attests.

SAMUEL PATCH

[1799–13 NOVEMBER 1829]

Today's skydivers and bungee jumpers have a progenitor in Patch, who took bold leaps almost two centuries ago, without any equipment. A failed entrepreneur and disgruntled factory worker, Patch seems to have found release— and a way to express class resentment—by plunging from bridges, cliffs, and other precipices. Patch's death-defying jumps made him a national celebrity, until he pushed his derring-do too far.

Samuel Patch, daredevil, was born in Reading, Massachusetts, the son of Mayo Greenleaf Patch, a landless farmer and cottage shoemaker, and Abigail McIntire, a daughter of a prominent landowner. Patch's eccentric adult life was a clear reflection of the failure of his father—a shiftless, contentious, conniving, ne'er-do-well—to prevent the family's descent into social and economic marginality during the transition of New England from an agrarian to an industrial society after the American Revolution.

After a series of migrations within Massachusetts prompted by financial and legal misfortunes, the family moved to Pawtucket, Rhode Island, in 1807. There Sam, at the age of eight, along with his mother and siblings entered the new industrial working class as laborers in Samuel Slater's cotton mill. His father, an abusive alcoholic, refused to work and abandoned the family in 1812. Early textile mills were located adjacent to waterfalls, and for Sam, like other boys, jumping into the pool at the base of the Pawtucket falls was a popular if dangerous form of recreation.

Jumping in the local style, feet first with arms clasped tightly against his sides at entry, Sam became a youthful legend by leaping from the roof of a four-story mill into the river. At an undetermined date, he capitalized on his childhood labor experiences and became a partner in a textile mill in nearby Central Falls, Rhode Island. But his partner soon absconded with the firm's money, and Patch, after a brief sojourn at sea and an unsuccessful attempt at owning a candlewick mill, moved in 1827 to Paterson, New Jersey, where he hired on as a boss spinner (mule spinner) at the Hamilton Mills adjacent to the falls of the Passaic River. Patch, who never married, was an alcoholic like his father and frequently beat the child laborers under his supervision.

During the summer of 1827 Patch, a twice-failed proprietor, watched with interest the efforts of Timothy B. Crane, a wealthy entrepreneur, to turn the north bank of Passaic Falls into a "commercial pleasure garden" connected to the town of Paterson by a toll bridge, Clinton Bridge. Whether as a reaction to his father's abandonment, an expression of anger at his loss of economic independence, an act of protest against the "civilization of nature" and the privatization of public space, or simply, as Paul Johnson put it, "an unhappy constellation of class consciousness and alcoholic resentment," Patch let it be known that he intended to spoil the opening ceremonies for Crane's Forest Garden. On 30 September 1827, as the townspeople watched the bridge being pulled into place along the cables spanning the chasm, Patch, who had been incarcerated but surreptitiously released, suddenly emerged at the edge of the cliff wearing the all-white cotton parade dress of the Paterson Association of Spinners and jumped seventy feet into the river.

Flushed by the cheers as he swam to shore and reveling in the notoriety of instant fame, Patch became a professional jumper. Whether the leap at Paterson was a conscious statement or an impulsive act is unknown, but his subsequent jumps were prideful exhibitions intended to recapture the sense of manhood and self-esteem that his father had lost. Patch called his falls jumping "an art," by which he meant performing, craftlike, an acquired skill that defined his identity. He proceeded to leap, after due public notice and newspaper coverage, from sundry heights—cliffs and bridges as well as bowsprits and masts of ships—in New Jersey and New York State, each time drawing large and enthusiastic crowds that both exulted in death-defying spectacle and contributed generously to the passed hat.

As Patch became a national celebrity, capturing the public's imagination with feats that were both brave and foolhardy, he sought ever greater heights. On 7 October 1829 he conquered Niagara Falls, jumping seventy feet from the lower end of Goat Island, a narrow islet that divided the American and

Horseshoe Falls, into the eddy at the base of the falls. Ten days later, with the aid of scaffolding, he dropped 120 feet into the Niagara River. He then moved on to Rochester, New York, where on 6 November he plunged 100 feet at the Genesee Falls. A 25-foot platform was erected, and on 13 November Patch set a new jumping record by dropping 125 feet into the Genesee. But, apparently becoming dizzy either from the new height or too many preleap brandies, he lost control in mid-fall and plunged awkwardly into the swirling torrent. On 17 March 1830, his body was found at the mouth of the river near Lake Ontario and subsequently buried in an unmarked grave at the nearby village of Charlotte.

Sam Patch passed into legend. Throughout the 1830s and 1840s and beyond, Patch was celebrated in ballads, poems, plays, folklore, and fiction. The prominent actor Danforth Marble portrayed Patch in two popular stage comedies, *Sam Patch; or, The Daring Yankee* and *Sam Patch in France.* Patch's jumps embodied the heroic and tragic elements from which myths are made. He was a megalomaniac, a tortured man whose life, aptly described by Johnson, was "an elaborate exercise in self-destruction." Comparing himself favorably with Napoleon and Wellington, he declared, "There's no mistake in Sam Patch." Prior to his fatal fall, he had made arrangements to sail to England (leaping daily off the ship's masts en route) to realize his ambition of jumping from London Bridge.

But just as there was more to the celebrated "Jumping Man" than senseless bravado or existential rebellion, so, too, was there more to his contemporary notoriety than titillation with deeds of derring-do. Caught in the throes of early stages of modernization, the United States in the first half of the nineteenth century was intrigued by the increasingly stark juxtaposition of nature and civilization, of untamed wilderness and urbanized, mechanized society. The search for individual place amid the clash of pastoral ideals and technological realities found expression in a fascination with waterfalls and dives. Sam Patch captured the fancy and imagination of the nation because he was a symbol of an age—an urban folk hero in the mold of the frontier's Davy Crockett and the river's Mike Fink.

L.R.G.

DAVID DOUGLAS

[25 JUNE 1799–12 JULY 1834]

While Johnny Appleseed spread orchards across pioneer country, European horticulturalists dug roots and seeds to transplant in the Old World. This seemingly gentle enterprise attracted men such as Douglas, a shy Scottish gardener's apprentice who gathered scores of species unknown in Britain, including honeysuckle and the giant fir named after him. But Douglas's sense of adventure and humble status in Britain drove him to undertake journeys well beyond the range of most plant collectors. His last trip, to the Hawaiian Islands, resulted in one of the most bizarre deaths in the annals of American adventure.

David Douglas, botanist, was born in Scone, Perthshire, Scotland, the son of John Douglas, a stonemason, and Jean Drummond. He spent a few years in the parish schools and was then apprenticed, at the age of eleven, at the earl of Mansfield's gardens. Through reading, field studies, and practical gardening, Douglas developed an enthusiasm for natural history, especially botany, which would be the single passion of his life. In 1820 he obtained a post at the botanical garden in Glasgow, and there met the famous botanist William Jackson Hooker. Hooker became his mentor and then his close friend, and the two went on many botanizing expeditions in the Scottish Highlands and Islands.

In 1823 Douglas entered the employ of the Horticultural Society of London and was sent on a journey to eastern North America to investigate fruit culture and send back samples of new trees and other specimens. He returned in 1824, and the society's officers were so pleased with his work that they sent him off within six months on what would be the first of two journeys to the American Northwest. In July 1824, he sailed on a Hudson's Bay Company ship, *William and Ann,* for the voyage around Cape Horn and arrived at the mouth of the Columbia River in April 1825. The purpose of his trip was to explore the region, study its plant life, and

The first botanist to make a comprehensive study of the flora of the Pacific Northwest, Douglas had an enthusiasm for natural history that took him thousands of miles from his home in Scotland.

send back seeds and specimens to the society. Hooker was very enthusiastic about the Northwest, saying it was "highly interesting country" about which there was little botanical knowledge.

Douglas, now twenty-five years old, was described as excessively modest and shy, but his contemporaries believed him to be a man of enthusiasm and intelligence. He also possessed a strong spirit of adventure and was well endowed with personal courage. The journey itself was a daunting prospect, and Douglas, at the time of departure, said he doubted he would ever see England again. However, his enthusiasm for botany was unbounded, and he combined this with a strong religious faith as his support in life.

Douglas spent two years in North America, years filled with difficult travel, interesting and sometimes dangerous encounters with Indians, and extraordinary successes in botanizing. He sent back to England collections of seeds and plants; included were many species new to English botanists—evening primrose, wild hyacinth, ocean spray, the Oregon grape, honeysuckle, and many others. He also described the giant fir, *Pinus taxifolia,* later given the name of Douglas fir (*Pinus Douglasii*), and further emended, in botanical nomenclature, to *Pseudotsuga menziesii.*

From Fort Vancouver on the Columbia, Douglas traveled across half the continent to York Factory on Hudson Bay; from there he sailed back to England, arriving in October 1827. He had traveled more than 10,000 miles in North America by canoe, on horseback, and on foot; had climbed peaks in the Rocky Mountains; and had fulfilled the mission of his journey beyond anyone's expectations.

Douglas spent the next two years as a public figure, the recipient of many honors, including membership in the Linnean Society and a fellowship in the Zoological Society of London. Douglas had introduced into England more plants than had ever been introduced into a single country by an individual hitherto. Much of the value of the Douglas contributions lay in the fact that they were readily adaptable to the English climate. Not only were society members relieved at his safe return, they were overwhelmed by the results of his expedition.

Toward the end of this period in his life, it became obvious that Douglas had no defined status in either the social or the scientific circles of his time. He was not well educated in a formal sense, and his humble origins gave him no social status at all. He did not qualify as a scientist, and there seemed to be no position that he could fill; in truth, many of his contemporaries regarded him as a successful plant collector, no more and no less. This situation caused him much distress, but he was rescued from it when his lifelong friend and patron William Hooker arranged for him to go on a second expedition to America. He sailed from England in October 1829 and, after a stop in the Sandwich (Hawaiian) Islands, he reached the Columbia River in June 1830. His new travels in the Northwest included what are now Washington and California. In the latter he spent nineteen months visiting Franciscan missions, collecting new specimens, and sending many back to England. Included were mariposa lilies, fairy lanterns, the scarlet bugler, bush poppies, and the blazing star. His new contributions were enthusiastically received by the Horticultural Society. On 15 May 1883, Hooker wrote to his friend John Richardson, "What a glorious collection has Douglas sent me from California." Douglas himself wrote that he hoped the new species would give his "good friend, Dr. Hooker . . . material for two new volumes of the Flora" (letter to Joseph Sabine, 26 October 1832).

Never to return to England, in the last two years of his life, Douglas made two more voyages to the Sandwich Islands, the second expedition sponsored by the Royal Horticultural Society with support from the Colonial Office and the Hudson's Bay Company. This was a land that held a great fascination for him; he thought it more interesting than California and suggested to Hooker that he might consider doing a "Flora of these Islands." Along with plant collecting on the island of Hawaii, he explored the island's mountains, including the active volcano Kilauea. He also made a trek to the summit of Mauna Loa, whose crater he measured. At this time, Douglas was ill, and his condition might have contributed to his death on Hawaii. His failing eyesight was his principal malady, and it is believed that, while on a trail, he missed his footing at a bullock pit (a large hole dug for the purpose of capturing wild cattle) and, falling into it, was gored to death by the captured beast.

News of Douglas's death produced an outpouring of praise and recognition of his special achievements. Not only had he introduced into Britain hundreds of new plants and an enormous fund of botanical information, he also was the first botanist to make a comprehensive study of the flora of the Pacific Northwest and made unique observations in the Hawaiian Islands. He was one of the preeminent natural history explorers of his generation of Europeans.

R.F.E.

An 1850 engraving of Sutter completed by J. S. Sartain two years after the mineral that would start a nationwide craze was discovered at Sutter's sawmill.

JOHN AUGUST SUTTER

[15 FEBRUARY 1803–18 JUNE 1880]

Sutter's name has become synonymous with his sawmill in the Sierra Nevadas where gold was discovered in 1848. But this was only one of many dramatic episodes in an elusive career that carried "Captain" Sutter from central Europe to St. Louis and across America to Hawaii and Alaska before he reached California. There, Sutter founded a multiracial settlement called New Switzerland, and seemed headed for great wealth—until the famous gold strike that proved, ironically, his undoing.

John August Sutter, pioneer, was born Johann Augustus Suter in Kandern, Baden, the son of Johann Jakob Suter and Christine Wilhelmine Stober (or Stoberin). His father—of Swiss rather than German ancestry—was the manager of a modest paper mill in the village. After a local common school education and probably a stay in a Neuchâtel Gymnasium, Sutter became an apprentice and then a clerk in a printing, publishing, and bookselling firm in Basel. When Sutter married Annette Dübeld in 1826, he opened his own dry goods and drapery store. In 1828 he volunteered for the reserve corps of the Canton of Berne's militia and by 1831 was a first under-lieutenant. Sutter never forgot his brief military experience and later exaggerated it into French army service under Charles X.

Sutter's shop was unsuccessful, and deep in debt, he showed the darker side of his complex nature by disappearing, abandoning his wife and five children along with his debts. He was pursued by a warrant for his arrest instigated by his creditors. Sutter stole away to Le Havre and took ship to New York (May 1834) and then joined the German colony in St. Louis. From there, he entered the Santa Fe trade in the 1835 and 1836 seasons but had very little success. He won the (deserved) reputation of a dead-beat and was even, erroneously, accused of murder. But he loved frontier life, and he began to call himself Captain John A. Sutter.

Once more, in 1838, Sutter seemingly started all over again, determined to try his luck in fabled California. Typically, he "skipped out" on some promissory notes when he left Westport, Missouri, fittingly on April Fool's Day. His trip to the penultimate Rocky Mountain fur trade rendezvous with Captain Andrew Drips of the American Fur Company was uneventful; as was his continuation of it to Fort Hall with Hudson's Bay Company bourgeois Francis Ermatinger and to Fort Vancouver with a party of Protestant missionaries.

Sutter made excellent use of his travels, from the Santa Fe Trail onward. He especially studied the British forts and their economic and diplomatic relations with the Indians. He filed away in his mind many ideas for his own planned colony in California.

Sutter hoped to drop down the trappers' Siskiyou Trail to San Francisco Bay, but he was dissuaded from doing so by James Douglas, the Hudson's Bay Company's acting chief factor at Fort Vancouver, who pointed out the dangerous combination of warlike Indians and snowy mountains separating Oregon from California. So Sutter sailed to California, the long way around, taking a company ship to Honolulu, where he was able to charter a vessel to San Francisco via Sitka, Alaska.

Sutter's luck finally changed. His calling on important individuals in government and business in the fur posts and in the seaports of Hawaii and Russian Alaska paid off. Sutter charmed his new friends, for he was endowed with a genuine charisma that was fueled by his ambition and his subtle talent for self-promotion.

Governor Juan B. Alvarado in Monterey was much impressed by Sutter's manner and his sheaf of letters to whom-it-may-concern. He allowed Sutter to choose a site for a colony on the American River near its junction with the Sacramento River in 1839, long before he formally granted him (in 1841) a rancho of eleven Spanish leagues, or 48,400 acres. Sutter's Nueva Helvetia ("New Switzerland"), in the heart of the as yet unsettled Sacramento Valley, would serve the governor as the eastern anchor of Alta California's Frontera del Norte. This northern frontier was meant to fend off hostile Indians from the settled San Francisco Bay region and, even more, to block the

Russians from penetrating to the bay from their (illegal) fur trade outpost of Fort Ross on the Redwood Coast. The commandant of the frontier was Alvarado's uncle, General Mariano G. Vallejo, who soon saw Sutter as more of a rival for military and political power than as an ally.

Sutter began his colony by having his *Kanaka* (Hawaiian) followers build simple *hale pili*, the grass shacks of the Sandwich Islands, but he was soon directing local Indians in constructing a strong, walled fortress of adobe. He garrisoned it with a bizarre army of former mountain men, sailors "on the beach," and other drifters, plus friendly Indians in hand-me-down Russian uniforms, for he bought Fort Ross from the Russian American Company in 1841. By imitating the Hudson's Bay Company's effective carrot-and-stick Indian diplomacy, Sutter largely pacified the Sacramento Valley. The paternalistic Sutter fed, clothed, and housed up to 1,000 "friendlies" at his fort and staged punitive raids against savages, or hostiles, with great severity.

Sutter's Fort, or New Helvetia, as the colony came to be called by arriving Anglo-Americans, became a great success, more of a plantation and ranch than a fort. It was ringed with wheat fields, orchards, and vineyards, all surrounded by great herds of longhorn cattle. The fort became a small community of varied enterprises, from a smithy and distillery to the headquarters for Sutter's beaver-trapping parties.

In 1844–1845, Sutter made a bad mistake when he led a foreign legion to rescue Governor Manuel Micheltorena from revolutionaries led by former governor Alvarado and General José Castro. (These *Californios* were tired of having governors imposed on them by Mexico City; they wanted an autonomous Alta California.) It was not just patriotism or his taste for military life that motivated Sutter; Micheltorena had awarded him a second rancho. The rebels defeated and captured Sutter. He was humiliated but was pardoned and released to resume command of his frontier fortress.

Sutter's finest hour came with his generosity toward, and succor of, trans-Sierra travelers, who usually were in rags and almost starving after the arduous crossing of the continent. For example, he aided explorer John C.

Frémont when he was in distress, and Sutter dispatched the first supplies to the snow-trapped Donner Party.

At this time, like his rival Vallejo, Sutter was becoming disgusted with California's political anarchy and welcomed the American takeover. But Frémont, who seized command of the *Osos* (or Grizzly Bears), American rebels who had seized General Vallejo, considered Sutter to be an enemy. When Frémont locked Vallejo and his lieutenants in Sutter's fort, he became so angered at Sutter's obvious concern for their health and comfort that he virtually placed Sutter under house arrest in his own fort. Sutter was not completely free again until the United States entered the Mexican War.

On 24 January 1848, Sutter's millwright discovered gold at his Sierra Nevada sawmill. Captain Sutter could not keep the find a secret, and, ironically, on the verge of great wealth, he was ruined by a tsunami of gold-hungry argonauts who soon became land-greedy squatters. They trampled his hopes and dreams as well as his crops, and they slaughtered his cattle as if they were wild game. After the pillaging squatters came lawyers and speculators to wrest more of his land from him in the land grant litigation of the 1850s.

Sutter was still widely respected, and he was honored by being chosen as a delegate to the 1849 California Constitutional Convention. Although he lost the gubernatorial race of 1850, the federal government made him an Indian subagent in that year. In 1853, the state legislature appointed him a major general and put him in command of California's militia. He had already fled devastated New Helvetia to his Feather River property of Hock Farm. There he lived in relative comfort, although in declining circumstances (and drinking heavily), through the Civil War years.

The last straw for Sutter was the 1865 destruction of Hock Farm by an arsonist. He again fled, this time to the quiet of Lititz, Pennsylvania. He survived on a pension of $250 a month paid to him (1864–1878) by the state of California in gratitude for his efforts in behalf of California's early American immigrants (the very people who had ruined him). Sutter spent his last years vainly trying to get a congressional pension. He died in a Washington, D.C., hotel.

Sutter is considered to be Anglo California's pioneer of pioneers, pre-eminent in the transition period when Mexican rule was giving way to American conquest. He was perhaps typical of the early non-Hispanic settlers of Mexico's most distant department (province), Alta California, but on a grander scale. He overcame flaws of character in order to secure a measure of greatness in western history. He was an adventurer but also a visionary and a builder. And his weaknesses were more than balanced by a strong sense of compassion, one that made New Helvetia or Sutter's Fort world famous for its hospitality to distressed travelers.

R.H.D.

Bridger was known by several names among the Indian tribes of the West: Blanket Chief, because of his alleged sexual prowess, Mysterious Medicine Man, because of his uncanny intelligence, and Big Throat, because of his goiter.

JAMES BRIDGER

[17 MARCH 1804–17 JULY 1881]

*Until about 1840, very few whites penetrated the Great Plains and Rockies,
except for fur trappers and scouts known as "mountainy men." Bridger, though
less famous than Kit Carson or Jedediah Smith, was among the toughest and
best-traveled of this rough-hewn breed. Born in a Virginia tavern and orphaned
as a boy, he headed West at the age of eighteen and kept scouting into his six-
ties. Like many frontiersmen, Bridger displayed contradictory tendencies. An
illiterate who loved literature, he was also a man who both fought and frat-
ernized with Indians, taking three natives as wives and living for three years
with an arrowhead in his back.*

James Bridger, fur trapper and trader, explorer, and scout, was born in
a tavern near Richmond, Virginia, the son of James Bridger, a surveyor
and innkeeper, and Chloe Tyler, a barmaid. Bridger and his family moved
in about 1812 to a farm near St. Louis, Missouri, where, on being orphaned
five years later, he became a blacksmith's apprentice. In 1822 he responded
to an advertisement calling for a hundred able-bodied young men to join
a fur-trapping expedition, lasting from one to three years, up to the headwaters of the Missouri River. The organizers of the expedition were William
Henry Ashley, then lieutenant governor of Missouri and a brigadier general in its militia, and his business partner Major Andrew Henry. Bridger
thus embarked on a lifelong career of trapping, trading, and exploring.

The Ashley-Henry group built a post called Fort Henry (later Fort Union)
at the junction of the Yellowstone and Missouri Rivers in Montana. In 1823
Hugh Glass, one of the members of the expedition, was horribly mauled
by a grizzly bear near what is now Grand River, South Dakota. Bridger
and another explorer, John S. Fitzgerald, agreed to stay behind with him
until he died. But they abandoned Glass, who survived his injuries, crawled
an alleged 300 miles to Fort Kiowa near the Missouri and White Rivers,

returned up the Yellowstone, and found and forgave Bridger on account of his youth. By this time, Bridger was among the first non-natives to see the geysers and other natural phenomena in the Yellowstone region. It is likely that a little later he was the first non-native to see the Great Salt Lake, perhaps in late fall 1824 or early spring 1825. Its salty taste convinced him that it was an arm of the Pacific Ocean.

In 1830 Bridger, with Thomas "Broken Hand" Fitzpatrick and other explorers, bought out Ashley and Henry and formed the Rocky Mountain Fur Company. Until 1834 they competed with rival concerns, including the Hudson's Bay Company from British Canada and John Jacob Astor's American Fur Company, for the lucrative beaver-pelt trade in the north central section of the country. In 1838 Bridger and his friend Louis Vasquez built a store on the Green River in southwest Wyoming and expanded it by 1843 into a trading post (later called Fort Bridger) for emigrants on the Oregon and California Trail.

By the 1840s Bridger had walked and was intimately familiar with most of the region bounded by Canada, the Missouri River, and the Colorado–New Mexico border. Evidently he possessed an unusually strong constitution, having been shot with arrows by Blackfoot Indians and having lived with an iron arrowhead in his back for three years. Bridger served as a guide on a variety of missions. In 1849 he led a railroad surveying party under Captain Howard Stansbury to Utah; in 1851 he scouted for a hunting party headed by Sir George Gore, a wealthy Irishman. During 1857–1858 he participated in Colonel Albert Sidney Johnston's campaigns against the Mormons, who in 1853 had driven Bridger from his trading post. He was involved in seeking a direct route from Denver to the Great Salt Lake in 1861 and took part in the expedition to measure distances along the 967-mile Bozeman Trail during 1865–1866. Among later acquaintances were scout Kit Carson; explorer John Charles Frémont; trapper Joe Meek; John August Sutter, the instigator of the California gold rush; and Mormon leader Brigham Young.

In 1835 Bridger married a Flathead Indian whom he named Cora and with whom he had three children. After Cora died in 1846, he married

Little Fawn later that year; she was the fourteen-year-old daughter of Washakie, the distinguished Shoshone chief. Called Mary Washakie Bridger, she died in childbirth in 1849. He then married, in 1850, a Shoshone Indian with whom he had two children. Some of Bridger's children were sent to Missouri to be educated.

Bridger spun tall tales about bizarre phenomena, such as petrified forests along the Yellowstone complete with petrified birds. Although illiterate, he could converse in French, Spanish, and a few Native American languages. He enjoyed having literature read to him; in one such instance, he listened to passages from Henry Wadsworth Longfellow's *Song of Hiawatha* until he objected to that poet's ignorance of Indian life. On being informed that William Shakespeare was the world's greatest writer, Bridger traded a team of cattle worth $125 for a book of Shakespeare's plays.

The names given to him by Indians included Casapy (Crow for "Blanket Chief," because of his alleged sexual prowess), Peejatowahooten (Shoshone for "Mysterious Medicine Man," because of his uncanny intelligence), and Big Throat (because of his goiter).

In 1865 Bridger received his discharge at Fort Laramie from service as an army scout and guide during the Powder River campaign against Sioux and Cheyenne Indians blocking the route to the Montana gold fields. Severely pained by his goiter, arthritis, and rheumatism, among other problems with his health, he returned in 1868 to his farm at Westport, Missouri. He requested back rent due him for the government's use of Fort Bridger, but he received nothing. By 1875 Bridger was totally blind. He died in Washington, Jackson County, Missouri. As much a legend as he was a genuine adventurer, Bridger can be counted among the most knowledgeable explorers who opened the West to pioneers from the eastern United States.

R.L.G.

SAINT JACOB NETSVETOV

ENLIGHTENER OF THE PEOPLES OF ALASKA

GO YE THEREFORE AND TEACH ALL NATIONS BAPTIZING THEM IN THE NAME OF THE FATHER AND OF THE SON AND HOLY SPIRIT

The first Native American Orthodox priest, Saint Jacob ministered to various native groups, vaccinated and dispensed medicine, and prepared specimens of various fish and other forms of marine life for the museums of natural history in St. Petersburg and Moscow.

JACOB NETSVETOV

[1804–26 JULY 1864]

One of the most extraordinary yet neglected chapters of American history is the hundred-year period when Russians oversaw a fur-trading empire stretching from the Aleutian Islands of Alaska to Northern California. While many Russian fur traders, known as promyshlenniki, *were brutal men who slaughtered and enslaved native people, their settlements also drew Orthodox priests such as "Saint Jacob," who ministered to remote Aleuts and Eskimos by kayak and dogsled.*

Jacob Netsvetov, Native American Orthodox priest and missionary in Alaska, was born Iakov Igorovich Netsvetov, the son of Igor Netsvetov, a Russian fur trader, and Maria Alekseeva, an Unangan Aleut from the island of Atka in the Aleutian chain. Hence he was a creole, of Native American and Russian blood. His birthplace was either Atka or the island of St. George in the Bering Sea, but he was raised on the latter island, where his father worked for the Russian-American Company, becoming a company manager there in 1818. Jacob was educated at home in his early years. In 1823 he entered the seminary in Irkutsk, Siberia. Two years later he married a Siberian creole woman, Anna Simeonovna; they had no children. In 1826 he graduated from the seminary with certificates in history and theology. On 4 March 1828, while still in Irkutsk, he was ordained to the priesthood in the Russian Orthodox Church, making him the first Native American Orthodox priest.

Netsvetov was immediately assigned to be the first resident pastor for the Unangan Aleuts living on Atka Island and the other islands of the western Aleutian archipelago. He and his wife reached Atka in June 1829. He soon discovered that most of the islanders had been previously introduced to Orthodox Christianity and had been baptized by laymen from Siberia associated with the extensive fur-trading operations in Russian

America. By the end of 1829, he had completed the baptism of hundreds of Aleuts through the administration of the sacrament of chrismation (anointing with holy oil).

For the next fifteen years, Netsvetov labored to strengthen and spread Christianity throughout the western Aleutian Islands, and he even made two trips to the Kurile Islands north of Japan. His parish stretched from Atka Island to Attu Island, a distance of about 700 miles. For his frequent trips among the islands, he traveled by kayak or on one of the Russian-American Company's sailing vessels and, wherever necessary, he held services in a portable "church-tent" that he constructed. In 1831 Netsvetov reorganized and began teaching in a bilingual (Russian and Aleut) boarding school on Atka Island, which graduated dozens of Aleut and creole students during his time there. He adapted for use among the Atkan Aleuts the translations of scriptural and liturgical texts done by Father John Veniaminov (who later became Saint Innocent) in the Unalaskan dialect of the Unangan language, since the Atkans spoke a different dialect of this language. Other scriptural, liturgical, and secular texts he translated directly into the Aleutian dialect, including the entire Gospel of Matthew. He also compiled a comprehensive dictionary for the Unangan language.

In 1844, Netsvetov, who had become a widower in 1836, was assigned by Bishop Innocent Veniaminov to the Kuskokwim–Lower Yukon River region of the southwestern mainland of Alaska. Although settling on the coast of the Bering Sea would have given him considerably more access to the outside world, he gained permission from Bishop Innocent to set up his headquarters in the village of Ikogmiut (now known as Russian Mission), on the Yukon River about 150 miles inland, in order to have more contact with the tribal peoples of the interior. He was only the second priest ever to minister to the Yup'ik Eskimos and the Athabascan Indians of this area. Through his efforts over the next eighteen years, Orthodox Christianity became firmly established as the faith of these peoples, which greatly helped to bring an end to the previous recurrent hostilities between the Yup'iks and the Athabascans.

Netsvetov's daily journals from this period, which he kept meticulously and faithfully, give detailed descriptions of his extensive missionary work in this vast wilderness of roughly 30,000 square miles. He learned the Yup'ik language and made the first translations of scriptural and liturgical texts into this tongue. When he ministered to the various Athabascan groups, he relied on creole interpreters. From his base in Russian Mission, in most years he made three round trips: in the spring, downriver and up the seacoast by kayak to St. Michael's Redoubt; in the fall, up the Yukon and Innoko Rivers; and in the winter, overland by dogsled to the Kuskokwim River. During these journeys, nomadic tribal men, women, and children gathered in the scattered villages along the rivers on hearing of Netsvetov's approach. In this way he proclaimed the Christian faith to and baptized hundreds of Native Americans and ministered regularly to them. He and his assistant, Constantine Lukin, a creole from Kodiak Island, vaccinated and dispensed medicine to the natives of this area, which helped them to resist the smallpox that had ravaged other parts of Alaska.

Netsvetov's journals also record his various ethnographic observations, which provide the first detailed view of the traditional Alaskan Eskimo culture. While in the Aleutians, he prepared specimens of various fish and other forms of marine life for the museums of natural history in St. Petersburg and Moscow.

His extensive missionary accomplishments are all the more noteworthy in light of the exceedingly rigorous and often dangerous climatic conditions in which he traveled and labored. Partly because of the bitter cold of the winters and partly because of undernourishment from occasional food shortages in the Alaskan interior, Netsvetov suffered from various debilitating chronic illnesses, beginning in 1848. Yet he carried on, even when the pain was virtually unbearable, for as he once wrote in his journal, "I was again bothered in increased degree by my illness in the cold. If it had not been for the natives, I probably would not have dared to celebrate [the church services]. It is for them that it was necessary to make the decision to celebrate."

In 1863, severely crippled by arthritis, nearly blind, and exhausted from his years of illness and exposure to the harsh climate of the Alaskan interior, Netsvetov—an archpriest since 1848 (a singular honor at that time)—

moved to Sitka (near Juneau), where he spent his last year serving the chapel for the Tlingit Indians. Long regarded as a saint by the peoples whom he served, in October 1994 this distinguished teacher, linguist, and missionary priest was officially canonized as a saint by the Orthodox Church of America, in a ceremony held in the cathedral in Anchorage. He is revered as Saint Jacob, Enlightener of the Peoples of Alaska.

D.C.F.

ELIZA HART SPALDING

[11 AUGUST 1807–7 JANUARY 1851]

Missionary work was one of the few fields of frontier endeavor open to women in the early nineteenth century. Long before wagon convoys trailed west, Spalding and another female missionary—who happened to be a competitor for the affections of Spalding's husband—became the first white women to cross the Rockies. They taught at a Nez Percé mission until beset by accusations of witchcraft and, eventually, a massacre.

Eliza Hart Spalding, pioneer and missionary, was born in Kennsington (now Berlin), Connecticut, the daughter of Levi Hart and Martha Hart, farmers who shared the same ancestor, Stephen Hart. When she was thirteen, the family moved to a farm near Holland Patent in Oneida County, New York. At home she learned the necessary crafts of spinning, weaving, and candle making. She attended Hamilton Oneida Academy and may have studied at Chipman Female Academy in Clinton, New York. Eliza was a serious and bright student. Slender and of medium height, she had dark brown hair and blue eyes and a "coarse voice." She was also very religious; baptized in August 1826, she joined the local Presbyterian church. For a while she also taught school. A friend of hers, known as Mrs. Jackson, suggested that she might wish to correspond with Henry Harmon Spalding of Prattsburg, New York, who had conveyed to Mrs. Jackson that he was looking for a woman who would "devote her life to educate the heathen." They began writing each other in 1830, and in the fall of 1831 they met.

Henry Spalding was a student at Western Reserve College in Hudson, Ohio, and Eliza moved there in 1832. In 1833 he graduated, and in October of that year they married; they had four children. Some years before, Henry Spalding had asked a woman named Narcissa Prentiss to marry him, but she rejected him. In an ironic twist, his bitterness and resentment over this rejection later complicated Eliza's and his missionary efforts. He was

Spalding Mission established 1836, At junction of Lapwai Creek & Clearwater River, On route of, Lewis & Clark.

A photograph of the mission in Idaho where Spalding taught English, spinning, weaving, knitting, and the Bible to the Nez Percé until 1847.

also virulently anti-Catholic, a feeling shared by Eliza, which later affected their efforts among the Indians. Their interest in religion bound them together, however, and her calm nature was a needed antidote to his contrary temperament.

After their marriage, the Spaldings moved to Cincinnati, Ohio; there Henry studied for the ministry at Lane Theological Seminary, where Lyman Beecher was president. While taking in students as boarders, Eliza studied at home from her husband's courses in Scripture and theology. In 1835 Henry was ordained, and he and Eliza received appointments from the American Board of Commissioners for Foreign Missions (ABCFM), composed of Congregational, Presbyterian, and Dutch Reformed churches. Their excursion west was delayed, however, while Eliza returned home to New York to give birth to a stillborn daughter.

In the meantime, in February 1835 Dr. Marcus Whitman and Rev. Samuel Parker had made an exploratory trip to present-day Idaho and Montana. Whitman, too, had applied for sponsorship from the ABCFM; he also married Narcissa Prentiss in early 1836. Whitman invited the Spaldings to join his expedition west, unaware that his wife had rejected Henry Spalding's marriage proposal years before. In March 1836 the two couples began an arduous trek west across the Rocky Mountains, through which Captain Benjamin Bonneville had taken wagons only recently. They stopped in St. Louis, Missouri, where the Spaldings (out of curiosity) visited the Catholic cathedral, and where, unbeknownst to them, two Nez Percé Indians were buried. They observed Mass being sung, which Eliza described as "heartless forms and ceremonies," and rejoiced that she and her husband had never embraced "such delusions."

Eliza was sick for most of the journey, and her husband was mortified that fate and their faith had brought them together with the woman who had spurned him. Along the way, they joined a caravan of the American Fur Company. The group later joined up with a convoy from the Hudson's Bay Company.

Having lost most of their possessions, the missionaries arrived at Fort Walla Walla on the Columbia River on 1 September 1836. The Whitmans founded their mission near there at Waiilatpu among the Cayuse Indians, who during this time were considered treacherous. The Spaldings, accompanied by 150 Nez Percé Indians, continued on to Lapwai, about 125 miles away from present-day Lewiston, Idaho, on the southern tributary of the Clearwater River. There they established a mission among the Nez Percés, a nomadic tribe from the Cascades to the Rockies, part of the Inland Empire. The Nez Percés had been evangelized by Jesuit missionaries and had received their name from French explorers because they wore bits of decorative shells in their noses. Eliza Spalding and Narcissa Whitman were the first white women to cross the Rocky Mountains and the Continental Divide.

The Indians assisted the Spaldings in constructing buildings. Eliza quickly learned their language and opened a school in January 1837 for both children and adult Indians; the school eventually had 225 students. She taught English, spinning, weaving, knitting, and the Bible. She also painted water colors depicting biblical stories, which her husband used in preaching to the Indians.

Meanwhile, the tension between Henry Spalding and Narcissa Whitman intensified. The ABCFM had heard of the ongoing troubles and had decided to dismiss the Spaldings, rescinding its decision only after Marcus Whitman traveled east and assuaged the board's concern. In 1844, Eliza painted the *Protestant Ladder,* a diagrammatic painting showing the history of Christianity and depicting Martin Luther and John Calvin as vital links between Christ and heaven. A colorful and polemical work, it was designed to counteract the teaching of the Jesuits and is the only one of her paintings that was extant at the end of the twentieth century (Oregon Historical Society).

Around this time, relations with the Indians began to deteriorate. More and more whites were migrating to the area, disrupting the nomadic way of life of the Indians and bringing measles, for which the Indians had no immunity. White children survived, but not Indian. The Indians accused the missionaries of witchcraft. Attendance at Eliza's school ceased and she and her family were threatened.

On 29 November 1847 a band of Cayuse attacked the mission at Waiilatpu; the Whitmans and twelve others were massacred and forty-seven others were taken prisoner. Eliza Spalding, whose husband was away at the time, was informed of the tragedy and was urged to leave by friendly Nez Percés. She agreed but insisted on waiting until Monday, the day after the Sabbath. She and her family were spared, but the Whitman massacre marked the end of the two missions. Her husband rashly accused the "Romanists" and Jesuit missionaries of the killings; yet no subsequent historical data has given any credence to his charges.

In 1848, the U.S. Congress created the Oregon Territory and appointed a governor of the area, which eventually became the states of Washington and Oregon. Meanwhile, Eliza's health deteriorated. With the mission closed, she and her family moved to the Willamette Valley in late 1847. They settled on the Calapooya River, near present-day Brownsville, Oregon, where Eliza Spalding died, probably of tuberculosis.

Spalding was an example of the indomitable spirit of faith and determination that characterized the American concept of territorial expansion during the 1840s, known as Manifest Destiny. Her husband later returned to the Nez Percé Indians near Lapwai, where he died. In 1913, Eliza Spalding's body was disinterred and buried next to her husband near their old mission home. In 1968, the site was incorporated into the Nez Percé National Historical Park.

G.G.

JOHN WISE

[24 FEBRUARY 1808–29 SEPTEMBER 1879]

Wise belongs to a long tradition of eccentric American inventors. An extraordinary blend of craftsman, meteorologist, and daredevil, he constructed—and piloted—elaborate flying machines, taking trips that resulted in crash landings, fires, and miraculous escapes. He also dropped cats and dogs in parachutes, and performed a similar descent himself, from 13,000 feet. Like many aeronautic adventurers, Wise kept pushing the envelope, setting a world record for distance travel and making 463 ascents before his luck ran out at the age of seventy-one.

John Wise, balloonist, was born in Lancaster, Pennsylvania, the son of William Weiss (occupation unknown) and Margaret Trey. Educated in both German and English, the nationalities of his parents, he attended local schools and graduated from the Lancaster high school. Following the custom of the third generation in immigrant families of Lancaster County, he anglicized his last name. From his sixteenth to his twenty-first years, he was apprenticed to a cabinetmaker, and until 1835, he was a piano maker. Then, from 1836 to 1847, he worked for a firm that produced scientific instruments.

Later in life, he claimed that his almost lifelong interest in ballooning sprang from an article he read on the subject in a newspaper written in German. He was fourteen at the time. Not until thirteen years later, however, in the spring of 1835 when he was living in Philadelphia, did he decide to make his first balloon. As he claimed, he did so without ever having witnessed an ascension or having any practical knowledge of how a balloon was constructed. He studied the atmosphere and contemporary technology, making the balloon of domestic sheeting muslin rather than the superior but more costly silk. Instead of expensive dopes and varnishes, he used birdlime suspended in linseed oil to cover the muslin and make it leakproof. His first flight took

Wise prepares to ascend in a balloon from Penn Square in Lancaster, Pennsylvania. He was the first to observe the "great river of air which always blows from west to east," an atmospheric condition now known as the jet stream.

place on 2 May 1835, carrying him from Philadelphia some nine miles to Haddonfield, New Jersey.

After several more flights in the muslin balloon, he attempted an ascent on 1 October 1835 in which his gondola hit the eaves of a two-story house, dumping him on the roof while the balloon continued on without him. "Thus ended," he remarked, "the experiments with a machine that had given me much more trouble than reputation as a skillful aeronaut."

It did not end his troubles. He acquired a silk balloon and launched it from Lancaster on 7 May 1836. He landed in Harford County, Maryland, about seventy-five miles away, after an uneventful flight, but as he emptied the hydrogen from the envelope, the gas remained close to the earth in the humid air and ignited from a lantern. Wise and several bystanders were severely burned. After this experience, he temporarily abandoned ballooning and became an instrument maker.

He did not, however, give up on the visions he had developed for the future of aerial transportation. Neither could he forget the thrill of flight despite the dangers he had encountered. He was moved to return to flying by the death of Robert Cocking while the English experimenter was testing a new, inverted parachute. Wise believed Cocking's concept was sound, so on 18 September 1837, he ascended in a balloon from Philadelphia, dropping a dog in a regular parachute and a cat in the Cocking variety. Both landed safely, although the aeronaut was swept against a three-story building and had to exit the balloon through a window.

Experiencing problems with the varnish he was using, in 1838 the balloonist experimented with different substances and discovered that linseed oil by itself proved an adequate treatment for the envelope fabric. He designed his next balloon with a line that enabled him to release all the hydrogen. Taking off from Easton, Pennsylvania, on 11 August 1838, he intended to release the gas and show that the envelope itself would act as a parachute when empty. When he reached 13,000 feet, however, the expanding envelope pulled the line taut, and the gas rushed from the opening "with tempestuous noise," as he recalled. Nevertheless, the empty bag did serve as a parachute, according to plan. On 1 October of the same year, Wise successfully repeated the experiment under more controlled conditions.

He continued his flights and experiments, and by 1847, he had become a professional balloonist rather than an instrument maker. Living in Lancaster from 1848 to 1872, he seems to have earned his livelihood from crowds in the Northeast and Midwest who observed his flights and/or paid to ascend in a tethered balloon. He also sold new and used balloons to other aeronauts. He was married, but there appears to be no information about the date of the marriage or his wife's name; his son Charles E. Wise became one of his students in the art of ballooning. Charles made his own first balloon ascent on 3 September 1853 when he was seventeen, and went on to become a professional balloonist.

John Wise was among those who observed the effect of solar heating on a dark balloon. He was interested in science, especially meteorology, and he appears to have anticipated the much later discovery of the jet stream, while underestimating its altitude. In Wise's own lifetime, his major claim to fame was a flight he made with three other men, including one of his students, from St. Louis, Missouri, to Henderson, New York, on 1–2 July 1859. They covered a distance of more than 800 miles, a world record that lasted several decades.

In 1871–1872 Wise served as librarian for the Franklin Institute in Philadelphia. He continued occasional balloon flights despite his advancing age and was involved for a time in 1873 in what proved to be an abortive scheme for a flight across the Atlantic. On 28 September 1879, Wise ascended from St. Louis on what turned out to be his last flight. The balloon with Wise and a companion aboard was last seen from the southern shore of Lake Michigan at 11:30 that night. A body identified as that of the companion was later recovered from the lake. Wise's body was not recovered, but he was presumed to have drowned sometime the following day.

During forty-four years as a balloonist, Wise made 463 ascents. He was the most experienced and distinguished American aeronaut of his day, and perhaps the greatest American balloonist of all time. According to the *Missouri Republican* of 6 October 1879, he did more than any other American to advance the cause of aerial navigation. Supplementing the influence of his many and notable flights were his writings, *A System of Aeronautics* (1850) and *Through the Air* (1873), as well as several articles for *Scientific American* in 1870 on ballooning and the use of balloons in meteorological research.

J.D.H.

Although commissioner of Indian affairs for the Confederacy in 1860, when Mathew Brady took this photograph, Pike found himself fleeing to the Ozarks a few short years later after being accused of treason by Jefferson Davis.

ALBERT PIKE

[29 DECEMBER 1809–2 APRIL 1891]

New England in the early nineteenth century produced a striking number of idealists and eccentrics. Few among them lived as strange and full a life as this alienated Boston intellectual. Forsaking Harvard, Pike headed to New Mexico and wrote poetry about his frontier exploits. Seesawing between vocations—lawyer, soldier, scholar, scoundrel—Pike also combined a deep sympathy for Indians with pro-slavery and anti-immigration views. This led to his involvement with extremist groups and secret societies, his indictment for treason, and to Pike's being branded by a Boston paper as the most "venomous reptile" who "ever crawled the face of the earth."

Albert Pike, lawyer, soldier, and Masonic scholar, was born in Boston, Massachusetts, the son of Benjamin Pike, a cobbler, and Sarah Andrews. The boy was torn between his father, whose irreverence and drinking scandalized neighbors, and his mother, who read the Bible to her only son daily and planned on his entering the ministry. In 1813, seeking to supplement his income by farming, Benjamin Pike moved the family to Newburyport, Massachusetts. In 1825, Albert was sent to live with his uncle, a teacher at Framingham Academy, who soon learned that Pike had a prodigious memory that enabled him to digest large volumes and recall their contents at will; the boy learned Hebrew, Latin, and Greek almost effortlessly. Eight months after his arrival in Framingham, Pike passed the entrance examination for Harvard College. He could not afford the tuition, however, so, instead of enrolling at Harvard, he taught common school at Gloucester. The following year Harvard agreed to admit him as a junior, but school officials insisted that he pay the first two years' tuition. Outraged, Pike abandoned his dreams of a formal education.

He returned to teaching, for a time at Newburyport; wrote poetry, most of which was published in Boston literary magazines; and began to regard himself as something of a Byronic hero, drinking too much wine and taking long walks with the "romping girls from Rowley," as he put it. When he was heard through an open window playing the violin on Sunday morning, the school board charged him with impiety and ordered him to apologize. He refused and was dismissed.

Pike resolved to break free from New England. In March 1831, using savings he had earmarked for Harvard, he set out for New Mexico. There he joined several hunting and trading expeditions. On one, his wagon train was caught in a snowstorm, and he nearly froze to death. On another, his party was attacked by Indians; Pike fled into the desert, became lost, and went without water for days.

Pike exulted in these hardships. During each crisis he pulled out his notebooks and unburdened his soul through poetry. "Dash the waves, bold Heart, that madly roll / Across thy path!" he wrote. In the end, however, Pike's adventures fell short of expectations. In 1833, having exhausted his savings, he was forced to teach school at Fort Smith, Arkansas, receiving payment in pigs. He also edited the Little Rock *Arkansas Advocate* and studied law, setting up practice in 1834, the same year he married Mary Ann Hamilton, whose money enabled him to buy the newspaper. Pike became active in politics, supporting the Whigs, advocating statehood for Arkansas, and proposing a railroad to connect the South with California. In 1837 he sold the newspaper and devoted himself to law, riding the circuit of rural courthouses throughout Arkansas.

Pike also organized a marching society, which, in 1847, volunteered for duty in the Mexican-American War. Pike was elected captain and led the regiment in the battle of Buena Vista. When Pike wrote an open letter to the *Little Rock Gazette* denouncing a regiment that had fled during a charge by Mexican lancers, one of its commanders, John Selden Roane, responded that Pike's unit had done little better. Pike challenged Roane to a duel, and on 29 July 1847 the two met on a sandbar in the Arkansas River. After each had fired pistols twice—and missed—friends persuaded the men to call off the duel.

During the 1850s Pike gained prominence as a politician and wealth as a lawyer. With the collapse of the Whig party, he organized the Order of

United Americans (Know-Nothings) in Arkansas and advocated immi-
gration restriction. On the great issue of the day—slavery—Pike combined
fatalistic metaphysics with practical politics. Slavery was a "disease" and
an "evil," he conceded, but the interplay of good and evil was part of "the
rule of God's providence" and thus beyond human attempts at reform.
Moreover, he reasoned, southern planters, if denied slaves, would import
as replacements "Lascars, Chinese, and Peons from Mexico."

Pike's facility for foreign languages enabled him to pick up Indian dialects
quickly, and this led to his representing the Creeks, Choctaws, and
Chickasaws in lawsuits against the federal government. Pike eventually won
multimillion-dollar settlements for the tribes and collected $192,000 in
gold as his fee. He built a mansion in Little Rock and became renowned
for lavish parties.

But as Pike's professional life flourished, his family life deteriorated. Seven
of his ten children died in their youth. Pike and his wife separated in 1853,
and he moved to New Orleans to practice law.

Pike's ties to the Indians led to the events that transformed his life. At
the outbreak of the Civil War he was named commissioner of Indian affairs
for the Confederacy. He succeeded in winning most of the Arkansas tribes
over to the Confederacy, and, after being commissioned brigadier general, he organized and armed several Indian regiments. In early March 1862,
over his objection that the Indians had agreed to fight only in defense of
their territory, Pike's regiments were ordered to take part in a Confederate
offensive. On 7 March, during the battle of Pea Ridge in northwestern
Arkansas, the Indians mutilated some Union dead, an infamy that haunted
Pike for the rest of his life. On 15 March 1862, the *Boston Evening Transcript*
doubted that "a more venomous reptile than Albert Pike ever crawled the
face of the earth."

Pike, meanwhile, became embroiled in controversy closer to home. On
31 July 1862, confronted with an order to release his units to another
command, he published an open letter to the Indians in which he
announced his resignation and indicted the Confederacy for neglecting
its treaty obligations. Jefferson Davis accused Pike of treason. In November

Pike's commanding officer, Major General Thomas C. Hindman, sent 200 soldiers to arrest him, but as the Confederate position in the West collapsed, Pike was released.

Worried that he would again be arrested and perhaps executed by the fleeing Confederate forces or murdered by Union soldiers intent on avenging the Pea Ridge atrocities, Pike slipped back to Little Rock only long enough to gather up his books. He then fled into the Ozarks, taking refuge in a cabin at Greasy Cove, Arkansas. What transpired during the next two years is the stuff of legend. Rumors abounded that he had stashed his gold in the mountains and that he had consorted with the devil in bizarre sexual orgies—stories that hill people in the Ozarks continued to tell a half-century after Pike's death.

What is known is that Pike turned his attention to secret fraternal ritual. He had joined the Freemasons in 1850, and the Scottish Rite branch of the order in 1853. At that time the initiations were simple—"for the most part a lot of worthless trash," Pike recalled—and he began to modify and greatly expand them, work that he pursued feverishly after 1863. Incorporating dramatic legends and esoteric philosophies from wide-ranging historical and religious traditions, he revised the twenty-nine initiations ("degrees") of the Scottish Rite. He also wrote *Morals and Dogma of Freemasonry* (1872, 1878, 1881, 1905), the great work of nineteenth-century Freemasonry, a monumental exegesis of the relation of Masonry to classical mythology, Oriental religion, and Medieval mysticism. (Pike did not claim authorship of this book, or of nearly anything else he wrote in his later years, explaining that his photographic memory had captured so many words of others that he could never determine which were uniquely his own.)

While Pike was at Greasy Cove, a federal district court indicted him for treason for his role in the Confederacy and confiscated his property. In 1866, after Masonic friends had interceded on his behalf, President Andrew Johnson officially pardoned Pike at a White House ceremony. During the next two years Pike practiced law in Memphis, Tennessee, and briefly served as editor of the *Memphis Appeal*. Pike may have written the ritual of the Ku Klux Klan, which originated about this time in Pulaski, Tennessee. In

1868 he moved to Washington, D.C., where he unsuccessfully attempted to resume the practice of law.

Pike increasingly devoted himself to Masonic affairs, and when he lost his home after the panic of 1873, he and his daughter Lillian took up residence in the Temple of the Supreme Council (governing body) of the Scottish Rite in Washington. The supreme council offered him an annual stipend of $1,800, which he accepted in 1879 and subsequent years.

Pike became a recluse, seldom venturing from his library in the temple. He produced, in addition to unoriginal poetry and several volumes of Masonic philosophy, some 13,000 manuscript pages of translations of the classic texts of Indian and Persian religions. He died in the temple. In 1899, the Supreme Council of the Scottish Rite erected a bronze statue of Pike at what is now Judiciary Square in Washington, D.C. In 1992 civil rights activists, alleging that Pike was an important figure in the early Ku Klux Klan, demanded that the statue be taken down. During weekly demonstrations at the statue they chanted, "Albert Pike, take a hike." (The charges, though plausible, have not been confirmed by extant fragmentary records.)

Pike was one of the most contradictory men of his or perhaps any age: a 300-pound gourmand who championed ascetic religion, a gun-toting lawyer who wrote lachrymose poetry, an apostle of human freedom who fought for slavery, a venial scoundrel to some and an exemplary moral philosopher to others. Pike, in short, embodied the extremes of nineteenth-century America; his peculiar genius was his ability to resolve these oppositions within the arcana of Masonic ritual.

M.C.C.

A remarkable man who captured, tamed, and trained eagles, wildcats, deer, elk, mountain lions, and wolves, Adams was the subject of an illustrated book published in San Francisco in 1860 entitled The Adventures of James Capen Adams, mountaineer and grizzly bear hunter, *of California.*

GRIZZLY ADAMS

[22 OCTOBER 1812–25 OCTOBER 1860]

*Like many adventurers who headed west in the mid-nineteenth century,
Adams wasn't just seeking his fortune; he was also running away from failure and debt back east. He fled humanity as well, preferring to live and work
among the wild animals of the Cascades and Sierra Nevadas. Though nicknamed for the fearsome* ursus horribilis, *Adams was the rare mountain
man who showed tenderness toward bears, beavers, and other creatures whom
others valued only for their pelts.*

G rizzly Adams, mountain man and wild animal tamer, was born John
Adams in Medway, Massachusetts, the son of Eleazar Adams and Sybil
Capen. Adams apparently served an apprenticeship as a cobbler, but when
he was twenty-one he began hunting and trapping animals for showmen
in the woods of Maine, Vermont, and New Hampshire. He delighted in his
work, which was cut short when he tried to control an unruly Bengal tiger.
In doing this favor for an exhibitor, Adams was badly mangled. When he
recovered his health, he went back to making boots and shoes.

In 1849 Adams suddenly left Massachusetts. The exact reason for his pre-
cipitous departure is unknown, but it seems to have been neither the shock
of his father's suicide nor the loss of his own savings in a speculation that
year. It was probably litigation over property or debts that caused him to
decamp. "I was dead broke," he told his first biographer, Theodore H. Hittell,
circa 1856. "The lawyers and judges ... contrived to rob me of everything
I possessed."

Out west, Adams tried mining, trading, and ranching, but nothing
seemed to work for him. He was as down on his luck in 1852 as he had been
when he arrived in California in 1849. Recalling his wonderful days in the
Maine woods and the Green and White Mountains, he determined to live
alone in the wilderness. Oddly, Adams took an alias (a common practice

in gold rush California), but one that only half hid his identity. He went by James Capen Adams, his brother's name. But he was soon called Grizzly Adams or Old Adams, although he was just forty when he headed into the Sierra Nevada.

In less than eight years of almost solitary living in the wilds, Adams won wide fame in the West. His prowess in catching and taming the much-feared California grizzly—the well-named *ursus horribilis*—was unique. He became a legend in his own time. Hittell wrote a best-selling biography of him, and melodramas based on his career were staged on both coasts. Adams even played himself at Tom Maguire's Opera House in San Francisco.

Adams, who was sometimes called the Wild Yankee, was an atypical recluse. Instead of hiding in a Sierra cave, he roamed about the Coast Range, Cascades, and Sierra Nevada as if he held a roving commission. Fur trappers and market hunters were common in California, but Adams did not run a trapline for beaver and river otter, bag wild ducks and geese for restaurants, or shoot deer and elk for their skins, venison, and tallow. He took animals alive. Using a lasso as well as box traps, he captured unharmed eagles, wildcats, deer, elk, mountain lions, wolves, black bears, and grizzly bears. He penned them up, tamed and trained them, and sold them to wild animal show entrepreneurs. Often in tight spots, he more than once was injured by grizzlies.

Grizzly Adams wandered the mountains either alone or with a single companion, often an Indian. He got along well with the Indians and treated them with respect. He made pets, "watch dogs," and beasts of burden of his grizzly bears, even showing off by riding them. Although he mixed kindness with discipline, he did not spare the rod. When he was asked how he controlled such strong and ferocious animals, Adams merely remarked that he was the "hardest" of the lot.

In 1855 Adams began to tour with his wild animal menagerie and, in 1856, opened his Mountaineer Museum in San Francisco, the ancestor of Woodward's Gardens and the Fleishhacker Zoo. He showed all sorts of animals, but the public came primarily to see his grizzlies, including mighty Ben Franklin, Lady Washington, and Samson. Adams became a celebrity, occupying prominent positions with his animals in civic parades such as that of 1858 celebrating the completion of the Atlantic cable.

In 1860 Adams moved his museum to New York, calling it the California Menagerie. P. T. Barnum, "the greatest American showman," bought a half-interest in it and made Adams famous in the East. Adams most likely brought eight or nine grizzlies with him, plus other "critters," including Old Neptune, Manhattan's first California sea lion.

Adams, who was suffering from the effects of many bear hugs, enjoyed his new fame only briefly. When Barnum examined Adams's head, he found his skull punctured and his brain showing. One of his grizzlies, Old Fremont, had reopened one of Adams's old head wounds. "I'm a used-up man," Adams admitted to Barnum. "I reckon I may live six months or a year, yet."

Adams was right. Although he managed to make a tour with his bears that summer, he took to his bed for the last time in October. *Harper's Weekly* (10 November 1860), noting the passing of the colorful mountaineer, observed, "His tastes led him to cultivate the society of bears, which he did at great personal risk, but with remarkable success, using them as pack horses by day, as blankets by night, as companions at all times."

R.H.D.

Count Haraszthy, from a portrait that was destroyed by fire in San Francisco. This photograph of the portrait hangs in the Portage Public Library in Wisconsin.

AGOSTON HARASZTHY
DE MOKCSA

[30 AUGUST 1812–6 JULY 1869]

*The failure of revolutionary movements in Europe between 1830 and 1850
sent a wave of political exiles across the Atlantic. Haraszthy, a high-born
Hungarian, brought his experience managing a family estate—and his taste
for European wines—to the pioneer settlements of Wisconsin, and later to
California. Along the way, he transformed viticulture in America by intro-
ducing grapes such as Zinfandel. But financial and political troubles forced
Haraszthy into exile again, leading to his bizarre death in the wilds of
Nicaragua.*

Agoston Haraszthy de Mokcsa, pioneer and winegrower, was born in
Futtak, in the county of Backsa, Hungary, the son of General Charles
Haraszthy de Mokcsa and Anna Halasz. According to tradition, he was
the descendant of a noble family long associated with agriculture, horticulture, viticulture, and even sericulture. After receiving a classical Greek
and Latin education, as well as experience in managing the family estate,
Haraszthy, at age eighteen, became a member of the imperial bodyguard
of Austria-Hungary's Emperor Ferdinand. In 1834, Haraszthy married
Eleanora Dödinsky, a refugee from the revolution that was crushed in
Poland in 1831. The couple had three children. By 1835 he had become
the private secretary to the viceroy of the palatinate of Hungary, Archduke
Joseph. Haraszthy was also said to have been the hereditary lord lieutenant
of his home county, a magistrate there, and an ex officio delegate to the
Diet. But he became involved in the revolutionary movement sweeping
Europe, and after his friend, the reformer Louis Kossuth, was arrested in
1837, Haraszthy had to retire to his estate. He apparently became per-
sona non grata, was virtually banished, and was consequently forced to
emigrate in 1840.

Settling initially in Wisconsin, Haraszthy founded a village on the Wisconsin River, naming it Széptáj (Belleview), although the name was later changed to Haraszthy, then to Westfield, and finally to Sauk City. With a partner, Haraszthy built a brick store and a schoolhouse and worked to attract immigrants, most of whom were German, English, or Swiss, rather than Magyar. With the help of General Lewis Cass, Haraszthy was able to return to Hungary in order to sell his estate and bring both his parents and his own family back to his village in Wisconsin in 1842. There he opened a brickyard, developed the state's first hopyard and kiln, established a ferry across the river, and later operated a packet boat, the *Rock River*. Haraszthy also grew wheat and corn, raised livestock, and set out a vineyard, although the climate was inhospitable to wine grapes. Haraszthy founded the Emigrant Association and the Humanist Society and wrote a popular book, *Utazás Eiszakamerikábu* (*Travels in North America*), in 1844.

The "Colonel," as he was called to distinguish him from his father, the "General," was a brilliant conversationalist who loved parties and was a perfect host. But he was "land poor," with great holdings (heavily mortgaged) but little cash. Business problems combined with his asthma to persuade Haraszthy to make a fresh start in the more benign climate of California. Before he left Wisconsin, the legislature honored him as an outstanding citizen with a dinner in the state capital, Madison. Haraszthy was elected captain and wagon master of a train that left St. Joseph, Missouri, in April 1849 and reached southern California over the Gila Trail by the year's end.

When San Diego County was formed in 1850, the self-titled "Count" Haraszthy was elected its sheriff and, shortly, was also made city marshal of the town of San Diego. He was an effective peace officer (although he was charged with a conflict of interest in the building of the county jail), and he cleaned up the rough little port while putting down an Indian uprising led by Antonio Garra in the interior. Haraszthy was also elected to the state assembly in 1852. He engaged in viticulture, and when Haraszthy found the San Diego climate too subtropical for vines, he set out two vineyards near San Francisco. But the cool, foggy, and windy climate there was better for brussels sprouts and artichokes than wine grapes.

In 1857, Haraszthy, who had done some private assaying, was appointed assayer and later smelter and refiner at the branch U.S. Mint in San Francisco. He was forced to resign, however, under charges of embezzlement after an investigation by Treasury agent J. Ross Browne, only to be acquitted in 1861. Meanwhile, Haraszthy bought land near General M. G. Vallejo's proven vineyard in Sonoma, building himself a grand, white Pompeiian villa, "Buena Vista," and planting 80,000 vines in one year. At Buena Vista he revolutionized the nascent wine industry by replacing the traditional but mediocre Mission grape vines with European varieties such as Zinfandel, Tokay, and Muscat of Alexandria. Zinfandel came to be the most widely planted varietal for red wine in the state. Haraszthy further violated tradition by deliberately planting his grape vines on the dry, thinly soiled hillsides of the Mayacamas Mountains rather than on rich and flat bottomland like his peers. His vintages, which won medals at the state fairs of 1858 and 1859, proved how right he was.

Haraszthy then wrote the first important California wine monograph, "Report on Grapes and Wines of California," for the 1859 *Transactions* of the California State Agricultural Society. In 1861 the governor of California appointed him to a three-man commission charged with reporting on ways to promote the improved culture of grapes in California. With the understanding that he had the legislature's blessing, Haraszthy paid his own way to Europe to survey the vineyards of France, Spain, Italy, and Germany, confident of being reimbursed for the expensive survey. He returned with notes for a Harper & Brothers book that consisted of his report in the form of a travelogue, plus an expansion of his earlier essay. The book, *Grape Culture, Wines and Wine-Making* (1862), was popular and influential. Along with his notes, Haraszthy also brought back 100,000 prime vines and cuttings of 1,400 different European varieties of *vinifera*. He also brought cuttings of choice almond, olive, fig, pomegranate, chestnut, orange, and lemon trees for propagation by grafting. The high quality of these imported species revolutionized viticulture and enhanced horticulture.

During the Civil War Haraszthy was mistakenly seen as a Confederate sympathizer by an ardently Republican legislature because he was a

Democrat. Perhaps because of this, the legislators refused to reimburse him for his $10,000 European venture. Hard-pressed, he was rescued financially in 1863 when his friend, San Francisco capitalist William Ralston, joined him to incorporate the Buena Vista Vinicultural Society. The corporation did well, but Ralston was interested in the "bottom line" of quick returns and large quantities of wine, while Haraszthy insisted on the careful (slow) making of limited amounts of high-quality wine. They were soon at odds, and the financier maneuvered the vintner out of the enterprise by 1866.

Once more Haraszthy had to start all over. By 1868, with partners, he bought a sugar plantation near Corinto, Nicaragua, clearing new land and planting more canes until he had the largest plantation in the country. He then built a rum distillery and planned a sawmill to take advantage of his hacienda's natural reserves of mahogany and other rare hardwoods.

On 6 July 1869 Haraszthy suddenly vanished, and searchers traced him to a stream where he planned to put up his sawmill. Haraszthy had tied up his mule and apparently attempted to cross the arroyo by means of a large tree whose branches extended to the other side. A large limb was broken in midstream. One of the count's sons wrote, "We must conclude that Father tried to cross the river by the tree and that, losing his balance, he fell, grasping the broken limb, and then the alligator must have drawn him down, forever."

R.H.D.

JOHN CHARLES FRÉMONT

[21 JANUARY 1813–13 JULY 1890]

Frémont was one of the last and most intrepid explorers of the continental frontier, and an exemplar of what de Tocqueville called the "strange unrest" of nomadic Americans. An illegitimate child who was expelled from college for "incorrigible negligence," Frémont sailed to South America and later determined to spend his life "among Indians and in waste places." Over the next twenty-five years he headed five expeditions to every corner of the West, served as a military man in several wars, and, though Southern-born, became the first presidential candidate of the anti-slavery Republican Party.

John Charles Frémont, explorer and presidential candidate, was born in Savannah, Georgia, the son of Jean Charles Fremon, a French émigré teacher, and Anne Beverley Whiting Pryor, a Virginia woman of patrician birth who left her elderly husband in 1811 to run away with Fremon. The couple, who apparently never married, moved frequently, living for a period in Savannah, where Jean Charles gave French and dancing lessons, and Anne took in boarders. In 1818, Jean Charles Fremon died, and the family, which by then included several younger children, eventually settled in Charleston, South Carolina, to a life of genteel poverty. The social and economic insecurity of his situation profoundly influenced Frémont. He grew up an outsider—proud, reserved, cautious in sharing his feelings, skeptical of rules and authority, and eager, at times to the point of recklessness, to prove himself.

As a youth, Frémont (who added the *t* and accent sometime after his father's death) worked in the law office of John W. Mitchell, who sponsored his preparatory education. In 1829, he entered the College of Charleston. Although he excelled in mathematics, in time he began to neglect his studies (he had fallen in love, he explained in *Memoirs of My Life* [1887]), and in 1831, a few months before graduation, he was expelled for

This 1856 lithograph of Frémont depicts a determined man who had already helped to survey the upper Missouri River and the Oregon Trail, and had made two attempts at finding an all-weather railroad route through the Rocky Mountains.

"incorrigible negligence." He applied for and was granted a B.A. some five years later. In 1833 the influential South Carolina politician Joel R. Poinsett secured him a place as a civilian mathematics instructor on the USS *Natchez*, bound for a two-year South American voyage. When Frémont returned, Poinsett arranged for a position with a topographical survey of a projected Charleston, Louisville, and Cincinnati Railroad route through the Carolina and Tennessee mountains and, in 1837–1838, with a reconnaissance of Cherokee lands, principally in Georgia. Frémont relished this wilderness work and in it discovered "the path which I was 'destined to walk.' Through many of the years to come the occupation of my prime of life was to be among Indians and in waste places" (*Memoirs*, p. 50).

In 1838, Poinsett, who had become U.S. secretary of war, assigned the French-speaking Frémont to assist Joseph N. Nicollet, a French scientist-explorer, in surveying the region between the upper Mississippi and Missouri Rivers. Several months later, Frémont received his commission as a second lieutenant in the U.S. Army Corps of Topographical Engineers.

During two successive expeditions (1838 and 1839), Nicollet gave Frémont an invaluable education in both the scientific and practical aspects of a wilderness survey. While in Washington, D.C., assisting Nicollet with the expedition map and report, he met advocates of westward expansion, including Missouri senator Thomas Hart Benton (1782–1858). Frémont's elopement with Benton's gifted seventeen-year-old daughter Jessie Benton (Jessie Benton Frémont) in 1841 provided him with both a devoted collaborator and, through her father, a powerful advocate in the halls of government. The couple had five children, three of whom lived to adulthood.

The following year, with the aging Nicollet too ill to travel, Benton arranged for his son-in-law to head a twenty-five-man, four-month expedition to survey and map the region of the emerging Oregon Trail through South Pass on the Continental Divide. A *Report of an Exploration... between the Missouri River and the Rocky Mountains ...* (1843), the lively, factually detailed government report that Frémont and his wife produced after the journey caught the public imagination: images of Frémont's guide, the then little-known Christopher "Kit" Carson, riding bareback across the prairie, and Frémont himself, raising a flag on a Rocky Mountain peak, entered the national mythology.

In 1843 Frémont set out on a far more ambitious journey to the Oregon region. Disregarding government orders to return by the same route, he went south to Nevada and, in a dangerous midwinter journey, over the snow-covered Sierra Nevada into Mexican-held California. By the time the expedition returned east across the southern rim of what Frémont defined as the Great Basin, they had completed a bold fourteen-month circuit of the West, traveling 6,475 miles by their own calculations. The Frémonts' account of the journey, *A Report of the Exploring Expedition to Oregon and California...* (1845), enthralled the nation. Skillfully combining adventure, scientific data, and detailed practical information for emigrants, supplemented by a valuable map prepared by expedition cartographer Charles Preuss, it was "monumental in its breadth—a classic of exploring literature" (William H. Goetzmann, *Exploration and Empire* [1966], p. 248). Powerful propaganda, it stirred Americans to head west, guided, as pioneer Sarah Royce stated, "only by the light of Frémont's *Travels*."

Initial instructions for Frémont's third expedition (1845–1847) limited him to a brief journey to the Rocky Mountains, but when expansionist James Polk assumed presidential office in March 1845, Frémont was given more funds and men, and his destination again became the Pacific Coast. Though the expedition was a scientific survey, the new administration doubtless thought it would be useful to have Frémont in California should war with Mexico occur, particularly since Polk and Benton feared that Great Britain might attempt to occupy the province.

When Frémont reached the Monterey, California, region in February 1846, the Mexican authorities were highly suspicious of his sixty-man armed expedition and ordered them to leave the country. Reacting defiantly, Frémont raised the American flag on a nearby mountain but, with the prudent American consul Thomas Larkin as intermediary, was persuaded to retreat. He moved north to Klamath Lake in southern Oregon, where, on 8 May, Polk's secret agent, Archibald Gillespie, reached him with messages, the contents of which historians have long debated, as well as news that war with Mexico was imminent. Frémont returned to the Sacramento Valley, where he encouraged and then joined American settlers in the Bear Flag Revolt, action, he told a congressional committee in 1848, that was "without expressed authority from the United States, and revolutionary in its character" (Jackson and Spence, vol. 2, p. 469).

When confirmed reports of war with Mexico reached the Pacific, the U.S. Navy seized California ports. Commodore Robert F. Stockton named Frémont commander of the California Battalion, which helped to occupy the province. In the winter of 1846–1847, during a revolt centered in Los Angeles, Frémont became entangled in a quarrel between Stockton and late-arriving General Stephen Watts Kearny of the army, both of whom claimed supreme authority in California. When Frémont, an army officer, rashly sided with Stockton, who had named him governor, Kearny marched him east in disgrace to face a court-martial. Despite widespread public support and Benton's personal defense of him during the long, rancorous trial, Frémont was found guilty and dismissed from the army. Although President Polk reinstated him for "meritorious and valuable services," Frémont bitterly resigned.

In October 1848 Frémont set out on his ill-fated fourth expedition, partially financed by St. Louis businessmen eager to locate a central, all-weather railroad route through the Rockies. During the unusually severe winter, the expedition lost its way in the rugged mountains of southern Colorado, and ten men, a third of the expedition, perished in the snow. While Frémont and several reliable men in his party blamed the guide, William S. "Old Bill" Williams, other members blamed Frémont himself.

Despite the tragedy, Frémont pushed on to California, where gold had been discovered at Las Mariposas, a seventy-square-mile tract near the Yosemite Valley that he had purchased sight unseen in 1847 for $3,000. Las Mariposas made Frémont rich, but he was not a shrewd businessman. Until he sold it in 1864, its legal entanglements and escalating costs diminished both his profits and his energy.

In December 1849 Frémont was elected California's first senator and began his term in 1850. During his brief tenure (he drew the short term), he voted for abolition of the slave trade in the District of Columbia and against stiff penalties for those who aided runaway slaves. When he ran for reelection in 1851, the state legislature deadlocked over his candidacy and eventually chose a proslavery Democrat.

In the winter of 1853–1854, Frémont headed his fifth and final expedition, again a privately financed journey, to find an all-weather railroad route through the Rockies. Although he believed he had found a suitable pass, he and his men, starving and pounded by blizzards, escaped disaster only when they stumbled to safety in the village of Parowan in southwestern Utah.

Frémont reentered politics in 1856. With crucial early support from Nathaniel Banks and Francis Blair, Sr. (1791–1876), he became the first

presidential candidate of the newly formed Republican party on a platform opposing the extension of slavery. Chosen more for his heroic image
than his political skills, he nonetheless inspired great enthusiasm in the
North, while in the South, he was branded a "Frenchman's bastard" and,
incorrectly, a secret Roman Catholic. Although Frémont gained the major-
ity of Northern votes, he was defeated nationwide by the Democratic candidate, James Buchanan (1.8 to 1.34 million, with an electoral vote of 174
to 114). Despite the loss, his candidacy established the Republican party's
dominance in the North and set the stage for Abraham Lincoln's victory
in 1860.

For the next four years, Frémont eschewed politics as he attempted to manage his increasingly debt-ridden gold mines. When the Civil War began,
President Lincoln appointed him major general commanding the
Department of the West with headquarters in St. Louis. Arriving in late July
1861, Frémont faced a chaotic and divided state, inadequate troops and arms,
and within two weeks, the disastrous battle of Wilson's Creek, when southwest Missouri fell under Confederate control. On 30 August 1861, without
consulting Lincoln, Frémont issued a limited emancipation decree, freeing
the slaves of Missouri rebels, but the president, concerned with Border State
loyalty, ordered him to rescind it. Over the next two months, continued
military defeats, corruption and war profiteering among his staff, and the
unexpected enmity of the powerful Blair family weakened Frémont's position. Although he personally led troops through southern Missouri in pursuit of the Confederate army, effectively driving them from the state, on 2
November, just before, Frémont claimed, he was about to face the enemy in
battle, Lincoln relieved him of his command.

Frémont's emancipation decree gained him a large following, particularly among radical Republicans critical of Lincoln's management of the
war. Bowing to their pressure, the president placed Frémont in command
of Union troops in western Virginia in the spring of 1862. When Frémont
fell victim to Thomas "Stonewall" Jackson's brilliant tactics, Lincoln reorganized his command, and Frémont resigned. He never received another
command, and by 1864, when he was nominated for the presidency by a

group of radical Republicans and other dissidents, his ineffective leadership along with rumors of business and personal scandal weakened his appeal. Nonetheless Lincoln viewed him as a threat. A bargain was struck, and on 22 September, Frémont withdrew from the race; the next day, Lincoln dismissed Frémont's enemy Montgomery Blair from the cabinet.

During and after the war, Frémont pursued railroad and other investments with no lasting success. His Memphis, El Paso, and Pacific Railroad venture ended in a financial scandal, for which he was at least partly responsible, and in the panic of 1873, he was reduced to near poverty. Appointed governor of Arizona Territory (1878–1881) by President Rutherford B. Hayes, Frémont used his position in a futile attempt to recoup his fortune through mining and land schemes and was eventually forced to resign. His *Memoirs*, the first of a planned two volumes, brought little remuneration. In 1890 Congress granted him a long-sought $6,000-a-year pension. A few months later he died suddenly in a New York City boardinghouse.

Frémont remains a controversial and somewhat elusive figure. While many were inspired by his stand against the extension of slavery during the 1856 election campaign and for immediate emancipation during the early Civil War, others suspected he was an ambitious poseur, more self-promoting than idealistic. Similarly, evaluations of his role in the conquest of California have ranged from hero to the fraud depicted by Josiah Royce in *California . . . A Study in American Character* (1886). A restless loner, Frémont disliked politics, found administrative work tedious, and lacked business acumen. He was at his best as the daring and resourceful leader of his early expeditions. The knowledge of the West and impetus to the westward movement that these journeys inspired remain a remarkable and enduring achievement.

P.H.

Recounting his mission to rescue Sir John Franklin, Kane would write in Arctic Explorations *in 1856, "Happily the day was warmed by a clear sunshine, and the thermometer rose to -4 in the shade; otherwise we must have frozen." This posthumous portrait by Alonso Chappel hardly suggests the hardship his expedition surely endured.*

ELISHA KENT KANE

[3 FEBRUARY 1820—16 FEBRUARY 1857]

*Curiously, ill health in childhood seems to have been the principal impetus
for Kane's brief but extraordinary career as a global adventurer. In just thirteen years, he traveled five continents, from Asia to the Arctic. Among his many
exploits, Kane descended volcanoes, snuck behind enemy lines in the Mexican
War, pursued a tumultuous love affair with a "spirit rapper," and survived a
hungry winter in the high Arctic by discovering an unlikely antidote to scurvy.*

Elisha Kent Kane, physician and Arctic explorer, was born in
Philadelphia, Pennsylvania, the son of John Kintzing Kane, a federal
judge, and Jane Duval Leiper. The Kane family was prominent in
Philadelphia and Washington, D.C., through Judge Kane's association with
President Andrew Jackson. Elisha's younger brother, Thomas Leiper Kane,
would become a general in the Union army and a hero in Mormon history. As a boy, Kane had a strong interest in natural sciences. While a
teenager, rheumatic fever seriously damaged his heart. After a long con-
valescence, Kane was expected to live for only a short time, but his father
suggested that he "die in the harness" rather than spend his life moping in
despondency. Young Kane embarked on a life of adventure.

Overcoming his ill health, Kane obtained a medical degree from the University
of Pennsylvania in 1842. His research thesis, "Experiments on Keisteine with
Remarks on Its Application to the Diagnosis of Pregnancy" (published in
American Journal of Medical Sciences, n.s., 4 [1842]: 13–37), was a remarkable
pioneering study about using urine samples to determine pregnancy and
became the leading research study in the field during the next two decades.

The Kane family believed that Elisha could not endure the rigors of a
normal medical practice, so Judge Kane secured his appointment as surgeon in the U.S. Navy. In 1844, while awaiting his commission, he joined
Caleb Cushing on the first U.S. diplomatic mission to China. During his

time in the Far East, he initiated bold adventures, including a descent into a Philippine volcano. In 1846, he officially began his naval duties with a cruise to Africa.

When Kane returned home in 1847, during the Mexican War, President James Polk sent him as a special courier to General Winfield Scott in Mexico City. Polk suspected Scott of insubordination and ordered Kane to cross enemy-infested territory to deliver his dispatch. Traveling with an allied group of Mexican partisans, Kane fought a bloody battle with the Mexican army. After the battle, the partisans seriously wounded Kane when he prevented their slaughter of the captured Mexican general Antonio Gaona. Kane's original mission proved futile because the president had already removed Scott from command. Kane's wounds left him near death, but General Gaona and his family nursed Kane back to health. Kane returned home as a war hero.

In 1850, after naval duty in the Mediterranean and South America, Kane joined an American expedition to search for the lost British explorer Sir John Franklin. The Franklin expedition had entered the Canadian Arctic in 1845 with two ships and 129 men, seeking the Northwest Passage, and had vanished in the Arctic. British, French, and American groups mounted an international rescue mission to find the missing explorers. Whaling magnate Henry Grinnell donated two ships for the American expedition while the U.S. Navy furnished personnel and supplies.

Lieutenant Edwin De Haven commanded the brig *Advance,* with Kane as surgeon and official historian. The *Advance* and a sister ship joined forces with the rescue fleet in Lancaster Sound, north of Hudson Bay. Kane quickly impressed British explorers with his intelligence and traveling experience. In August 1850 the fleet located Franklin's first winter base on Beechey Island, along with the graves of three of Franklin's men. Further searches by the *Advance* failed to locate Franklin's expedition. The *Advance* returned to the United States in September 1851.

Kane's belief that Franklin might have gone farther north persuaded Grinnell and the U.S. Navy to support a second expedition to search for the lost explorers. Kane led this new expedition in the *Advance* to seek a more northerly route near Greenland. During the preparations for the voyage, thirty-two-year-old Kane fell in love with a teenaged spiritualist, Margaret Fox. Margaret and her sister were the famous "spirit rapping" team that performed seances for mid-nineteenth-century celebrities. Both the Kane and the Fox families opposed the relationship between the socially prominent physician and the scandalous girl who supposedly communicated with the dead. Before departing on his polar expedition, Kane and his aunt placed Margaret in a private home for tutoring. When he returned from his expedition, Kane believed that Margaret would complete her transformation into a socially accomplished young lady.

Kane's expedition departed in 1853, traveling northward along the Greenland coast. As the ship entered Smith Sound, the channel separating Greenland from Ellesmere Island, Canada, heavy ice stopped its progress. Rather than retreat to the south, Kane elected to keep his ship in Smith Sound. The ice soon froze around the ship, trapping Kane and his men in the high Arctic for the winter. When spring arrived, Kane sent exploring parties to the north along Smith Sound. One of his men, William Morton, discovered a broad expanse of open water, which he thought was an ocean. Morton's report led Kane to the erroneous conclusion that there was an open polar sea. Kane did chart many new discoveries in what later became known as "the American route to the pole."

The 1854 summer thaw failed to release the ship from the ice. Some of Kane's men, fearing that they would not survive another winter in the Arctic, demanded to go south to reach the Greenland settlements. Kane, unable to quell the mutiny, refused to abandon the ship and his sick men. The dissenters, who included Isaac Hayes, then insisted that Kane supply food and equipment for their escape. Kane reluctantly complied.

Kane and his remaining men faced a second bleak winter in the Arctic. While strong men wilted, Kane, the invalid, became a pillar of strength. The innovative doctor traded with the local Inuit for food. He also used the bountiful supply of the ship's rats for food and as a remedy for scurvy. When Kane learned that the deserters were starving, he sent them food and assisted their return to the ship.

During the summer of 1855 Kane successfully led his men south to the Greenland settlements. He quickly became the United States' first Arctic hero. Reports to Congress and lectures seriously disrupted Kane's happy reunion with Fox. His parents continued to oppose the marriage of their son to the notorious spirit rapper. Seeking to become financially independent from his family, Kane labored to complete his book. He juggled a few brief interludes with Fox while struggling against publication deadlines.

From across the Atlantic, Franklin's wife implored Kane to come to England to organize a new search for her husband. The British government and the prestigious Royal Geographical Society also wished to honor the American hero. In October 1856, Kane reluctantly sailed to England, where his health rapidly deteriorated. Seeking a warmer climate, Kane sailed to Havana, Cuba, in December 1856, but his physical condition worsened. Kane died in Havana. Margaret Fox never obtained a widow's share of his estate, despite her claim that they had secretly married. When Kane's remains arrived in the United States, thousands gathered in each city, from New Orleans to Philadelphia, to express their grief. In American history, only the funeral processions of Abraham Lincoln and Robert Kennedy have approached the public tribute given to America's first Arctic hero.

During his short life, Kane experienced travel and adventures that rivaled Marco Polo. His extensive travels on five continents yielded major contributions to medical research, Arctic exploration, and international understanding. He inspired and blazed the trail for future American explorers such as Charles Hall, General A. W. Greely, Admiral Robert Peary, and Dr. Frederick Cook. Even more remarkable was the high esteem he earned from the people and nations around the world.

T.H.

EDWARD ZANE CARROLL JUDSON

[20 MARCH 1823–16 JULY 1886]

Restlessness—occupational as well as geographic—came with the territory in mid-nineteenth century America. In a nation on the move, Judson went everywhere and did everything, including stints as a sailor, Civil War soldier, and showman who popularized Buffalo Bill. Judson was just as restive in his family and political life, gaining notoriety as a bigamist and proselytizer for a range of dubious causes. He also displayed a very American flair for self-promotion, turning his adventures—real and imagined—into trashy best-sellers known as "shilling shockers."

Edward Zane Carroll Judson, adventurer and writer known as "Ned Buntline," was born in Stamford, New York, the son of Levi Judson, a schoolmaster and, later, an attorney; his mother's name is unknown. After his father moved the family to Philadelphia, the adolescent Judson rebelled and ran away to sea as a cabin boy. He served for about five years on voyages to various Caribbean and South American ports. Judson's life and career—one might say lives and careers—epitomize a restlessness that made him thirst for adventures and misadventures in- and out-of-doors, and they show that he had a keen eye for the chance to promote himself as heroic in sensationally fictionalized accounts of his own adventures. The list of epithets he inspires is almost encyclopedic: sailor and U.S. Navy officer; soldier; magazine editor; writer of several hundred "shilling shockers," dime novels, and other "continuous" stories; temperance lecturer (and drunkard); superpatriot to those of Know-Nothing (Buntlinite) persuasion, jingoist bigot to others; expert marksman and angler; bigamist; "discoverer" of Buffalo Bill; playwright; proselytizer; generic showman; and, occasionally, outright con artist. To these might be added still others.

Ned Buntline's Own.

EXTRA.

NED never before has had occasion to get out an extra, but he deems it necessary to say that he was not participating in the *riot* at the Astor Place Opera House on the night of the 10th; that he merely walked over there from the bed-side of a sick wife, to see if the reports were true which had reached him in regard to there being a mob—and without knowing a single man in the crowd, while standing in silence on the side-walk, he was arrested. The reason of that arrest can perhaps be accounted for by those who have read his articles in regard to the police lately. They were determined to show their *efficiency* upon an unharmed, unoffending, quiet person, who, at the moment of his arrest, not having been *five minutes* on the ground, was turning to go home to the presence of his sick wife. The article in my paper, (which was *already published* when this affair occurred, it having gone to press at *three o'clock* on Thursday afternoon,) referring to the riot of the 8th, and the Macready quarrel, will at once explain my sentiments in regard to riots, and prove that I am not one to countenance them by word or deed.

I now beg all of my friends to watch the manner in which my foes, and those whom I have spoken so boldly and freely of, are endeavoring to work my ruin. They cannot succeed—I am "firm in the right cause," as ever, and so both friends and foes will find me! I shall issue, either on Saturday or Monday morning, an extra, large size, price three cents, containing a complete account of this sad affair, and also showing how I have been wronged and imposed upon. If the wife of my bosom, who is now on a sick-bed, dangerously ill, should die from this shock, there shall be more than one man held responsible for her murder! At the present writing, though ready to give bail to any amount, I have been a prisoner for over fifteen hours, and it is only through the kindness of Captain Cunningham, the *gentlemanly* and generous Captain of the Ninth Ward, that I am afforded facilities for writing this article. To him and his gentlemanly clerk, with the exception of Officer Bumstead of the 10th Ward, and the clerks of the Essex-street Court, and Mr. Stewart of the Tombs, do I owe and return thanks for anything like courtesy!

This extra is struck off for gratuitous circulation among my friends, to refute the gratuitous lies of the Herald and other papers!

EDWARD Z. C. JUDSON,

THE

"NED BUNTLINE."

An *"Extra"* from one of Judson's monthly journals hints at his turbulent relationship with the law—charges of bigamy, drunkenness, and leading a mob landed him in jail on no fewer than five occasions.

At fourteen, Judson, impulsive and impetuous, enlisted in the U.S. Navy, hoping to be part of an Antarctic expedition. He had to settle for ships that took him, first, to the Mexican coast and, later, to Florida and the exciting prospect of the Seminole wars. Though he saw no actual combat, he mined imaginary battles for two decades in essentially trashy fictions. Resigning his midshipman commission in mid-1842, he remained unaccounted for until May 1844. His interests had turned inland and literary.

Two attempts to establish monthly literary journals, first in Pittsburgh and then in Cincinnati, failed. Almost immediately he resurrected his first journal as *Ned Buntline's Own*, a magazine he enriched with a continuing narrative of his own "actual" adventures and a pietistic guide for travelers about how to avoid a variety of confidence games. At the same time he had published in Lewis Gaylord Clark's *Knickerbocker* two stories and had an agreement with Clark for a serialized narrative of sea adventures, "Ned Buntline's Life-Yarn." His hankering for a literary career led him into publicity stunts. In a typical escapade he fabricated his single-handed capture of two of three murderers near Eddyville, Kentucky. Any notoriety seemed welcome, even that attached to real-life events. In Nashville, Judson was suspected of seducing a teenaged bride; when the husband came after him firing several shots, Judson shot him in the forehead. Falsely accused by the victim's friends of shooting the man in the back, Judson fled the courtroom with a serious chest wound when they opened fire. Trying to escape through a hotel's third-story window, he fell, as he later put it, "forty seven feet three inches, (measured), . . . and not a bone cracked!" He was in fact seriously crippled. Recaptured and taken to jail, that night he was put upon by a lynch mob and hanged in the public square; he was saved, he reported, when a friend cut the rope. A grand jury later accepted his plea of self-defense. Meanwhile, his wife, Seberina, virtually abandoned, died in childbirth.

A year later, back in New York, Judson became aware of the emergence of a new reading class of uneducated, relatively poor people engrossed in shilling shockers, the kind of melodramatic adventure trash he had earlier panned in his magazine reviews. Some writers, he learned, were turning out one and two dozen such volumes annually, and Judson took them as his models. The titles of his earliest narratives are typical of all of them: *The Last Days of Calleo; or, The Doomed City of Sin*, *The King of the Sea: A Tale of the Fearless and Free* (1847), and *The Queen of the Sea; or, Our Lady of the Ocean: A Tale of Love, Strife and Chivalry* (1848). His output in the next twenty years was prodigious; he once boasted that he had written a book of more than 600 pages in just sixty-two hours. By the 1860s he was said to be earning $20,000 yearly. Though some of these shockers and dime novels sold in the hundreds of thousands, none is seen in twentieth-century literary histories. Judson himself, in his reformist zeal, put more stock in his *Mysteries and Miseries of New York: A Story of Real Life* (1848), a melodramatic exposé of gambling, prostitution, and various forms of gangsterism done up with a sociological air. By 1869, when he met William F. Cody near the North Platte River and began creating the legend of Buffalo Bill in a series of dime novels and a play in which Judson himself took a role, Judson was a celebrity as one of the creators of the Beadle's and the Street and Smith genre.

Judson by no means had to cloister himself to write so many volumes. In 1849, he led a mob to New York's Astor Place Opera House to protest English actor William Macready's performance of *Macbeth*. Twenty-three people were killed, and Judson was tried, found guilty, and sentenced to a year in prison. Concurrently, Annie Bennett, whom he had married in 1848 and with whom he had one child, was divorcing him for infidelity and drunkenness—while Judson was achieving further notoriety on the temperance lecture circuit and was reported by several scandal sheets as having six mistresses in the city. The next year found him in St. Louis, and by 1852, he was in jail there for leading a mob of enthusiasts of the "nativist"—America for Americans—movement. He jumped bail, only to be rearrested on the charges twenty years later when touring with Buffalo Bill in *The Scouts of the Plains* (1872). In 1853, while campaigning for his Know-Nothing party, he married Lovanche Swart as well as a young actress, Josie Juda. He was charged with bigamy and again jailed.

After he was released by New York's governor, Judson lectured on temperance in Maine. He was charged with shooting and wounding a black man (thinking him to be a Greek) and was jailed and tried, but this time he was acquitted. The middle and late 1850s found him retreating to cabin life in the Adirondacks—hunting, fishing, and writing—while, around 1857, eschewing both Lovanche and Josie for another teenaged bride, Eva Gardiner, who died in childbirth in early 1860. By the end of that year, he had both entered into a clandestine relationship and married still another wife, Kate Myers.

The unhappiness of the match probably influenced Judson's decision to enlist in the Union army in late 1862. Because of his superb marksmanship, he was quickly made sergeant, and he acted ably in one skirmish before being imprisoned for desertion when he overextended a furlough. Released, he was given an honorable discharge in late 1864 and returned home telling his readers he had served as "Chief of Scouts with the rank of a Colonel." He mythologized his war experiences in *Life in the Saddle; or, The Cavalry Scout.*

After the Civil War, Judson concentrated on the Buffalo Bill legend and launched a successful tour of *The Scouts of the Plains*. In 1871 he married Anna Fuller, with whom he had two children. In 1884 Lovanche publicly accused him of bigamy again. On a second trip west, he traveled to Dodge City to present Wyatt Earp and Bat Masterson with "Buntline Specials," guns which Colt had made for him. He retired to "Eagle's Nest," a luxurious home in Stamford, New York, built with his considerable literary profits. There he lived as a family man, expert angler, and writer for numerous New York newspapers and magazines, especially *Turf, Field and Farm.* Ever the boyish patriot, he prided himself on the pyrotechnic displays he put on for July Fourth celebrations. He died in Stamford.

J.D.C.

Limitless aspirations for adventure led Walker from Nashville to the Tropics of Central America where his expansionist dreams were extinguished when British naval forces captured him in Honduras.

WILLIAM
WALKER

[8 MAY 1824–12 SEPTEMBER 1860]

A lawyer, doctor, duelist, and journalist, Walker was also an example of Manifest Destiny gone mad. He belonged to a small but determined band of swashbucklers who sought to extend the Plantation South to Latin America, often by force. (They were called "filibusters," a term that migrated to American politics in 1854 when a minority of senators delayed passage of the Kansas-Nebraska Act.) In a mere seven years, Walker invaded Baja, annexed a Mexican state, declared himself president of Nicaragua (as well as of the nonexistent "Republic of Lower California"), and repeatedly broke neutrality laws before Hondurans extinguished his expansionist dreams.

William Walker, adventurer, was born in Nashville, Tennessee, the son of James Walker, an insurance executive, and Mary Norvell. While the family was not especially affluent, the parents were determined that William receive a good education. Accordingly, he graduated from the University of Nashville at fourteen years of age and received a medical degree in 1843 from the University of Pennsylvania. Shortly thereafter he journeyed to Europe, where he pursued additional medical studies. He returned to Nashville in 1845. He practiced medicine for a while but evidently did not enjoy the profession, so he studied law. Late in 1845 he moved to New Orleans, where he practiced law a short time. He may have been unsuccessful in the occupation, for he soon turned to yet another profession. In 1848, he became assistant editor of the *New Orleans Daily Crescent*. He seemed to enjoy this profession more than his previous ones, but evidently he became bored after a while. Seeking new adventures, he headed for California's gold fields, arriving in San Francisco in 1850. There he took employment as an associate editor of the *San Francisco Daily Herald*.

As a newspaper editor he expressed contempt for the corruption in the California judicial system, especially that of Judge Levi Parsons, who subsequently had Walker arrested for commenting editorially about Parsons. Released as a consequence of a public outrage, Walker fought a duel with one of Parsons's supporters. Although slightly wounded, Walker recovered and moved in 1851 to Marysville, California, where he again briefly practiced law. Possibly influenced by the French filibustering efforts into northwestern Mexico, led by such men as Raousset Boulbon and Charles de Pindray, Walker decided to establish American colonies in Sonora and Baja California, with or without Mexican cooperation.

Walker's Mexican adventure began in 1853, when he attempted to secure a permit from Mexican authorities to bring American colonists to Baja California. Mexico wanted no American settlement on its northern frontier and thus refused Walker any cooperation. Walker was not discouraged, however, for he and law associate Henry P. Watkins planned a takeover of Baja California and possibly Sonora. Walker recruited adventurous men in California, and he found many eager volunteers. He acquired the use of a small brig, and on 3 November 1853, after what he considered careful planning, the party landed at La Paz, Baja California. Walker quickly proclaimed the creation of the Republic of Lower California and named himself president.

Walker's future as president of Lower California was far from secure. Mexican authorities dispatched a small fleet with enough men to drive Walker out of La Paz. Somehow Walker learned of the approaching Mexicans, and with his party numbering only forty-five men he decided to move north toward the international border. Since the brig that had deposited the Walker party had headed back to California, Walker had to lead his men overland. Moreover, his associate, Watkins, who was supposed to bring reinforcements, had been detained by U.S. authorities and could not come to Walker's assistance. After a long and difficult march, the party reached Ensenada, approximately 100 miles south of the border. By this time, Mexican forces were pursuing him overland as well as by sea. On 18 January 1854, although his position was precarious, Walker grandiosely annexed the Mexican state of Sonora and told his men they would march north and east into Sonora, where his government could be established.

Walker then led his men northward, trying to avoid Mexican troops and aiming to cross into Sonora near the mouth of the Colorado River. When he arrived at the international border, he discovered that Mexican troops had arrived first and blocked his path. He could only surrender or fight the Mexicans. He chose the latter and charged the Mexican line. The line parted sufficiently for the men to escape, and Walker's party got to safety in the United States.

Walker's troubles were not over, for U.S. Army authorities immediately arrested him and his men. He was brought to trial in California for violation of U.S. neutrality laws, but he was easily acquitted. Californians were more in sympathy with Walker than with the government. After his acquittal, Walker returned to San Francisco but did not give up the idea of being president of some Latin American country. He set his sights next on Nicaragua. He chose Nicaragua because of the constant political turmoil in the country. Between 1830 and 1855, Nicaragua had been engulfed in constant civil war. Visitors from the United States had written of the chaos in the country, and it struck Walker that this instability might offer an opportunity for his designs. He raised money from hopeful entrepreneurs, recruited men eager to participate in such an adventure and, by 1855, he was ready to launch his expedition to Nicaragua.

In January 1855, one of the warring factions in Nicaragua, the Democrats, faced a crisis. Honduran president General Trinidad Cabañas withdrew troops he had sent to help the Democrats. Francisco Castellón, the leader of the Democratic faction, signed two contracts with Byron Cole, an associate of Walker's, authorizing Walker to bring a number of armed Americans to Nicaragua to serve the Democratic party. The first contract signed in the fall of 1854 authorized Walker to bring 300 men to Nicaragua for military service. After their service, the men would be given land grants. Meanwhile, Nicaragua would pay these troops and provision them. Upon reading the contract, Walker suggested to Cole that Nicaragua give him a colonization grant. The second contract gave Walker permission to bring the colonists, who were authorized to bear arms as long as they remained in the country. These contracts were the basis for Walker's expedition.

In his Nicaragua venture, Walker also received help from Cornelius Vanderbilt's Accessory Transit Company, a firm established in Nicaragua in 1850. The company carried passengers between the United States and Nicaragua. Men who worked for the company participated with Walker in his military activities. Walker led his force to Granada, Nicaragua, in 1855 and captured this city. He had taken the city by surprise and thus established himself in the enemy's capital, losing few men in the process. Walker then ordered a cabinet minister of the opposing government shot, making clear that the families of the city would be held hostage. They would not be harmed as long as opposing forces cooperated. Soon Walker obtained a peace treaty that ended fighting and established a provisional government for the country. In this treaty Walker agreed to representation in the government of the major opposing faction.

Walker soon named himself president of the country and head of the Nicaraguan army. In 1856, the United States recognized his government. Walker wished to cooperate with the United States in the construction of an interocean canal across Nicaragua. He proclaimed slavery to be in existence in the country, as he was a southerner by birth, but there is no evidence that his activities were part of any conspiracy to expand the institution into Latin America, although he was clearly favored by southerners. And he solicited southern support when he later attempted a return to Nicaragua.

Walker's government in Nicaragua was short-lived. He involved himself in an attempt to take over the Accessory Transit Company, headquartered in New York. He chose the losing side in his support of this takeover effort and thus became the target of Cornelius Vanderbilt. Vanderbilt maintained control of the company and then set about obtaining the cooperation of Central American republics to overthrow Walker's regime. Surrounding republics fielded forces and sent them to Nicaragua. Vanderbilt sent agents to the region to assist. With the specific assistance of Costa

Rica, Walker's supply routes to the United States were severed, making his military defeat easy.

On 1 May 1857 Walker surrendered to U.S. naval authorities off the coast of Nicaragua. Walker's support from the U.S. government as well as some special groups had eroded since he had become the president of Nicaragua. In June 1857 the frigate *Wabash* arrived at New York with 138 survivors of Walker's party, including thirteen women and five children. These refugees were in wretched condition and bitterly criticized Walker for deserting his followers in their desperate situation. Walker was in New York when their complaints appeared in the newspapers, but he chose not to answer the charges. By November, Walker had returned to the United States and was once again plotting to return to Nicaragua. Shortly thereafter Walker attempted to lead another group of men to Nicaragua, but U.S. naval authorities intercepted him and forced his return to the United States. President James Buchanan, in an address to Congress during December 1857, struck out against filibusters as being detrimental to U.S. interests.

Meanwhile, Walker had returned to New Orleans, and in June 1858 he was brought to trial there for violating the U.S. neutrality laws of 1818. Once again a jury acquitted him. From June 1858 until well into 1859 Walker toured the South to raise money to lead yet another expedition to Nicaragua. During this time he also wrote a book, *The War in Nicaragua,* describing his activities in that country.

Walker planned to lead an expedition to Honduras during 1860, and from there to march to Nicaragua. He formulated this strategy to avoid U.S. naval vessels patrolling off the coast of Nicaragua. Walker returned to Central America in late August 1860. On 3 September 1860, while traveling along the Honduran coast toward Nicaragua, Walker fell captive to British naval forces in the region. The British commander turned Walker over to Honduran authorities, who evidently asked Nicaraguan authorities what to do with him. The Nicaraguans wanted Walker to bother them no longer. It might be that he was court-martialed for violation of Honduran sovereignty. In any case, what was certain was that the Hondurans executed Walker by firing squad at Trujillo, Honduras.

Walker was not successful in that he did not achieve his personal aims as a filibuster. His activities surely were injurious to private capital in the United States, they caused property and life loss in Nicaragua, and added to the suspicions that Latin Americans had long held about U.S. expansion and its desires to control areas south of its international border.

J.A.S.

CALIFORNIA JOE
[8 MAY 1829–29 OCTOBER 1876]

Though nicknamed for the Golden State, this legendary hunter and scout honed his skills as a log-cabin Kentuckian in the tradition of Daniel Boone. Leaving home at fourteen, he hunted and trapped his way across the continent, earning a reputation as a crack shot who felled Indian warriors at a distance of four hundred yards. The rest of California Joe's life is the stuff of old-time Westerns. He spent his honeymoon in a covered wagon train, drank with Wild Bill Hickok, scouted for George Custer, and died near a frontier fort with a bullet in his back.

California Joe, plainsman and army scout, was born Moses Embree Milner in Standford, Kentucky, the son of Sarah Ann and Embree Armstead Milner, planters. Plantation life in the Kentucky wilderness was hardly genteel; the Milner home was a log cabin, as was the schoolhouse where the young Milner was an able student. Along with "book learning," Milner excelled in tracking and hunting, which meant his family always had fresh meat to eat. Even as a boy he was known for his skill in shooting his father's long-barreled rifle, a talent his family regarded as wholly in keeping with his father's past military experiences in George Washington's revolutionary army and in the War of 1812. Like Daniel Boone, another woodland-wise Kentuckian, Milner honed his natural abilities with patient practice until, at age fourteen, he and his muzzle-loading rifle were a nearly unbeatable pair. The precision of his shooting, especially, would come to be legendary and, if true, could be matched today only by experts using high-powered rifles. In any event, he was a crack shot and a stealthy hunter well at home in the wilderness.

Milner found the wilderness surrounding his family's home was becoming less wild, so, to his parents' distress, he quit school, and, one August morning in 1843, headed out for a few days' hunting that became five years.

Colonel George Armstrong Custer, who chose Milner as his chief scout in 1868, noted that Joe was an "inveterate smoker... The endurance of his smoking powers was only surpassed by his loquacity."

Milner may not have intended to leave home, but once into the forest he just kept going west until in September he found himself in St. Louis, the center of fur trade in America. Milner latched on to a party of fur trappers heading for Independence, Missouri, and a hunting trip up in the Platte River valley. He learned how to trap well, and his rifle skills were appreciated by the other trappers. During that long autumn and winter of trapping, the boy shared and survived hardships with the older trappers, listened to their tall tales of adventure, and gained knowledge and experience that he would soon parlay into a colorful and peripatetic career.

In the spring of 1844 the trappers met an agent from the American Fur Company in Fort Laramie who convinced them to sell their furskins there instead of traveling back to Independence. Located in Oglala Sioux country near the Platte River of the Wyoming Territory, Fort Laramie was the most famous and notorious of the fur trading posts, "home" to famous and infamous trappers, frontiersmen, and mountain men. A few days after arriving in Fort Laramie, Milner joined another group of trappers, led by Jim Baker, heading for the Yellowstone River to trade with the Indians there and to provide escort back to Fort Laramie for other trappers coming in with their winter catches. When they reached the Powder River, they discovered a band of Blackfoot, who were considered "hostiles." There were more Blackfoot than trappers, and Baker, who had had many such encounters before, ordered a surprise attack on the Indians. It was a rout, and a bloody one. The trappers killed eighteen Blackfoot warriors and destroyed their nearby village, though the women and children managed to escape to the hills. The fifteen-year-old Milner killed three of the warriors. One of those men he shot from a distance of 400 yards, a phenomenal shot that won him the admiration of his comrades and the beginnings of a reputation as an Indian fighter.

The rest of the journey was uneventful, with successful trading among the Indians of the Yellowstone Valley. Upon the trappers' return to Fort Laramie in the spring of 1846, Milner parted with them and signed on as a hunter for the American Fur Company. Yet again his skill with a rifle added to his reputation, this time as a buffalo hunter. On his hunting trips he would often camp nights at Sioux villages, and over the course of two years he learned to speak the Sioux language. Milner eventually moved from Fort Laramie to Fort Bridger and came under the employ and tutelage of Jim Bridger himself, working as a livestock herder and muleskinner. It was also at Fort Bridger that Milner, still a teenager, acquired his reputation as a very hard drinker—he shot the man who drank his shot of whiskey, or so the story goes. Further exploits and adventures followed—including service as an army guide during the Mexican War. Some may be true, some garnished, but what was becoming clear was that Milner was making a name for himself in the Wild West.

While young Milner had been gone, the Milner family had moved from Kentucky to Warren County, Missouri. Being an expert tracker, Milner found them and, in 1848, just suddenly reappeared, ending his five-year absence. One other skill he had developed while away from home was how to tell a whopping story. He had also begun to develop into a rather eccentric character, with his flyaway hair and charming loquaciousness. Whether he had yet acquired his ever-present briar pipe is unknown, but he was already good at attracting attention. One person who attracted *his* attention was Nancy Emma Watts, and in 1850 they married. Their honeymoon trip was a covered wagon journey across the Great Plains to California. For the next twenty-six years there would be years at a spread when Nancy would not see him. Nevertheless, she adored Milner, and they had four sons, who also adored him. When he was home he told wonderful and exciting stories. And when he was away he wrote thrilling letters, sporadically. During one of his trips back to California, he moved his family to Corvallis, Oregon, where he had built them a new home. Sometimes, later on, he took his older sons with him on his wanderings.

It may have been after his move to California with his new bride and his subsequent return to the western frontiers of Idaho and Montana and the Indian territories that his name became California Joe. How he acquired the name is unclear, but a logical story holds that, upon being asked his identity by some less than trustworthy characters, Milner circumspectly said he was called "Joe" and came from California. At any rate, few if any of his contemporaries ever knew him by any other name. And he was certainly known throughout the West—as an incredible rifle shot, a superb guide, a clever Indian fighter, a roustabout, and a very hearty drinker. His skills as a scout were often sought by the army, and when he was not scouting he tried his hand at ranching and mining, the latter endeavor gaining him some unhappy enemies.

One of Joe's closest friends was another army scout with a reputation, Wild Bill Hickok. Joe and Hickok probably met at Fort Riley, Kansas, in 1866, in the course of their scouting duties. The men held each other in high regard, with Hickok perhaps the more coolly dangerous of the two. They were not often together (contrary to what has become popular myth), and when Hickok was backshot by John McCall in a Deadwood, South Dakota, saloon on 2 August 1876, Joe was not there to save his friend. When he did return to Deadwood and found out not only that Hickok was dead but that a rigged jury and court had let his killer go, Joe turned murderously mad and went after McCall to challenge him to a gunfight. McCall, being cowardly but not stupid, fled, only to be later arrested, tried, and hanged for Hickok's murder. But that was in March 1877, after Joe's own death.

In 1868, two years after California Joe and Wild Bill met, the U.S. Army, in the person of Colonel George Armstrong Custer and the Seventh Cavalry, again required Joe's services, this time for the winter campaign along Oklahoma's Washita River. Joe made quite a first impression on Custer. In *My Life on the Plains,* Custer gives a wonderfully full physical description of Joe: "[He was] over six feet in height, and possessing a well-proportioned frame. His head was covered with a luxuriant crop of long, almost black hair (Custer, pp. 234–236). Custer also noted that Joe was an "inveterate smoker. . . . The endurance of his smoking powers was only surpassed by his loquacity," and there "was but little of the western country from the Pacific to the Missouri River with which California Joe was not intimately acquainted" (Custer, pp. 237–238).

This was the man Custer chose to be chief scout. On his first night in his new job, Joe led a column of soldiers out to search for Indians. To celebrate his promotion, Joe had filled his canteen with rotgut whiskey and

was imbibing steadily as, in the dark, his mule led him away from his column. Suddenly the soldiers heard violent screams ahead of them. Thinking
they were about to engage a frenzied enemy, they instead discovered their
scout, roaring drunk and so frantic to fight Indians that the soldiers had
to hog-tie him to his mule to get him back to camp. Custer removed Joe
as chief scout, but he kept him as a regular scout and as one of his favorite
companions. At every opportunity, Joe would entertain Custer with "peculiar but generally correct" ideas about how to conduct an Indian campaign (Wheeler, p. 97). Around January 1869, Joe wandered off yet again,
but he kept up a lively and erratic correspondence with Custer and his wife,
Libbie, for the rest of his life.

In the summer of 1876, Joe was in the Black Hills—ostensibly to chase
out prospectors, but also doing some clandestine prospecting of his own—
when Custer engaged in his last Indian campaign, but without his rowdy
scout. Joe lost two great friends that summer, Custer and Hickok. On 26
October, drunk and angry, Joe beat up several unarmed agency Indians at
Fort Robinson, Nebraska, shouting, "I'll show you how you killed Custer!"
(Wheeler, p. 97). Three days later and sober, Joe had an argument with
Thomas Newcomb, one of the quartermaster's employees. The reason for
the argument is unclear, but it was serious enough that both men drew
their pistols. Joe, however, managed to convince Newcomb "to put up your
dam' gun and have a drink" (Milner, p. 279). Folks in the vicinity thought
that that was the end of the matter, but Newcomb returned later with a
Winchester rifle and shot Joe in the back, killing him as he was talking to
some friends. Newcomb was arrested and set free when no civil charges
were made against him, and then disappeared. Joe's true name was discovered when the fort's doctor, V. T. McGillycuddy, emptied Joe's pockets
and found a packet of letters addressed to Moses Milner of Kentucky,
"and under that name I buried him the next day on the banks of the
White River" (Milner, p. 281). Joe's headstone in the fort's cemetery identified him simply as "Moses Milner, Scout."

California Joe was a singular and extraordinary example of the kind of
man who both tamed the West and made it wild. He did not go down in

legend the way others did, but in his own time he was as famous. What makes his story worth preserving is not merely his real and elaborated exploits—some of which are abhorrent while others are hilarious—but his voice. That someone as unrooted as he would leave behind any trace, would maintain a relationship of reciprocal love with a wife and children, would maintain a substantial correspondence with them and with the Custers over a period of many years (indeed, Joe's letter-writing and letter-saving is remarkable) and from many places, *and* would make such a vivid impression on a man who was only briefly his commanding officer bespeaks someone extraordinary and worth remembering. California Joe's voice offers a unique and genuine look at a time both vibrant and deadly. For better and for worse, California Joe was America's West.

E.D.L.

Known for his scrappiness in the ring, "Old Smoke," as he would come to be called, took his fearlessness and ferocity all the way to the West Coast, wagering that he could turn a profit with his pugilistic prowess.

JOHN MORRISSEY

[12 FEBRUARY 1831–1 MAY 1878]

Anyone who thinks today's political scene is nasty and corrupt should study the career of this bare-knuckles New Yorker. A street gang leader and professional pugilist, Morrissey stowed away to California and tried to seize Canadian gold fields with a group of armed thugs. He later ran gambling houses, saloons and racetracks, and rode his luck and connections all the way to the House of Representatives.

John Morrissey, gambler, prizefighter, and U.S. congressman, was born in Templemore, County Tipperary, Ireland, the son of Timothy Morrissey, a factory worker, and Julia or Mary, whose maiden name is unknown. He immigrated with his family to Canada in 1834 and then moved with his family to Troy, New York, where he grew up. As a youth, Morrissey joined several street gangs in Troy and was constantly involved in brawls and gang fights. He worked briefly in a wallpaper factory and in the Burden iron works. He was the leader of a gang called the Downtowns, which engaged in continuing fights with the Uptowns. By 1848, at the age of seventeen, Morrissey began to consider a career in prizefighting after beating a gang of six Uptowns in one afternoon. He got a job as a deck hand on a Hudson River steamer, and about 1849 he married Sarah Smith, the daughter of the ship's captain. They had one child who died in childhood.

In 1849, Morrissey issued a challenge to "Dutch" Charley Duane, a New York City prizefighter. Duane ignored his challenge, and Morrissey traveled to New York to find him at the saloon of Isaiah Rynders, a Tammany Hall politician. Finding that Duane was not there and that no prizefighters were available, Morrissey challenged "any man in the house." He was immediately set upon and beaten up by a group at the saloon, including one man who knocked him down with a spittoon. Rynders was impressed and nursed Morrissey back to health.

After a return to Troy, Morrissey went to work for Rynders as a "shoulder hitter," one who would get out the vote for Tammany. He was just under six feet tall and extraordinarily powerful, with huge hands and arms and a deep chest. He would keep fighting long after others would have given up. Morrissey earned the nickname "Old Smoke" in a fistfight with a hoodlum named Tom McCann over a madam, Kate Ridgely, who operated a popular New York brothel. The two fighters overturned a stove, and glowing coals rolled out on the floor. McCann held Morrissey down on the coals, which burned through his clothes, filling the room with smoke. Eventually Morrissey overcame McCann and kicked and beat him to defeat.

In 1851, Morrissey saved enough money to journey to California, traveling at least part of the distance as a stowaway. In San Francisco he opened a gambling game and amassed a bankroll. He appeared for the first time in a professional boxing ring on Mare Island, California, defeating George Thompson in August 1852 for a purse of $4,000 and a side bet of $1,000. According to some reports, Thompson, intimidated by Morrissey's followers, threw the match. While in California, Morrissey led an abortive expedition to seize gold lands in the Queen Charlotte Islands off British Columbia, outfitting a schooner with weapons, cannon, and a crew of thugs.

Although Morrissey called himself the "Champion of America" following the fight with Thompson, the title was not confirmed until 1853, when he defeated "Yankee" Sullivan in a fight in Boston Corners, New York, in thirty-seven rounds.

Morrissey organized a gang that fought for Tammany and led a group that engaged in fights with a Know-Nothing political gang led by Bill Poole. Eventually Morrissey and Poole challenged each other to a fight on the New York docks on 26 July 1854, in which Morrissey was defeated. A vendetta between the two gangs ensued, with several fatalities and serious injuries. On 8 March 1855 Poole was shot and killed, allegedly by one of Morrissey's men. Morrissey was arrested for the murder but was released.

In October 1858 Morrissey fought John C. Heenan, "the Benicia Boy," a fellow resident of Troy, New York, in Long Point, Canada, and won a side bet of $5,000. All of these fights were without gloves, with a round lasting until one or the other fighter fell to the ground. The fight ended only when one fighter could not return to the center of the ring on his feet.

After his defeat of Heenan, Morrissey retired from boxing and gave his attention to saloon ownership, gambling, and politics. He briefly operated two saloons in New York, and with the profits from the saloons and his prizefight winnings, he took over a gambling house on Barclay Street in New York. This "resort" became very popular among politicians and the gambling "sporting" community of New York. He reputedly banked a net profit from this house of $1 million within five years. He continued to work several other gambling houses in New York as well. Although faro-houses and casinos were illegal at the time, they were widely tolerated by the police in return for generous cash payments. In the late 1850s, Morrissey emerged as one of the most successful and well-known proprietors of such resorts in New York City.

Morrissey invested in real estate and a gambling casino in Saratoga and held controlling interest in the Saratoga race track after 1863. In 1866 he was elected to the U.S. Congress as a Democrat from New York's Fifth District and, reelected to a second term, served from 4 March 1867 through 3 March 1871. He took up residence in Saratoga, continuing improvements to the track and gaming house there. In 1875 and 1877 Morrissey was elected a state senator. In politics, he became known as an opponent of William M. Tweed. He died in Saratoga Springs, New York. Morrissey's colorful life as a brawler, boxer, political tough, gambling house owner, and politician illustrates the connections between the rough sporting life and the political machines of the 1850s to the 1870s.

R.P.C.

MARY ANN
BROWN PATTEN
[1837–18 MARCH 1861]

*The mid-nineteenth century saw the brief but brilliant era of clipper ships:
elegant vessels that swept around Cape Horn to California in a fraction of
the time it took to reach the West Coast by land. As a pregnant nineteen-
year-old, Patten accompanied her husband, a clipper-ship captain, on the San
Francisco–bound Neptune's Car. When he became delirious with "brain fever,"
Patten lashed her husband to a bunk and took command of the ship, navigating it through storms and near-mutiny in a voyage that made her an
early feminist heroine.*

Mary Ann Brown Patten, navigator and sailor, was born in Boston,
Massachusetts, the daughter of George Brown and Elizabeth
(maiden name unknown). Married in April 1853 at the age of sixteen, she
accompanied her husband, Captain Joshua Adams Patten, on two voyages
aboard his ship, the major shipbuilders Foster & Nickerson's big vessel,
Neptune's Car, becoming the first woman to command a clipper ship around
Cape Horn. She was eighteen when she first went to sea and took advantage of long stretches of time becalmed in the Pacific by teaching herself
the art of navigation. She also studied medical procedures, knowledge
that came in handy when *Neptune's Car* was struck by lightning and several crew members were injured. During this voyage her husband remarked,
"Mrs. Patten is uncommon handy about the ship, even in weather, and
would doubtless be of service if a man."

On 1 July 1856, *Neptune's Car* departed again from New York City, bound
for San Francisco. At about the same time, two other swift clippers set sail,
the *Intrepid* and *Romance of the Seas,* and many bets were placed as to which
would reach San Francisco harbor first. Early on in the voyage, *Neptune's
Car's* first mate proved himself a troublemaker, sleeping on watch and being

A Currier and Ives lithograph of a clipper ship from the late nineteenth century. Having captained such a ship through hurricane-force winds, Patten later remarked, "I have endeavored to perform that which seemed to me, under the circumstances, only the plain duty of a wife towards a good husband."

abusive to other crew members. Captain Patten was quick to discharge him, confining the man to his cabin for the duration of the trip. The ship's second mate was willing but unable to assume navigational duties because he was illiterate. So Mary Ann Patten, who by this time knew that she was pregnant with her first child, became the clipper's navigator.

Before long, Captain Patten, ill with advanced tuberculosis (then called "brain fever"), became exhausted. As they neared Cape Horn, he became delirious, then lapsed into a coma, leaving his wife to take command. The first mate, hearing of his captain's illness, sent a message to Mary Ann, warning her of the enormous costs and responsibilities involved in completing the voyage; he offered to take control of the ship if he were set free. She refused, knowing that her husband did not trust him. When he threatened to incite the crew to mutiny, she appealed to the men directly. No doubt touched by the plight of this slight, pregnant nineteen-year-old who asked for their loyalty, the crew members gave her their unanimous support.

The winter was an especially harsh one, and as the clipper neared Cape Horn, gales and hurricane-force winds lashed the vessel. Patten spent some fifty days navigating the clipper through the dangerous waters off the cape. As they beat against towering waves and relentless seas, she was unable to navigate using the sextant; the skies were never clear. Instead, she approximated *Neptune's Car*'s speed and draft, plotting the course as closely as possible on a chart.

Patten was rarely able to rest for more than a few hours and used what little free time she had to attend to her husband. Mopping his feverish face, trying to ease his delirium, she read every medical journal she could find in his cabin. Finally, after shaving his head to cool his fever, she lashed her young husband to his bunk so that the pounding seas would not pitch him to the floor.

At last *Neptune's Car* rounded the cape, and Patten set a north-by-northwest course to sail up the Pacific Coast toward San Francisco. With a slight improvement in the weather, her husband was better, too, experiencing some lucid spells during which time, still severely weak, he was able to help with navigation. Seeing his wife's exhausted state, Captain Patten decided to give the first mate another chance and freed him from his cabin. When the mate set a new course toward Valparaiso, however, the captain discharged him once again, and the man was returned to his quarters.

As the clipper approached San Francisco, Joshua Patten relapsed, sinking into a deep coma and losing his sight entirely. Finally, on 15 November, following a 134-day journey, Mary Ann Patten safely sailed the 1,600-ton clipper into San Francisco harbor. (She arrived before the *Intrepid* but was twenty-two days behind *Romance of the Seas*.) There, Patten quickly transferred her husband to a steamer and returned with him to New York, where he was carried from the vessel on a stretcher, his wife at his side. As soon as possible, she took him home to Boston.

Following her heroic voyage, which saved the clipper ship's insurers some $100,000, Patten received a letter of thanks from the New York Insurance Officers along with a check for $1,000. In reply, she wrote, "I have endeavored to perform that which seemed to me, under the circumstances, only the plain duty of a wife towards a good husband, stricken down by what we now fear to be a hopeless disease." Praised by local feminist groups who collected additional money to help their hero, Patten modestly declined to join their ranks. Two weeks after writing to thank the insurance company, she gave birth to a son on 10 March 1857. Joshua Patten died in July, never knowing that he had become a father.

Newspaper accounts of the time hailed Mary Ann Patten's bravery and skill in commanding the clipper so ably. The *New York Herald Tribune* reported on 18 February 1857: "Among the noble band of women who, by their heroic bearing, under great trial and suffering, have won for themselves imperishable fame, Mary A. Patten may claim a prominent position."

Four years after her husband's death, having contracted his tuberculosis, Patten died in Boston at the age of twenty-four.

A.W.M.

William "Buffalo Bill" Cody (left) poses with Gordon "Pawnee Bill" Lillie and "Buffalo Jones"
(right) for a studio portrait. In 1908, Cody and Lillie joined forces in Buffalo Bill's Wild West and
Pawnee Bill's Great Far East Show.

BUFFALO JONES

[JANUARY 1844–1 OCTOBER 1919]

*The conquest of the West exposed warring impulses in the American charac-
ter. Even as pioneers were still busy plowing, logging, and hunting their way
into every corner of the continent, some of them mourned their own destructive powers, and sought to preserve the wilderness they were rapidly van-
quishing. Buffalo Jones's career straddled this contradictory moment in the
closing days of the American frontier. So-named because of his skill as a buffalo hunter, Jones began conserving rather than killing the dwindling bison.
He went on to do the same with mountain lions, wild mustangs, and Arctic
musk oxen, as well as becoming an early park warden at Yellowstone, and a
game-catcher in Africa.*

Buffalo Jones, frontiersman, rancher, and conservationist, was born
Charles Jesse Jones in Tazewell County, Illinois, the son of Noah
Nicholas Jones and Jane Munden; the exact date of his birth is unclear.
His father often served as an election judge and reportedly once hired
Abraham Lincoln as an attorney. Charles, the second of twelve children,
grew up a backwoods farm boy on Money Creek, in McLean County near
Springfield, Illinois. From an early age he developed a passion for wild creatures and often kept several as pets. Although he studied for two years at
Wesleyan University in Bloomington, a bout with typhoid fever cut short
his college education. Subsequently, "itchy feet" prompted Jones to move
west, and in 1866, he settled at Troy, in Doniphan County, Kansas. There
he set up a fruit tree nursery and married Martha J. Walton. They had
four children, two of whom died when they were young.

Despite some moderate success with his fruit orchard and vineyard, the
lure of the wilderness spurred him onward. By 1869 Jones had sold his Troy
interests and moved his growing family to what would later become
Osborne County, Kansas, where he built a sod house. There he began

hunting buffalo, initially for his own family's needs and later to market the hides. These early hunting exploits eventually took him into West Texas, where he became acquainted with Pat Garrett and John R. Cook. He also had his share of encounters with Indians. According to some accounts, Jones was a participant in the battle of Yellowhouse (or Thompson's) Canyon against Black Horse's recalcitrant Comanches near present-day Lubbock, Texas, on 18 March 1877. His hunting prowess soon earned him the sobriquet "Buffalo" Jones. Even as he was hunting bison, on occasion he captured and tamed several buffalo calves, selling them for $7.50 a head or exhibiting them at county fairs.

In 1878, along with the brothers J. R. and W. D. Fulton and others, Jones laid out the town of Garden City, Kansas, and was elected its first mayor. In that capacity he came to know such legends as Wyatt Earp and "Buffalo Bill" Cody. He also became involved in real estate and occasionally drove a team of buffalo calves through the streets of Garden City as a promotional stunt.

Increasingly concerned with the threat of extinction of the buffalo, Jones set out from Kendall, Kansas, in April 1886 toward the Texas Panhandle to see if any were left in that area. On finding several, he lassoed eighteen calves and took them back alive. That and similar such feats brought him increased publicity, particularly from writers like Emerson Hough. Having apparently learned of pioneer rancher Charles Goodnight's success at raising buffalo, Jones established a ranch across the Arkansas River from Garden City. There he experimented at crossing buffalo with cattle to produce the cattalo, a sturdy breed with good qualities but too often sterile. Between 1886 and 1889 Jones accumulated more than fifty head, including the buffalo herd he purchased in 1888 from Sam I. Bedson of Winnipeg, Manitoba, and shipped them with some difficulty to Garden City. From this herd Jones began selling a few choice animals to zoos, parks, and other ranchers interested in preserving the bison. Once he personally delivered ten buffalo to a purchaser in Liverpool, England, who paid him $10,000 for his efforts. However, financial difficulties brought on by the panic of 1893 and compounded by the failure of a second ranch in Nebraska forced him, by 1895, to sell off his herd to ranchers in Montana and California.

In 1897, Jones and several companions journeyed to the Canadian arctic to capture the musk oxen, an animal then seen by few Americans. Despite
opposition from local Indians, who considered the oxen sacred, the party
wintered in a cabin they had built near the Great Slave Lake until February
1898, when Jones figured the icy weather had driven the oxen south.
Eventually he and John R. Rea roped five calves, but these were killed by
superstitious Indians and afterward were devoured by wolves. Jones returned
to Kansas via Alaska and the Aleutian Islands, and while he realized little
profit from that venture, his feats as a game catcher had extended his fame
worldwide. In 1899 he captured a bighorn sheep for the National Zoological
Park in Washington, D.C., and, with Henry Inman, published an autobiography, *Buffalo Jones' Forty Years of Adventure*. Jones's story of how he and
his party shot and fended off a hungry wolf pack near the Great Slave Lake
was verified in 1907 by Ernest Thompson Seton and Edward A. Preble when
they discovered the wolves' remains around the abandoned cabin.

On hearing of the proposed buffalo herd at Yellowstone National Park,
Jones offered his services to President Theodore Roosevelt and, in 1902,
was made a park game warden. (The story of how he roped an unruly
bear to a tree and spanked its behind "to teach it some manners" added
another dimension to the Jones legend.) But while he successfully developed the Yellowstone buffalo herd from Texas and Montana imports, his
strict rules against drinking, smoking, and gambling led to dissension with
the men working under him, and by 1906 he was discharged.

Undaunted, Jones next started a new buffalo preserve and experimental
ranch on the Kaibab Plateau, north of Arizona's Grand Canyon, bringing
in animals by rail from Montana and California to Lund, Utah, and trail-
ing them to the new site in June 1906. These became the nucleus of the
herd now maintained in the House Rock Valley, east of the Kaibab. In the
summer of 1907 Jones led the aspiring writer Zane Grey on a hunting trip
in which he roped mountain lions and captured wild mustangs. Grey subsequently launched his writing career by publishing his impressions of Jones
in *The Last of the Plainsmen* (1908). Jones also engaged in nationwide lecture tours, which increased after his wife's death in October 1907. Eastern

audiences, particularly those of the Camp Fire Club and other conservation groups, eagerly absorbed his colorful narratives, which he sometimes embellished.

Late in 1909 Jones persuaded industrialist Charles S. Bird of Willapah, Massachusetts, to finance a game-catching expedition to East Africa. With two cowboys, Marshall Loveless and Ambrose Means, plus twelve cow ponies and several hounds, Jones arrived at Nairobi, Kenya, on 3 March 1910. In the Kenyan savannahs they managed to rope warthogs, elands, zebras, a rhino, and a lioness (which lived at the New York Zoo until 1921). Then, in 1913, in company with Means, Dallas McDaniel, and Ohio business magnate William Moguey and his wife, Jones traveled to the Belgian Congo (now Zaire) to capture gorillas, but that effort was less successful; finances ran out, and the expedition broke up in disarray, resulting in bad feelings between Jones and his sponsors. Weakened after contracting "jungle fever" on that escapade, Jones died of a heart attack in Topeka, Kansas, at the home of a daughter. He was interred in the Valley View Cemetery in Garden City, next to his wife and sons. Flamboyant in personality, Buffalo Jones was a true pioneer in the establishment of America's game preserves and wildlife refuges.

H.A.A.

JOSHUA SLOCUM

[20 FEBRUARY 1844–NOVEMBER 1909?]

Marriage to a seafarer has never been easy, but the second wife of Joshua Slocum may have got more than she bargained for. The couple's wedding sail in 1886 ended in a bloody mutiny and stranding in Brazil. No matter: Slocum turned the damaged vessel into a sail-rigged canoe and piloted his bride 5,500 miles back to America. He later embarked on a solo sail around the world in a converted oyster boat. Slocum survived delirium and other setbacks to complete the world's first single-handed circumnavigation. Still restless at age sixty-five, he set off one last time, on a solo sail in search of the source of the Amazon.

Joshua Slocum, circumnavigator, shipbuilder, and author, was born in Wilmot Township, Nova Scotia, Canada, the son of John Slocombe, a farmer and bootmaker, and Sarah Jane Southern. Slocum attended school only until age ten, when he was set to work to earn his keep. He left home permanently after the death of his mother when he was sixteen, working as a deep-water sailor. From that time on his life, for better and for worse, was defined by the sea.

His first command (in 1869, the same year he became a U.S. citizen) was of a coastwise schooner between Seattle and San Francisco, after which he commanded the bark *Washington*, sailing to Sydney, Australia, in 1870. In 1871, in Sydney, he married Virginia Albertina Walker, an American. The well-matched couple spent most of the next thirteen years together at sea, accompanied, ultimately, by their four children, until Virginia died in 1884.

During those years Slocum captained several large ships, carrying various cargos mostly to Pacific ports. His last command was the bark *Aquidneck,* which he also owned. Not only a sailor and navigator, Slocum built the hull of an eighty-ton steamer in Subic Bay, the Philippines. Though

Slocum had only just returned from his 46,000-mile circumnavigation when this 1899 portrait was taken, probably about the same time he was finishing Sailing Alone around the World, *a classic of nautical literature.*

he was paid for the job with a small schooner, the money he was promised never materialized—the first of several financial disappointments.

In 1886, in Boston, Slocum married his cousin Henrietta "Hettie" Miller Elliott. Their wedding trip on the *Aquidneck* (with two of his children along) included a mutiny, in which the captain shot two men, killing one, and it ended in disaster when the uninsured ship became stranded in Brazil and was a total loss. Saving what he could from the wreck, Slocum built by hand a 35-foot "canoe," rigged it with sails sewed by Hettie, named it *Liberdade* because of its being launched on the day Brazil's slaves were freed, and sailed it 5,500 miles to Washington, D.C. That was the end of Hettie's seafaring.

It was also the end of Joshua Slocum's career as a merchant captain. He was a wind sailor, and the age of sail was almost over—too few sailing ships, too many captains. Slocum, who despite his lack of formal education had read widely, turned to authorship, publishing *The Voyage of the Liberdade* in 1890 but not realizing a profit. Odd jobs took up the next few years.

In 1892, an acquaintance gave him the decrepit hulk of a 37-foot oyster sloop named *Spray*. Slocum, who had said that "next in attractiveness, after seafaring, came ship-building," rebuilt it himself. When he launched it, he thought it "sat on the water like a swan." Once more he had a vessel—but not an occupation. In 1893 he was commissioned to deliver the iron gunboat *Destroyer,* built by John Ericsson (designer of the Civil War *Monitor*), to naval authorities in Brazil. He brought the vessel into Bahia, turning it over to Brazilians who, for uncertain reasons, soon sank it. Once again, Slocum received no money for the job. Hoping to benefit somehow from the misadventure, he published *Voyage of the Destroyer from New York to Brazil* in 1894. It was well reviewed in Boston but earned him nothing.

Ultimately Slocum decided on what he thought would be a gratifying and remunerative endeavor: to take the *Spray* around the world, alone. On 24 April 1895, he left Boston on his solo voyage, reportedly with only $1.50 in his pocket. Other less-than-ideal conditions included the absence of a chronometer (for calculations of longitude)—considered essential in his day. Altering his intended track according to local conditions (such as the threat of piracy in the Mediterranean), Captain Slocum sailed across the Atlantic to Gibraltar and then recrossed it, entering the Pacific through the Strait of Magellan. He traversed the South Pacific to Australia, sailed through the Coral Sea and the Indian Ocean, rounded the Cape of Good Hope, and crossing the Atlantic for the third time, returned to the United States after 46,000 miles under wind power on 27 June 1898, having accomplished the world's first single-handed circumnavigation. *Sailing Alone around the World* (serialized in 1899–1900 and then published as a book in 1900) is the justly admired record of his seamanship, character, and navigational skill, a classic of nautical literature.

Readers remember Slocum's delirium off the Azores, in which he saw the pilot of Columbus's *Pinta* steering the *Spray*; they recall his protecting himself from Fuegians by sprinkling the deck with carpet tacks and writing, "Now, it is well known that one cannot step on a tack without saying something about it." Such dry wit is a prominent feature of his writing, as in his encounter with an American warship at sea after the Spanish-American War had broken out. The *Spray* signaled, "Let us keep together for mutual protection." And in the minds of most readers must linger the captain's repeated expressions of love and admiration for his vessel: "There the *Spray* rode, now like a bird on the crest of a wave, and now like a waif deep down in the hollow between seas; and so she drove on."

With proceeds from the book and from lecturing about his experiences, Slocum bought a house on Martha's Vineyard in 1902. It was no doubt what Hettie wanted, but Joshua was not happy. Clearly ill at ease, he began making solitary trips in the *Spray* to spend winters in the Caribbean. Returning from the first of these, he stopped to lecture at Riverton, New Jersey, where he was arrested on a charge of raping a twelve-year-old girl. Though rape was medically disproved and the charge was ultimately reduced to one of indecency, Slocum, insisting he had no memory of the incident, did spend more than a month in jail. Not long after his release after a plea of no contest, he was delivering a rare orchid from the Caribbean to a cordial President Theodore Roosevelt.

Finally, at age sixty-five, the captain conceived another extraordinary plan: he would sail the *Spray* to South America, up the Orinoco and Rio Negro to the still unknown source of the Amazon, down the Amazon to the sea and to New England again. The *Spray,* according to some observers, was in bad repair and the captain negligent. Whether those were contributing factors or not, the weather was stormy when he left, and Captain Slocum and his boat were never seen again. He was finally declared by a court to have officially died the day he set sail, 14 November 1909.

H.S.

This photograph from a Joy family genealogy captures the other side of a woman who once wrote of a scrape with death, "I was more annoyed than frightened because it is far too stupid to shoot at a woman alone, as if I could have assaulted their battery. My first impulse was to ride into those cowards and to beat them with my riding whip on their long ears."

AGNES ELISABETH WINONA LECLERCQ JOY SALM – SALM

[25 DECEMBER 1844–21 DECEMBER 1912]

While women in nineteenth century America rarely traveled far from home except with their husbands, this mysterious adventuress made the most of her marriage. Born to a Vermont farm family, she wed an aristocratic Prussian soldier and accompanied him to the front of three conflicts on two continents, acting as a nurse and intermediary between warring parties. Left penniless by his death in battle, she continued her travels as a European princess acquainted with the pope and the German emperor.

Agnes Elisabeth Winona Leclercq Joy Salm-Salm, princess, adventurer, and wartime humanitarian, was born in Swanton, Vermont (or southern Canada), the daughter of William Leclercq Joy, a farmer, and his second wife, Julia Willard. Salm-Salm always remained secretive about her youth, thereby feeding romantic rumors about her age, ancestry, and past. After spending some time in Cuba, as she asserted in her autobiography, she arrived in Washington, D.C., in the fall of 1861, a vivacious, pretty young woman. There she attracted the attentions of Prince Felix zu Salm-Salm, the adventurous younger son of an old aristocratic German family. After serving in the Prussian and Austrian armies, the prince had left Europe to escape his debts and to seek employment in the American Civil War.

Without the consent of his family to an obvious mésalliance, Felix and Agnes were married on 30 August 1862. The energetic bride immediately took charge of her husband's career and succeeded in obtaining his appointment as colonel in the Eighth, later the Sixty-eighth, New York Infantry Regiment and eventually his commission as brigadier general. Spirited and adventuresome but soon taking interest in the plight of wounded soldiers, Agnes accompanied her husband on his tours of duty in Virginia, Alabama, and Georgia, where Felix Salm-Salm was appointed military governor of Atlanta in 1865.

Seeking further military honors, Felix Salm-Salm left in February 1866 to join the staff of Archduke Maximilian of Austria, who had become emperor of Mexico. The princess again followed him, soon to witness the collapse of the imperial government. In the weeks after the fall of Querétaro in May 1867, Agnes used every effort to mediate between the doomed emperor and his staff and the republican generals, personally persuading Benito Juárez to postpone Maximilian's trial. Together with her husband, who shared the emperor's captivity, she made plans for Maximilian's escape, trying to bribe officers of the republican army. When their schemes were discovered, Agnes was exiled to San Luis Potosí, where Juárez refused her desperate pleas for Maximilian's life but promised that her husband would be spared. In January 1868 Agnes joined her husband in Europe. She did not return to the United States for more than three decades.

After a brief meeting with the Salm family, the couple proceeded to Vienna in February. Although the prince failed to draw the attention he expected as a close companion of Maximilian's final days, Agnes was graciously received by the Archduchess Sophie, Maximilian's mother, and granted an annual pension for her valiant efforts on behalf of the unfortunate emperor. Felix Salm-Salm subsequently obtained a commission as major in a Prussian Regiment of Guards stationed at Koblenz. At the outbreak of the Franco-Prussian conflict in summer 1870, Agnes again accompanied her husband to war, this time securing permission to join a medical unit attached to the Prussian First Army. In the ensuing months, she exerted herself to the utmost in caring for the wounded and consoling the dying, assisting in operations, supervising the kitchen staff, and organizing hospital supplies. After the cease-fire, Agnes returned to private life, receiving thanks and an imperial decoration for her charitable work.

Salm-Salm's husband, however, had been killed in battle, and her personal situation proved difficult. Since she had no means—nor the Salm family the intention—to pay the prince's old debts, she felt compelled to repudiate her husband's inheritance. Much to the family's dismay but with characteristic initiative, she appealed to the German emperor for help, which was granted, thus enabling her to establish herself independently at Bonn. Although at times toying with plans to work in a hospital or even to enter a convent—an idea she abandoned after an audience with Pope Pius IX— she spent the next years traveling in Europe and writing her memoirs.

In 1876 Salm-Salm married Charles Heneage, the younger son of a respectable Lincolnshire family and a minor British diplomat with literary ambitions. However, the couple separated, and Agnes, childless from both marriages, continued to live in retirement in Germany as Princess Salm-Salm. She made headlines again in 1899, when she visited the United States to present the survivors of her husband's old regiment with the flags of their Civil War unit. The Boer War tempted her to resume her army relief work, but its brief duration prevented her from doing so.

Salm-Salm spent her last years mostly at Karlsruhe and nearby Herrenalb at a residence she named "Minnehaha." When she died at Karlsruhe, newspapers in Europe and the United States as well as novelists and playwrights later remembered her as the somewhat enigmatic, courageous, and warmhearted woman who had managed to play an active role in three wars on two continents. She shares a grave in the old cemetery in Bonn with Louise Runkel, an associate during the Franco-Prussian War who had remained her confidante.

M.L.F.

RAILROAD BILL

[?–7 MARCH 1896]

The Civil War ended slavery, but failed to free rural blacks from economic peonage. While many Southern blacks sharecropped cotton, others toiled as migrant laborers in the timber industry and at turpentine camps. One such itinerant was Railroad Bill, a freight-jumper who became a fugitive and folk hero after hijacking a train and vanishing into Murder Swamp, evading blood-hounds and posses.

Railroad Bill, thief and folk hero, was the nickname of an African-American man of such obscure origins that his real name is in question. Most writers have believed him to be Morris Slater, but a rival candidate for the honor is an equally obscure man named Bill McCoy. But in song and story, where he has long had a place, the question is of small interest and Railroad Bill is name enough. A ballad regaling his exploits began circulating among field hands, turpentine camp workers, prisoners, and other groups from the black underclass of the Deep South, several years before it first found its way into print in 1911. A version of this blues ballad was first recorded in 1924 by Gid Tanner and Riley Puckett, and Thomas Dorsey, a blues singer from the 1920s, took Railroad Bill as his stage name. The ballad got a second wind during the folk music vogue of the 1950s and 1960s, and in 1981 the musical play *Railroad Bill* by C. R. Portz was produced for the Labor Theater in New York City. It subsequently toured thirty-five cities.

The name Railroad Bill, or often simply "Railroad," was given to him by train men and derived from his penchant for riding the cars as an anonymous nonpaying passenger of the Louisville and Nashville Railroad (L&N). Thus he might appear to be no more than a common tramp or hobo, as the large floating population of migratory workers who more or less surreptitiously rode the cars of all the nation's railroads were labeled. But Railroad Bill lim-

An 1863 photograph of Federal boxcars waiting at a depot in Chattanooga, Tennessee. Railroad Bill was a frequent nonpaying passenger on the Louisville and Nashville Railroad around this time.

ited his riding to two adjoining South Alabama counties, Escambia and Baldwin. Sometime in the winter of 1895 he began to be noticed by trainmen often enough that he soon acquired some notoriety and a nickname. It did not make him less worthy of remark that he was always armed, with a rifle and one or more pistols. He was, as it turned out, quite prepared to offer resistance to the rough treatment normally meted out to tramps.

An attitude of armed resistance from a black man was bound inevitably to bring him into conflict with the civil authorities, who were in any case inclined to be solicitous of the L&N, the dominant economic power in South Alabama. The conflict began on 6 March 1895, only a month or two after trainmen first became aware of Railroad Bill. L&N employees discovered him asleep on the platform of a water tank in Baldwin County, on the Flomaton to Mobile run, and tried to take him into custody. He drove them off with gunfire and forced them to take shelter in a nearby shack. When a freight train pulled up to take on water, he hijacked it and, after firing additional rounds into the shack, forced the engineer to take him farther up the road, whereupon he left the train and disappeared into the woods. After that, pursuit of Railroad Bill was relentless. A month to the day later he was cornered at Bay Minette by a posse led by a railroad detective. A deputy, James H. Stewart, was killed in the ensuing gunfight, but once again the fugitive slipped away. The railroad provided a "special" to transport Sheriff E. S. McMillan from Brewton, the county seat of Escambia, to the scene with a pack of bloodhounds, but a heavy rainfall washed away the scent.

In mid-April, a reward was posted by the L&N and the state of Alabama totaling $500. The lure of this reward and a rumored sighting of the fugitive led Sheriff McMillan out of his jurisdiction to Bluff Springs, Florida, where he found Railroad Bill and met with death at his hands. The reward climbed to $1,250, and the manhunt intensified. A small army with packs of dogs picked up his scent near Brewton in August, but he dove into Murder Swamp near Castelberry and disappeared. During this period, from March to August, the legend of Railroad Bill took shape among poor blacks in the region. He was viewed as a "conjure man," one who could change his shape and slip away from pursuers. He was clever and outwitted his enemies; he was a trickster who laid traps for the trapper and a fighter who refused to bend his neck and submit to the oppressor. He demanded respect, and in time some whites grudgingly gave it: Brewton's *Pine Belt News* reported after Railroad Bill's escape into Murder Swamp that he had "outwitted and outgeneraled at least one hundred men armed to the teeth." During this period a Robin Hood–style Railroad Bill emerged, who, it was said, stole canned goods from boxcars and distributed them to poor illiterate blacks like himself. Carl Carmer, a white writer in the 1930s, claimed that Railroad Bill forced poor blacks at gunpoint to buy the goods from him, but Carmer never explained how it was possible to get money out of people who rarely if ever saw any. Railroad Bill staved off death and capture for an entire year, a virtual impossibility had he not had supporters among the poor black population of the region.

Sightings became infrequent after Murder Swamp, and some concluded Railroad Bill had left the area. The "wanted" poster with its reward was more widely circulated. The result was something like open season on vagrant blacks in the lower South. The *Montgomery Advertiser* reported that "several were shot in Florida, Georgia, Mississippi and even in Texas," adding with unconscious grisly humor, "only one was brought here to be identified." That one arrived at Union Station in a pine box in August, escorted by the two men from Chipley, Florida, who had shot him in hopes of collecting the reward. Doubts about whether he remained in the area were answered on 7 March 1896, exactly a year and a day after the affair at the water tower when determined pursuit began. Railroad Bill was shot without warning, from ambush, by a private citizen seeking the reward, which by now included a lifetime pass on the L&N Railroad. Bill had been sitting on a barrel eating cheese and crackers in a small Atmore, Alabama, grocery. Perhaps he was tired as well as hungry.

Railroad Bill's real name probably will never be known. At the time of the water tower incident and up to the killing of Deputy Stewart, he had only the nickname, but in mid-April the first "wanted" posters went up in Mobile identifying Railroad Bill as Morris Slater, who, though the notice did not state it, had been a worker in a turpentine camp near Bluff Springs, Florida. These camps were often little more than penal colonies. They employed convict labor and were heavily into debt peonage. People were not supposed to leave, but Slater did, after killing the marshal of Bluff Springs. When railroad detectives stumbled on this story their interest was primarily in Slater's nickname. He had been called "Railroad Time," and "Railroad" for short, because of his quick, efficient work. The detectives quickly concluded, because of the similarities in nicknames, that Slater was their man. The problem, of course, is that the train men called their rider Railroad Bill precisely because they had no idea who he was and well before railroad authorities heard about Slater. If the detectives were right, then it follows that the same man independently won strangely similar nicknames in two different settings, once because he was a good worker, and again because he was a freeloader.

No one from the turpentine camp who had known Slater identified the body, but neither the railroad detectives nor the civil authorities involved questioned the identification. The body was taken to Brewton, on its way to Montgomery, where it would go on display for the public's gratification, but it was also displayed for a time in Brewton and recognized. The *Pine Belt News* reported that residents recognized the body as that of Bill McCoy, a man who would have been about forty, the approximate age of the corpse, since he had been brought to the area from Coldwater, Florida, as a young man eighteen years earlier. McCoy was remembered as a town trouble-maker who two years earlier had threatened T. R. Miller, the richest man in town, when he worked in Miller's sawmill and lumberyard. He had fled the scene hastily, not to be seen again until his corpse went on display as Railroad Bill. But, apart from the local newspaper stories, no one disputed the Slater identification, and the local Brewton people seem to have con-cluded that Morris Slater must have been a name used by Bill McCoy after he fled the town. The problem with that conclusion is that when the inci-dent at Miller's sawmill occurred Morris Slater had already earned the nick-name "Railroad Time" in a Florida turpentine camp.

J.L.P.

I S H I
[1862?–25 MARCH 1916]

This Native American made an astounding journey that should be measured in millennia rather than miles. The lone survivor of an Indian tribe that possessed a Neolithic material culture, Ishi emerged from the chaparral to become known as the "Wild Man" of northern California. Though alone in a world where no one knew his language or customs, Ishi adapted as best he could to modern society, enjoying the ferries and streetcars and shops of twentieth-century San Francisco.

Ishi, the last "Stone Age" Indian in California and, probably, in the entire United States, was a member of the Yahi people of northeastern California. He was encountered in a slaughterhouse corral in Oroville, California, on 29 August 1911, thirty-eight years after the last major Indian conflict in the state. When taken into custody by Sheriff J. B. Webber of Butte County, Ishi was naked save for a scrap of old wagon canvas, worn like a cape, and very weak from exposure and near starvation. Communication with him, other than in sign language, was impossible, although English, Spanish, and several Indian tongues—such as Maidu and Wintun—were tried.

When the story of the "Wild Man of Oroville" broke in San Francisco, University of California professors Alfred Kroeber and T. T. Waterman were immediately interested. They remembered the 1908 rumor of "untamed" Indians scattering before a surveying party in the Mount Lassen foothills. Waterman had subsequently tried to find the mysterious natives but had failed. Kroeber telegraphed the sheriff: "Hold Indian till arrival professor State University who will take charge and be responsible for him. Matter important account aboriginal history."

Waterman escorted the Neolithic Californian to San Francisco, where it became obvious that this "missing link" was a lone survivor of a primitive, and presumed extinct, subtribe of the Yana band, or tribe, the Yahi.

A staged photograph taken by anthropologist Alfred Kroeber at Deer Creek, California, in 1914 shows Ishi in traditional Yahi dress with a fishing spear.

California's first ethnographer, Stephen Powers, as early as 1874 had remarked on the Yana's determination to resist civilization "to the last man, squaw and papoose." The Yana and Yahi were then virtually exterminated by settlers avenging thefts of property and livestock and a few murders by the so-called Mill Creek Indians.

Kroeber and Waterman gave their charge a sanctuary in the university's Museum of Anthropology. The Yahi's rescue gave the budding science of anthropology a wealth of information. The Yahi had a name, but no one ever learned it. It was a quasi-religious custom of the tribe not to reveal one's name. So the professors dubbed him Ishi, meaning "man" in Yahi. Kroeber and Waterman picked up his language quickly, but Ishi, intelligent enough, was reluctant to learn more than pidgin English.

The story of Ishi's life was shocking. His doomed people had been hunted down like deer by whites. He had seen his people reduced by guns and disease from about 300 to 400 souls to just five individuals in 1908. When surprised by the surveyors, they had scattered, and Ishi never saw or heard of his fellow tribe members again. They simply disappeared. Apparently the sole survivor of his people and of Neolithic Native American life, Ishi was driven to the white settlements—and into the twentieth century—by hunger as game grew scarce in the chaparral of the volcanic canyons of Mill and Deer Creeks. Thus ended what Ishi's biographer, Theodora Kroeber, called the Long Concealment.

In San Francisco, Ishi came to enjoy riding on ferryboats and streetcars and loved to shop and to roam the city, once he overcame his initial fear of crowds. When taken to a theater, he showed more interest in the audience than in the actors performing on the stage. But some aspects of civilization distressed him. He would never enter the Old Bone Room of the museum. He was frightened by the hospital's anesthesia because he believed that one's soul left the body during an unconscious state. And he was horrified by the dissection of cadavers in the medical school.

The University of California faculty protected Ishi from those who would have exploited him as a sideshow savage. He was found to be anything but savage and was quite the reverse of the dirty, miserable Digger Indian of white stereotyping. He was so concerned with cleanliness that he was put on the museum payroll as an assistant janitor. Gentle, kind, and warm-hearted, he was more reserved than shy and welcomed (well-behaved) visitors. He patiently submitted to their photographs and even early motion pictures. He was particularly interested in visiting Chinese and those Caucasians who wore any sort of uniform. Ishi had few friends, but they were all very close: Waterman; Kroeber; Saxton Pope of the medical school; assistant curator Edward Gifford; the janitorial staff, museum guards, and preparators; and a Papago Indian, Juan Dolores, who liked to visit him.

Ishi was much better at showing than telling. He demonstrated his accuracy with bow and arrows, his skill at making fire with a drill, and his proficiency in napping (flaking) razor-sharp arrowheads from obsidian, flint, and even beer-bottle glass. He taught archery so well to Pope that the doctor later hunted lions in Africa with a bow and arrows. Ishi guided his new friends to his old hunting grounds in 1914 and there practically reenacted his life in a sort of extended pantomime. Kroeber scheduled special trips with him for an annual acorn harvest and a salmon run, extremely important events in aboriginal life. But World War I forced a postpone-ment that became indefinite as Ishi's health declined.

A common cold brought on pneumonia that led to tuberculosis. Ishi was given the very best medical care but died. He was cheerful and content, sto-ically awaiting death without self-pity. The professors were devastated by Ishi's death. Waterman wrote to Kroeber, away in New York, "He was the best friend I had in the world." Kroeber ordered his colleagues to give their friend the last rites of his religion and to prevent any autopsy. "As to the disposal of the body, yield nothing, at all, under any circumstance. If there is any talk about the interests of science, say for me that science can go to hell! We propose to stand by our friends."

But Kroeber's allies could not prevent the ultimate indignity of a post-mortem. However, after the autopsy, the anthropologists did their best to make amends to Ishi's spirit. They placed with his body a bow and five arrows, some acorn meal and tobacco, shell beads, and obsidian chips for his last journey. They then cremated the last Stone Age man in America in accordance with Yahi custom. As a last gesture of friendship, they spurned the standard urn of Mount Olivet Cemetery and placed his ashes in a black pottery jar of Pueblo design.

R.H.D.

DAVID FAGEN

[1875–1 DECEMBER 1901?]

At the end of nineteenth century, with the closing of the American West, the United States extended its power across the Pacific to Hawaii and the Philippines. Fagen, a black soldier sent to subdue Filipino nationalists who opposed American imperialism, seems to have identified with islanders' quest for independence. He switched sides and became a guerrilla captain, ambushing American forces and taunting them with racial jibes, until his apparent capture and gruesome end.

D avid Fagen, captain in the Filipino nationalist army, was born in Tampa, Florida. Little is known about either his parents or his early life. In the summer of 1899, just after the United States ended the war with Spain, Fagen was a corporal in the Twenty-fourth Infantry of Company I. He was among the black soldiers of the Twenty-fourth and Twenty-fifth Infantries and the Ninth and Tenth Cavalries dispatched to the Philippines in the U.S. effort to enforce territorial concessions granted by Spain in a peace treaty signed in February 1899. Emilio Aguinaldo, an ardent Filipino nationalist, led a guerrilla war resisting what he considered the United States replacing Spain as colonizer.

Letters written by African-American soldiers to newspapers and family members indicate that some of them sympathized with the Filipino cause, and a few even joined its ranks. Fagen's actions in the fall of 1899 mark the beginnings of an extraordinary expression of African-American solidarity with Filipino nationalist aspirations for independence. He defected from the U.S. Army, accepted a commission with the Filipino nationalists, and participated in a two-year guerrilla war against the American forces.

Prior to Fagen's defection, his company had clashed with Filipino nationalists in the Nueva Ecija province on the island of Luzon, pushing them out of the towns and into the foothills and mountains on the outskirts of settled areas. Fagen "slipped away and mounted a horse" on 17 November

The Ninth Regiment, U.S. Cavalry, Camp Wikoff, Montauk Point, Long Island, September 1898. Fagen was among the black soldiers of the Twenty-fourth and Twenty-fifth Infantries and the Ninth and Tenth Cavalries dispatched to the Philippines in 1899.

1899 while his company was preparing to relocate its station to another town. A U.S. Army report, "Information Slip on David Fagen," states that he was assisted by a nationalist officer who had a horse hidden near the company's barracks. Fagen joined General Urbana Lacuna's forces, which were located at Mount Arayat and in the surrounding area. His immediate commander was José Alejandrino. Fagen is not known to have written a statement detailing the reasons for his defection. Military records note that he had "continual trouble" with his company's commanding and noncommissioned officers and was often assigned extra work duty as punishment. The tenacity of Fagen's resolve to combat his former compatriots, however, suggests that discipline problems were probably not the sole basis for his decision. In fact, U.S. soldiers who clashed with him recall that in the midst of raging, pitched battles, Fagen enjoyed shouting "taunting boasts," some of which had racial overtones. On one occasion, he reportedly yelled, "Captain Fagen done got yuh White boys now" (Ganzhorn, pp. 172–73).

Fagen's claim of captaincy was not mere self-indulgence. Indeed, in September 1900 his nationalist commanders promoted him from lieutenant to captain, and from that time until December 1901 (the purported date of his death), Fagen was engaged in a protracted and relentless guerrilla war. The U.S. Army's inability to capture Fagen swiftly earned him a reputation as a shrewd and cunning adversary. John Ganzhorn, a member of General Frederick Funston's elite scouts, recalls violent confrontations with Fagen. Ganzhorn related that in one close encounter Fagen "ambushed two four-mule wagons" (Ganzhorn, p. 172). After killing all but one of the soldiers, Fagen and his men set the wagons on fire and ambushed another group of American soldiers who were drawn by the smoke.

Perhaps out of embarrassment, American military leaders generated various excuses for their inability to capture Fagen. Remembering an incident when Fagen killed one of his comrades, Ganzhorn wrote: "I've heard Fryburger's cry for me to kill Fagen. God I wanted to! But when I could see to shoot, Fagen was not in sight" (Ganzhorn, p. 177). Similarly, General Funston described a battle with Fagen, "In this fight I got a fairly good look at the notorious Fagen at a distance of a hundred yards, but unfortunately had already emptied my carbine" (Funston, p. 376).

As time progressed, Fagen's comrades began to buckle under the continuous onslaught of the U.S. Army and an embargo that prevented them from receiving aid and supplies from abroad. Aguinaldo, the charismatic nationalist leader, was eventually captured. Fagen, unwilling to turn himself in, remained in northern Luzon with a small group of nationalist soldiers. General Funston offered a bounty of $600 for Fagen's head. On 5 December 1901 Anastacio Bartollome arrived at Bongabong, in the Nueva Ecija province, carrying a black man's head that he claimed was Fagen's. However, U.S. military officers who reviewed the report of Fagen's death were not totally convinced and referred to it as a "report of the supposed killing of David Fagen." Historians have pointed out that the question of whether Fagen survived the manhunt should not overshadow the historical significance of his rebellion as an expression of African-American militant resistance to American imperialism.

S.N.B.

This posed photograph of Livingstone (seated) with her secretary, Joan Davies, was taken at a New York Federal Court in 1931 and printed in the newspaper along with a story about her arrest for running an illegal salon of "culture, wit and bonhomie" during prohibition. Her bail was set at $5,000.

BELLE LIVINGSTONE

[20 JANUARY 1875?–7 FEBRUARY 1957]

If Livingstone's life were a movie, she'd be played by Mae West. Raised in a conventional Kansas family and educated at a convent school, Livingstone's sharp wit and "poetic legs" carried her as far as she could go from her strait-laced Midwestern upbringing. She became, in turn, a showgirl, a risqué hostess known as "the most dangerous woman in Europe," a Bohemian traveler who once bet friends she could circle the globe on five pounds sterling, and a speakeasy owner in New York and Nevada. Married four times, and arrested just as many, Livingstone lived by her devil-may-care dictum: "Spend it while you've got it."

Belle Livingstone, showgirl, adventuress, and Prohibition Era saloon-keeper, was a foundling, purportedly discovered under a clump of sunflowers in Emporia, Kansas, in the summer of 1875 at approximately six months of age. She was adopted by newspaperman John Ramsey Graham and his wife, Anne M. Likly, and they named her Isabelle Graham.

Even Livingstone admitted that the sunflower story sounded a bit far-fetched. "Of course, I bedeviled my foster parents with questions," she wrote in her memoirs. "But they always clung to the sunflower story, and since it's a good story I may as well cling to it too." She had a conventional upbringing in Emporia. Her father was the editor and co-owner of the *Emporia News*, and he later founded the *Emporia Gazette*. When speculative business ventures caused him to lose the *Gazette*, he took a job with the *Chicago Dispatch*, and the family moved to Chicago. After her family's move, Livingstone attended a convent school in Oldenburg, Indiana.

After she left school, Livingstone frequently attended theatrical productions with her father. She became stage-struck and began making audition rounds. She eventually landed a job in the chorus of the second road company of the comic opera *Wang* and left home on the sly, knowing that her parents would never give her permission.

Livingstone's father followed her to the company's first stop, Saginaw, Michigan, and told her that he and her mother would never allow their unmarried daughter to live away from home. She circumvented that edict by asking a newfound acquaintance, Chicago-based paint salesman Richard Wherry, to marry her. After a ceremony in Saginaw, Livingstone and Wherry went their separate ways. To avoid embarrassing her family, Livingstone adopted the stage name of Belle Livingstone, after missionary-explorer David Livingstone.

Livingstone appeared as a member of the chorus in several stage productions, settled in New York, and was dubbed "the girl with the poetic legs." She also showed a flair for making herself known. Among her acquaintances were Diamond Jim Brady and Theodore Roosevelt. Then, legend has it, her in-name-only husband died, and Livingstone unexpectedly inherited $150,000 from his estate. According to Livingstone's memoirs, Wherry had reluctantly divorced her a year earlier, which makes the unexpected inheritance seem even more unlikely. Whatever the true story, Livingstone did receive enough of a windfall to set sail for Europe in the summer of 1897. She settled in London, where she used her looks, her money, and the novelty of her forthright American ways to establish herself in London society. It was during her years in London that she coined the phrase "Spend it while you've got it," a dictum that she followed throughout her life.

In 1902, after being swindled with forged stock certificates and discovering that her investments in an Australian mine were worthless, Livingstone found herself broke. She bet friends £5,000 that she could make her way around the world on nothing more than a £5 note. Traveling east, she got as far as Japan. In March 1903, in Yokohama, she married Count Florentino Ghiberti Laltazzi, an Italian diplomat; they had one daughter. After their marriage, they headed in opposite directions, she to the United States to visit her family, he to Europe to resume his diplomatic duties. He died shortly thereafter in St. Petersburg, Russia. When Livingstone returned to Europe, she learned that his family had had their marriage declared invalid.

To support herself, Livingstone published her first volume of memoirs, *Letters of a Bohemian* (1906). In 1906 she married an American millionaire,

Edward Mohler of Cleveland, Ohio. They lived in Paris and had a son. She divorced Mohler in 1911 and married Walter James Hutchins, a British engineer, in 1912. They lived in Paris, and Livingstone became a prominent hostess, noted for ignoring social barriers. It was during this period that a journalist dubbed her "the most dangerous woman in Europe."

In 1923 Livingstone learned that she had gone through virtually all of Hutchins's money. They separated with vague plans to resume their marriage once they had recovered financially. In 1925 Livingstone was paid well by *Cosmopolitan* magazine for a series of memoirs that were the basis of her second book, *Belle of Bohemia* (1927), and the marriage temporarily resumed, but they once again found themselves broke in 1927 and separated again. They were still separated when Hutchins died some five years later.

In 1927 Livingstone returned to the United States after thirty years abroad. She declared New York dull and announced an antidote: she would open a salon where luminaries could meet. Her salon proved to be a thinly disguised speakeasy. One Man House, membership for which cost $200, opened shortly after her return to New York and failed in 1928. A new "salon," the Silver Room, opened in the fall of 1929. By April 1930 Livingstone had been arrested three times in three months for violating the Volstead Act, which prohibited the sale, manufacture, and transportation of alcoholic beverages, and the colorful Livingstone's flip attitude and ability to turn a phrase had made her a newspaper favorite. Throughout 1930 and into 1931, federal agents would raid her saloons, rounds of court appearances would begin, and Livingstone would settle into another location. In 1931, however, she spent thirty days in prison.

After filing for bankruptcy, Livingstone left New York and moved to Reno, Nevada. Problems with liquor deliveries put an end to that venture, and she had subsequent short-lived clubs in Dallas, San Francisco, Phoenix, and East Hampton, New York. "Those who operate outside the law of the land find themselves perforce under the law of the jungle, where the strong prey on the weak and the fittest survive," she wrote in her final memoir, *Belle Out of Order* (1959). "The idea was finally being borne in upon me that perhaps I was not one of the fittest."

The repeal of Prohibition put an end to her career as saloon hostess and headline grabber. Her last nightclub, the Reno, opened in New York City in December 1934 and closed ten days later. After that, she lived modestly in a small New York City apartment and worked on her final memoirs, which were published posthumously. She suffered a heart attack in 1949, and, after a second heart attack in 1955, she moved to a nursing home in the Bronx, where she died.

Belle Livingstone is one of those historical curiosities—a woman undeniably famous in her own era but for reasons subsequent generations cannot quite fathom. Throughout her life, Livingstone showed a knack for keeping her name in the limelight. Her ability to embellish, however, has made it difficult to ascertain what parts of the Livingstone legend are fact and what parts are fiction.

L.H.

HIRAM BINGHAM

[19 NOVEMBER 1875–6 JUNE 1956]

Born to a prominent missionary family, and reared to carry on his parents' work, Bingham instead became a professor, philanderer, pilot, and turn-of-the-century version of Indiana Jones. Drawn to the wilds of South America, he retraced the steps of earlier travelers, "discovered" Machu Picchu in Peru, and appears to have looted the country's Incan relics. Bingham's political career was just as colorful, and controversial. He arrived at one press conference in a blimp, and was later censured by the Senate for cozying up to business interests.

Hiram Bingham, explorer, was born Hiram Bingham III in Honolulu, Hawaii, the son of Hiram Bingham (1831–1908) and Clarissa Minerva Brewster, missionaries. Bingham's family assumed he would constitute the third generation of missionary service to the natives of the South Pacific and constantly pressured him to live the godly life. His few efforts as a missionary literally made him sick, and he seems to have had little interest in the salvation of the natives. Bingham (he appears to have dropped the III about the time his father died) instead sublimated the family's missionary zeal into a broad variety of interests.

In 1892, he was enrolled in Phillips Academy, Andover, Massachusetts. Once a stronghold of Congregationalism, Phillips had recently separated itself from its theological school and in many other ways was secularizing the curriculum as well as the student body. Hiram now dared to take such bold steps as to manage the football team, study Latin on Sunday, and participate in the burgeoning Student Volunteer Movement, an evangelical organization made up largely of eastern college boys who worked among the urban poor; it was much too liberal-minded for his family.

Bingham moved even farther from the missionary field when, in the fall of 1894, he enrolled at Yale University. There Hiram experimented with many new interests, none to his parents' liking. He joined a fraternity and

An assistant history professor who longed to acquire firsthand knowledge of his subject matter, Bingham had just finished retracing a centuries old Spanish trade route when he stumbled upon the "city in the clouds."

a debating society; he enjoyed sports. He wrote home criticizing the visiting evangelical preachers and lauding the exhilarating ideas of his teachers. He determined to become a college professor.

He also fell in love with Alfreda Mitchell, daughter of Alfred and Annie Mitchell, whom he had met in both Connecticut and Hawaii. The Mitchells, heirs to the Tiffany fortune, felt that a potential missionary might prove unable to support their daughter and withheld their approval of a marriage until Hiram had acquired an advanced college degree.

In 1899, Bingham commenced graduate work in history at the University of California at Berkeley. In 1900 he began his Ph.D. program in Latin American history at Harvard. That same fall he and Alfreda were married at the Mitchell estate in New London. He acquired his doctorate in 1905, occasionally teaching at Harvard and Princeton while completing his studies. In 1909 he received an appointment to Yale as assistant professor, rising through the usual ranks until 1922, when he entered politics.

The Tiffany wealth allowed him to acquire firsthand knowledge of his teaching subject matter. In 1906 he traveled to Venezuela and Colombia, attempting to retrace the routes of Simon Bolívar's military campaigns.

For the next few years exploring dominated his life far more than teaching. In 1908 and 1909 he traced old Spanish trade routes throughout southern South America, pausing long enough to serve as U.S. delegate to the first Pan American Scientific Congress at Santiago, Chile. In 1911 he made a major discovery high in the Peruvian Andes, the mysterious fortress, temple, and residence of ancient Incas—Machu Picchu. Unknown to all but a few Indians for hundreds of years, Machu Picchu made Bingham famous, and in spite of many other achievements, he continued to think of himself as an explorer for the rest of his life. He made many more trips to South America, finding new trails, climbing unknown mountains, and directing Yale's frequent Peruvian expeditions.

Prior to America's entrance into World War I, Bingham privately obtained his pilot's license and in 1917 obtained a commission in what was then called the U.S. Army Air Service. He organized schools of military aeronautics for the United States, then went to France as chief of air personnel, later commanding the Allies' largest flying school.

In 1922, he was easily elected lieutenant governor of Connecticut. After one term he won the gubernatorial campaign but served only two days; an incumbent U.S. senator committed suicide, forcing a special election that Bingham won. He was reelected in 1926 for a full term but lost in 1932. In the Senate he specialized in measures concerning the Caribbean, the Pacific Islands, and air power. His behavior was often unusual. He once arrived at a press conference in a blimp and left another in an autogiro. In 1929, he became one of the few senators ever censured by the Senate, bringing to that body "dishonor and disrepute" for permitting a manufacturer's lobbyist to sit in on price-setting legislation. After the Democratic landslide of 1932, Bingham spent much of his remaining life pursuing business interests, including publishing.

In 1951 he was called from retirement by President Harry S. Truman to chair the new Loyalty Review Board, the final appeal of civil service loyalty cases. In the early years of the domestic Communist scare, Bingham received much criticism from liberal circles for his decisions, making it easier for the government to dismiss employees, among whom were several famous "old China Hands," accused of losing China to the Communists.

Bingham's role in his several careers was usually marked by controversy, often bitter. Even his explorations, which he considered his chief contribution, invoked complaints from Latin American nations; the government of Peru once accused him of smuggling Incan artifacts out of the country. In the Senate, where he considered himself an authority on the Far East, he opposed the independence of the Philippines on grounds of political immaturity, and he frequently upbraided other senators for their ignorance of Latin America. He favored sending the marines to Nicaragua, again because of what he viewed as the natives' backwardness. In his book *The Monroe Doctrine: An Absolute Shibboleth* (1913), Bingham called the Monroe Doctrine obsolete, provoking a national discussion among scholars and politicians. He later changed his mind, saying that the doctrine must still be applied to the small Caribbean states but not to the large nations of the southern cone of South America, which he thought had matured beyond the need for U.S. intervention.

Bingham was the author of a dozen or more books and many articles, mostly on his Latin American explorations, and he received many medals and honors from several Latin American governments. He frequently represented the United States in international congresses, especially those of a scientific nature.

His prolonged absences from home provoked serious family problems. He told Alfreda that their married life was better because of his absences and that he hoped she understood his need for other female companionship; he boldly acquired a mistress. In 1937, Alfreda divorced him, their seven children generally supporting their mother in the hearings. He died in Washington, D.C.

Bingham is highly praised in academic circles as a pioneer in Latin American history and geography. His major reputation lies in the exceptional and often solitary geographical discoveries he reported in *Across South America* (1911), *The Discovery of Machu Picchu* (1913), and *Inca Land* (1922). He had many "firsts," but in particular he should be recognized as the person who first popularized Latin America for the North American public.

T.L.K.

Hines, pictured here with his wife, Clara, turned a passion for food into a successful series of books, writing of his recommended restaurants in 1935, "I am passing this information on to you, hoping that it may yield enjoyment and delectation, should you find yourself in the vicinity of one of these 'harbors of refreshment' as you travel hither and yon."

DUNCAN HINES

[26 MARCH 1880–15 MARCH 1959]

Nineteenth-century European visitors to America often lamented the young nation's cooking, as well as the speed and lack of decorum with which travelers dispatched their meals. "The dinner hour," Frances Trollope tartly observed, "was to be anything rather than an hour of enjoyment." With the arrival of the automobile in the twentieth century, road food became a consumer item for millions of Americans who had never traveled widely before. Hines, all-too familiar with "leathery eggs" and "dishwater soup" from his decades as a business traveler, discovered a late-life vocation in guiding motorists to plain but high-quality American cooking. From humble beginnings, his Adventures in Good Eating *grew into a gastronomic publishing empire that made Duncan Hines a brand name.*

Duncan Hines, author, editor, and publisher of travel and restaurant guidebooks for motorists, was born in Bowling Green, Kentucky, the son of Edward L. Hines, a former Confederate army captain, schoolteacher, lawyer, and housebuilder, and Cornelia Duncan. Hines was raised by his grandmother after his mother died, and he attributed his appreciation of the art of dining to his grandmother's southern cooking. Though he would achieve widespread name recognition as a restaurant critic, his career did not involve food until he reached his mid-fifties. In 1896, he enrolled in Bowling Green Business University but left after two years. For the next forty years he worked in a variety of jobs, mostly public relations; he designed, wrote, and produced corporate brochures, traveling widely from his home in Chicago to visit clients around the country. In 1905 he married Florence Chaffin; they had no children.

Hines, whose hobby was eating well, became expert at sniffing out good food while he was on the road. Because of the dearth of clean restaurants serving tasty food, Hines applied himself assiduously to the search; he sought recommendations and filled notebooks with his findings. Traveling with his wife on weekends, he took busman's holidays, driving as much as 500 miles on gastronomic safaris. His reputation as a restaurant hunter began to spread, and a growing contingent of Chicago business travelers consulted him before daring to venture out of town.

Beleagured by queries, he came up with a scheme to silence his phone. In 1935, he printed a list of 167 favorite spots in thirty states and mailed off 1,000 copies as Christmas greetings. But the gesture failed to accomplish its goal; the barrage of requests for restaurant reconnaissance only escalated. In self-defense, Hines expanded the card into an inexpensive, pocket-sized guidebook called *Adventures in Good Eating*, adding more restaurants with short descriptions for each; the price is variously reported to have been $1.00 or $1.50. From this modest beginning would erupt a quarter-century publishing phenomenon that would make "Recommended by Duncan Hines" a household—or, rather, a car-seat—phrase.

Hines was an advocate of plain American cooking, which, in his view, could be "the best in the world" and also "the worst." He liked simple, wholesome fare true to its geographic origins. The author grumbled publicly about restaurants that served "leathery eggs or vegetables in billboard paste or dishwater soup," and he railed against inns that ignored regional specialties in favor of steak and chicken. Once, when asked how he made his menu selections, he snapped, "I steer clear of hashes and meat loaves with fancy names, and from dishes disguised with French names that don't mean anything in a Midwest hotel."

Even more demanding were his standards of cleanliness. Before entering a restaurant, Hines often surveyed the back door, using his nose to detect malodorous garbage and other sanitary lapses. He then asked to inspect the kitchen. If satisfied, he entered the dining room and ordered a half-dozen entrées. Restaurants that pleased his sensibilities and his palate were added to the annual (eventually semiannual) update of *Adventures in Good Eating*. Although Hines included some well-known big-city restaurants in the book, he focused on uncharted territory—the uncelebrated small-town establishments that his urban readers needed to know about in order to eat well when driving from one city to another. He reviewed these places without a trace of snobbery or literary affectation in a style that exuded humor and humility. Restaurants included in the book could hang his seal of approval: a sign that boasted "Recommended by Duncan Hines." Hines retained ownership of the signs and would retrieve one when he judged that a restaurant's quality had fallen. He snubbed all offers of advertising, fiercely guarding his independence and his anonymity. The only photograph he used was a twenty-year-old portrait.

Financially, *Adventures in Good Eating* was at first a disaster, netting the author-publisher a $1,500 loss on 5,000 copies sold. But in 1938 a feature article in the *Saturday Evening Post* helped put him in the black. After publishing *Lodging for a Night* (for travelers seeking a bed) and *Duncan Hines' Vacation Guide*, he quit his job and moved back to Bowling Green. His books catered to motorists at a time when owning a car was coming to be regarded as an American birthright. By the end of 1939 Hines's books were moving at a brisk 100,000 copies a year. Eventually, with the addition of *Adventures in Good Cooking* and *The Art of Carving in the Home*, combined annual sales would reach half a million. According to a chef cited in *Scribner's Commentator* in 1941, Hines had done "more in four years to raise the level of the American cuisine than chefs had done in the previous forty." As business soared and mail poured in (more than 50,000 letters a year), Hines found it necessary to assemble a volunteer corps of several hundred "dinner detectives" who pioneered new ground and revisited the old. His army of culinary lieutenants included bank presidents, university professors, corporate chiefs, and many well-known personalities.

Hines's first wife died in 1939, and his second marriage, to Emelie Elizabeth Daniels, that same year ended in divorce. In 1946, he married Clara Wright Nahm, a widow who embraced his hobby-turned-profession. He had no children with any of his wives. The two of them toured the United States, Mexico, the Caribbean, Hawaii, and Western Europe for gastronomic pleasure. Hines claimed to have logged over two million miles for the love of food.

In 1948 Duncan Hines was approached by Roy H. Park, a businessman in upstate New York who was seeking a brand name for clients interested in marketing food products. Park broke down Hines's resistance to endorsements, and the two men established Hines-Park Foods to license the Duncan Hines name. It soon appeared on 200 different items from bread and jam to canned fruit, ice cream, and cake mix. To administer publication of Hines's books, the partners established the Duncan Hines Institute at Ithaca, New York, in 1953. Two years later, the institute brought out the *Duncan Hines Food Odyssey* and the *Duncan Hines Dessert Book*, which included his thoughts on courtesy, safe driving, and cooking methods. After a vigorous promotional campaign complete with television appearances and the proclamation of "Duncan Hines Days" in dozens of cities, the food champion slowed down. In 1956 Procter & Gamble purchased all the Duncan Hines interests, and Hines went into semiretirement.

The guidebooks outlived their creator, who died of lung cancer in Bowling Green eleven days before his seventy-ninth birthday. Procter & Gamble discontinued the book series in 1962 and later dropped most products bearing the Duncan Hines name. The notable exception was cake mixes, and for these, rather than guidebooks or restaurant recommendations, the name Duncan Hines has lived on. Highway travelers, who now take for granted the availability of appetizing food prepared in sanitary kitchens, owe a debt of gratitude to Duncan Hines. He demanded a level of quality and cleanliness that was uncommon in his day. Gradually it became the norm, perhaps because, for more than two decades, the nation's best-known advocate of fine dining would accept nothing less.

D.M.S.

ANNETTE KELLERMAN

[6 JULY 1887–5 NOVEMBER 1975]

Encumbered by Victorian mores and modest clothing, women in the late nineteenth and early twentieth centuries were largely excluded from water sports. Kellerman, a polio-afflicted Australian, challenged this orthodoxy in dramatic fashion. She became a champion swimmer and daredevil diver who railed against corsets and boldly wore a one-piece racing suit, leading to her arrest for indecent exposure. A vaudeville and film star in movies such as Diving Venus, *Kellerman also served as a traveling apostle for women's athletics, helping to create notions of female freedom and physical fitness that are taken for granted today.*

Annette Kellerman, swimming, vaudeville, and film star, was born in Sydney, Australia, the daughter of Frederick Kellerman, a musician, and Alice Charbonnet, a concert pianist. A weak child, Kellerman began swimming as physical therapy for a mild case of polio. Feeling more graceful in water than on land in her leg braces, swimming literally became her life. As the strength in her legs increased, she also learned to dive. In 1902, she won her first title as Swim Champion of New South Wales and set a world record of 78 seconds for 100 yards using the newly introduced racing technique of the double-over arm crawl and scissors kick. By her own admission, she also reigned as the champion girl diver of Australia the same year. The next year, she set a world record for the mile at 32:29 minutes, subsequently lowering it to 28:00 minutes. Her first of many record-setting distance swims covered 10 miles in Australia's Yarrow River. She began professional swimming and diving exhibitions in Sydney, then toured Melbourne and Adelaide.

In 1904 her father took her to England to promote her aquatic skills. Sponsored by the Harmsworth newspapers, she swam 17 miles down the Thames and attempted to be the first woman—and the first person

In addition to her stunts on- and off-camera, Kellerman published two books that were among the first to offer women a regimen of physical fitness.

in thirty-six years—to swim the English Channel. Her three attempts failed, but her covering of three-fourths of the distance in 10.5 hours remained a women's record for many years. After more swimming stunts—notably a 7-mile swim in the Seine through Paris and a 22-mile swim in the Danube from Tuln to Vienna—garnered her more publicity, she signed with Arthur Collins, the "Prince of Showmen," to star in his London music hall. Her swimming and diving act then toured Great Britain with great success.

Kellerman's arrival in the United States in 1907 erupted in scandal when she appeared on Boston's Revere Beach in a one-piece bathing suit, a style of racing suit she always wore even when she was not competing. Arrested for indecent exposure, her court case brought her instant fame as the progenitor of modern swimwear. Women began to abandon the cumbersome and heavy wool skirts, blouses, and stockings Victorian mores dictated they wear. After her charges were dismissed in Boston, she traveled to Chicago for her first American playdate at the White City Amusement Park, where she did fifty-five shows a week for seven weeks. B. F. Keith then engaged her as a headliner in his Keith/Orpheum vaudeville circuit for $1,250 a week. She remained with Keith for two years, performing fourteen shows a week. Her act consisted of singing, dancing, playing the violin, tightrope walking, diving, and swimming in a large glass tank. In 1910 she signed with William Morris to manage her vaudeville career (resulting in a lawsuit by Keith/Orpheum), and in 1912, when she married James Sullivan, she decided to let her new husband manage her career (requiring her to sue William Morris). Under Sullivan's management, they built a small fortune in vaudeville (including five world tours between 1914 and 1929 and numerous appearances at New York City's Hippodrome) and moved into filmmaking.

Kellerman had made her U.S. film debut in a Vitagraph short, *Diving Venus* (1909), for which she received the largest salary the studio had ever paid and her own glass tank. She demonstrated some exercises, dives, and swimming techniques. Her first feature film, *Neptune's Daughter* (Universal, 1914), won major acclaim. She played a mermaid granted legs so that she could seek out the humans who killed her younger sister. The film, shot on location in Bermuda, fully exploited her diving and swimming skills featuring a 45-foot solo dive, a 30-foot tandem dive, and much underwater swimming. She followed this success with *A Daughter of the Gods* (Fox, 1916). Shot on location in Jamaica, the film took nine months to shoot, featured a cast of 20,000, required the construction of two cities (one underwater), employed a camera in a diving bell, and cost more than $1 million (a record budget). As before, the film functioned as a showcase for Kellerman's abilities; her greatest stunt was a 92-foot dive—for which she was bound hand and foot. She made three more feature films, *Queen of the Sea* (1918), *What Women Love* (1920), and *Venus of the South Seas* (1924). *What Women Love* won her the title of "the Douglas Fairbanks of the Screen Girls Athletic Association." Of these five films, only ten minutes from *Neptune's Daughter* seems to have survived.

In 1918 Kellerman published two books designed for women, *Physical Beauty* and *How to Swim*. *Physical Beauty* railed against the corset while extolling the virtues of exercise and diet (she was a vegetarian) to achieve proper posture, strength, and body tone. She demonstrated through illustration and direction how to achieve her world-renowned physical perfection. *How to Swim* followed the same tack, advocating swimming as an excellent form of exercise. These books were among the first to offer women a regimen of physical fitness.

After her last world tour ended in 1929, she limited her activities to the always popular "Swimologues" (physical fitness lecture tours featuring underwater films shot by her husband), running a health food store in Long Beach, California, and relaxing on Pandamus Island, an island inside Australia's Great Barrier Reef that she and her husband owned. During World War II, she devoted her talents to charity benefits (as she had during World War I) and established and ran an Australian Red Cross theatrical unit. Her life came full circle in 1952 when MGM released *Million Dollar Mermaid,* starring Esther Williams. A fictionalized biography of Kellerman, she served as technical adviser on the film. *Million Dollar Mermaid* follows Kellerman's life from her early years as a crippled child to the spectacular Hippodrome shows to her severe accident when an 8,000-gallon glass tank broke during the filming of *Neptune's Daughter*.

After her husband died in 1953, she moved to Southport, Queensland, Australia, where she lived for more than twenty years, until her death there. In 1974 she was inducted into the International Swimming Hall of Fame in Fort Lauderdale, Florida, for "doing more to popularize swimming (especially for women) than any other person in the early years."

Kellerman's aquatic skills set numerous records and served as the basis for many years of a successful international vaudeville career—a career in which she helped introduce synchronized swimming with her Acquabelles and women's high diving. Her move into film stardom established the tradition of Hollywood's exploitation of successful athletes (for example, Johnny Weissmuller, Sonja Henie, Esther Williams, and Arnold Schwarzenegger) in films tailored to showcase their unique talents. The publicity surrounding her one-piece bathing suit altered the course of women's swimwear design toward the contemporary styles of the maillot, tank, and bikini. She was an athletic feminist, and her lectures, books, performances, and films encouraged and inspired women to break away from the antiathletic tradition of their gender to pursue health and beauty through exercise and diet. As "swimming's greatest saleswoman," Kellerman took an esoteric sport and moved it into popular culture.

G.S.F.

After the last member of her family died in 1920, Boyd devoted her time and money to travel. Ten years after this photograph was taken in 1928, she would venture north to the highest latitude then reached by an American expedition, and the second highest seagoing latitude reached in history.

LOUISE ARNER BOYD
[16 SEPTEMBER 1887–14 SEPTEMBER 1972]

As a governess-educated debutante, and a grower of prize camellias, Boyd seemed destined for a life of domestic ease. Instead, this California heiress became an unlikely explorer of glaciers and fjords, leading multiple expeditions to the Arctic in a Norwegian sealing ship. Her discoveries included a remote stretch of Greenland named Miss Boyd Land. An accomplished writer and photographer, Boyd won countless honors and appointments from the traditionally all-male world of geographical and exploratory societies. She also became the first woman to fly over the North Pole—at the age of seventy-eight.

Louise Arner Boyd, Arctic explorer, photographer, and author, was born in San Rafael, California, the daughter of John Franklin Boyd, Sr., and Louise Cook Arner. Boyd was born to one of the wealthiest families in turn-of-the-century San Francisco. Her maternal grandfather, Ira Cook, had built a fortune in the mid-nineteenth century, and her father ran the family gold-mining business and an investment company. Boyd was educated privately, first by governesses, then at Miss Stewart's School in San Rafael and Miss Murrison's in San Francisco. She did not attend college or university and made her social debut in 1907. Throughout the next decade, during which her father trained her to become the financial manager of the family business, Boyd stayed busy with family concerns and community interests, helping care for her invalid brothers and emerging as a leading patron of music, art, and charitable causes in San Rafael and San Francisco. She also became expert at growing prize camellias.

Events in the 1920s propelled her toward a career as an Arctic explorer. Her father's death in 1920 had been preceded by the deaths of her brothers and her mother. Thus Louise Boyd was the sole survivor, unmarried, and heiress to a fortune at age thirty-two. Thereafter she channeled her grief, her money, and her time into travel. In 1924, after several European tours, she took a pleasure cruise that included Spitsbergen, an archipelago in the Arctic Sea between Norway and East Greenland where she fell in love with the Arctic. "Far north," she wrote, "are lands that hold one spellbound. . . . One enters another world where men are insignificant amid the awesome immensity of mountains, fiords, and glaciers" (Olds, p. 234). Boyd organized, financed, and led seven Arctic expeditions between 1926 and 1941. Each expedition had a specific mission and carried the latest scientific equipment.

On the first two voyages, in 1926 and 1928, Boyd developed her expertise as a photographer and expedition leader that earned her a place in the circles of the American Geographical Society. In 1926 she chartered the Norwegian sealer MS *Hobby*, once the flagship of Roald Amundsen's polar expedition, for a voyage that combined sport with science. Boyd and her six-man team hunted polar bears and studied Arctic flora and fauna in Franz Josef Land, the northernmost point of land in the Eastern Hemisphere. More important, the 1926 voyage launched Boyd's career as a photographer. Thereafter, as official photographer for her expeditions, she was not only patroness but part of the scientific team.

In 1928, Boyd was preparing for another voyage when she learned that Roald Amundsen, "Norway's cherished hero of Arctic and Antarctic exploration," had disappeared in his hydroplane *Latham* on a mission to rescue General Umberto Nobile, whose dirigible *Italia* had crashed while trying to fly to the North Pole (Olds, pp. 239, 240). Boyd immediately changed her plans and committed herself to the search for Amundsen. In the course of the search Boyd and the *Hobby* covered 10,000 miles of Arctic seas between 1 July and 22 September. Although Amundsen was never found, Boyd's rescue mission brought her international publicity as a serious explorer who had scrapped her expedition for a noble cause. That year she received high civilian honors from the nations sponsoring the search: she was the first non-Norwegian woman to receive the Knight Cross of St. Olaf, First Class, and France made her a chevalier of the Legion of Honor. The instant fame also brought her to the attention of Scandinavian Arctic experts and notable American scientists such as Isaiah Bowman of the American Geographical Society.

The four expeditions in the 1930s, in the 125-foot oak-ribbed Norwegian sealer *Veslekari*, added significantly to the knowledge of the fiords and sounds of East Greenland. The 1931 expedition was Boyd's first exploration of the Franz Josef and King Oscar fiord regions of East Greenland, which had been surveyed by Denmark but never studied closely. On this voyage she discovered the true end of Ice Fiord, in the Franz Josef region between De Geer and Jaette glaciers. Previous explorers had misjudged the fiord's terminus. The new area was an important glaciological find, as "one of the three principal sources of icebergs in the entire fiord region." The Danes honored her discovery by christening it "Weisboydlund" (Miss Boyd Land) (Olds, p. 246). On the steamer home from that expedition, Bowman and others from the American Geographical Society convinced Boyd to take a multidisciplinary team of experts on subsequent voyages with the society as official sponsor.

The next voyage, in 1933, mapped the inner reaches of Franz Josef Fiord. Photography became Boyd's top priority, and this expedition yielded the first of her three books, *The Fiord Region of East Greenland* (1935), coauthored with the expedition's scientists. It featured 350 of Boyd's photos and several new maps, including the first echo sound map of the floor of Franz Josef Fiord.

Isaiah Bowman now held Boyd's work in such regard that he named her a delegate to represent the American Geographical Society, the American Academy of Sciences, and the U.S. State Department at the 1934 International Geographical Congress in Warsaw, Poland. The trip resulted in a second book, *Polish Countrysides* (1937), featuring her classic photographs of a vanishing culture.

The 1937 and 1938 Arctic voyages were planned as a unit with a dual agenda, one exploratory, the other scientific. Boyd wanted to go as far north into East Greenland as possible and to continue the study of glacial margins begun in 1933. Unfortunately, the 1937 expedition (4 June–27 September) was trapped by ice in Franz Josef Fiord and had to return by a 100-mile detour through King Oscar Fiord and Sona Sound in order to avoid disaster. Nevertheless, Boyd discovered the western peak of an unknown ocean bank between Bear and Jan Mayen islands, later named Louise A. Boyd Bank.

In 1938, aboard the *Veslekari,* Boyd succeeded in reaching the Isle de France, at 77° 48" north latitude, only about 800 miles from the North Pole—the highest latitude reached by an American expedition and the second highest seagoing latitude reached in history. For "the notable contribution which her expeditions have made to geography and its related sciences," the American Geographical Society awarded her its Cullum Geographic medal in 1938. She was only the second woman in the society's eighty-six years to receive the medal, joining the ranks of such illustrious recipients as Admiral Robert E. Peary and Captain Robert F. Scott.

By the summer of 1940, Boyd was preparing to publish the results of her 1937–1938 voyages. But Hitler had conquered Denmark, making the Danish island of Greenland strategically important. Consequently, she complied with the War Department's request to forestall publication and turn over all of her records and data on Greenland to them for the duration of the war. In 1941, she financed and led an expedition, sponsored by the U.S. Bureau of Standards, to Canadian Arctic waters to gather data on military uses of long-range radio transmission in the Arctic ionosphere. In 1942 and 1943 she served as a civilian consultant to the Military Intelligence Division of the War Department. After the war, she published the accounts of the 1937 and 1938 expeditions in her third book, *The Coast of Northeast Greenland* (1948). Between 1943 and 1955, when not exploring, Boyd lived at Maple Lawn, her San Rafael estate, and hosted lavish social events. She also worked diligently for the arts and for her favorite charity, the Red Cross.

Her final expedition was by air. On 16 June 1955, she and her American crew made exploration history with a flyover of the North Pole. At age seventy-eight she was the first woman to undertake this endeavor, the first in a nonmilitary plane, and the first by privately financed expedition.

Boyd has been called "the only woman to achieve an outstanding position in Arctic exploration" (Olds, p. 234). However, two obstacles frustrated her bid for recognition as a scientist. First, she was a woman in a field dominated by men, some of whom resented her intrusion into their brotherhood. Second, she was an explorer among scientists. The botanist on her 1937 expedition, Henry J. Oosting, described the dilemma from the scientists' standpoint: "We fear she [Boyd] will develop wanderlust when we hope to concentrate all endeavors on one localized area associated with a single glacier" (Oosting diary, 14 July 1937, p. 46). Because Boyd had no professional credentials, some scientists dismissed her as a wealthy socialite simply indulging a hobby. "Louise had absolutely no scientific training or background," wrote her friend and colleague Walter A. Wood. "I think that Louise tried her hardest to become a member of the scientific fraternity. I'm glad she didn't [succeed]. She was a far better advocate of science in her social environment" (Trussell, p. 12). It was as an explorer, photographer, and friend of science that she joined the inner circles of the American Geographical Society in the 1930s. In 1960, she became the first woman named to its executive council. Twelve years later, Boyd died in a San Francisco nursing home, without enough money to satisfy her request that her ashes be scattered over the North Pole. Devoted friends flew her remains as far north as funds permitted, scattering them over the Canadian Arctic.

C.F.J.

The father of modern surfing and an ambassador of Hawaiian culture, Duke once said, "I have never seen snow and do not know what winter means. I have never coasted down a hill of frozen rain, but every day of the year where the water is 76°, day and night, and the waves roll high, I take my sled, without runners, and coast down the face of the big waves that roll in at Waikiki."

DUKE PAOA
KAHANAMOKU

[24 AUGUST 1890–22 JANUARY 1968]

Early European explorers of the Pacific marveled at the swimming skills of islanders, and also at their fondness for riding waves atop wooden boards. But it wasn't until the twentieth century that surfing became common outside Polynesia. No one did more to popularize the sport than Duke Kahanamoku, a three-time Olympic swimmer and movie actor who acted as the "missionary of surfing."

Duke Paoa Kahanamoku, Olympic swimming champion and world-recognized surfer, was born and raised in the old Kalia District of Honolulu near the present location of the Hawaiian Village Hotel, the son of Halapu Kahanamoku, a police officer, and Paakonia Lonokahikini Paoa, or Julia. He was named after his father, who had been christened "Duke" by Princess Bernice Pauahi in 1869 for Queen Victoria's second son, the duke of Edinburgh, who was visiting the islands. Kahanamoku and his friends grew up as beach boys in Waikiki. They would gather under a big hau tree near the Moana Hotel, and there, in 1911, they formed Hui Nalu (Surf Club), which is still active today. At the beach Kahanamoku developed the skills that would lead him to prominence as both a swimmer and a surfer.

While swimming was a competitive sport at that time, surfing was not. Those who surfed did so just for the pleasure and thrill of riding the waves. Even in Hawaii, recognized as the birthplace of modern surfing, the sport did not enjoy a large following because existing surfboards were very heavy and unmaneuverable. Through Kahanamoku, however, surfing gained widespread popularity, and although he never intended to be known as a missionary of surfing, that is what he became. He wanted to be able to surf even when he was away from Hawaii, so he made a surfboard of redwood, which was much smaller and lighter than those currently in use, and took it with him wherever he traveled to participate in swimming events. During a trip to Australia in 1915 he introduced the sport there. As his travels continued, word of his skill spread. England's Prince of Wales heard of the young athlete's surfing ability, and during a visit to Hawaii in 1920 he asked to meet with "the much-heralded Duke Paoa Kahanamoku . . . to witness some of his fabulous surfing" (Brennan, *Father of Surfing*, p. 14). A close friendship developed between the two men, and before the Prince left the islands, he knew how to surf.

Kahanamoku rode his board on both coasts of the mainland United States, and during a visit to Corona Del Mar, California, in 1925, he won national acclaim for himself and his surfing skill. A fishing boat capsized in a raging surf, and Kahanamoku, using his surfboard as a rescue vehicle, paddled twelve people to safety in repeated trips between the wreckage and shore. J. A. Porter, chief of police of Newport Beach, called Kahanamoku's feat "the most superhuman rescue act and the finest display of surfboard riding ever seen in the World" (Luis, p. B3).

It was considered a fair exchange that Kahanamoku introduced surfing to Australia, because it was from studying the swimming style of Australians visiting Hawaii that he developed his famous flutter kick. This style, which was a flexible-knee version of the stiff-legged "Australian Crawl," provided the extra speed needed to make him a champion. He called this modified Australian style the "Hawaiian Crawl," and later, when Kahanamoku had gained world recognition, it became known as the "American Crawl."

Kahanamoku's competitive swimming career was launched in 1911 during the first swimming meet of the newly formed Honolulu Amateur Athletic Union. In the meet, which took place in Honolulu Harbor's Alakea Slip, the 21-year-old Kahanamoku set a world record of 55.8 seconds in the 100-yard freestyle—although his time was not recognized by the AAU, possibly because the race was held on a temporary course rather than in the controlled setting of a regulation pool. He traveled to Chicago to try out for the U.S. Olympic team that would compete in the 1912 games in Sweden. He made the team on 14 March with an impressive 57-second record in the 100-yard freestyle event.

In July 1912 in Stockholm, Kahanamoku continued to excel, winning the gold medal in the 100-meter freestyle with a world-record time of 63.4 seconds. His performance brought attention to his American Crawl, which was soon imitated by swimmers the world over. King Gustaf of Sweden was so impressed with Kahanamoku that he motioned the new record holder to the royal box, where he addressed him in English, saying, "My heartiest congratulations," and presented him to the queen.

Eight years later, in 1920, Kahanamoku swam in his second Olympiad, in Antwerp, Belgium, and continued his mastery of the 100-meter freestyle. On 24 August, he won the event in 61.4 seconds, another world-record time. The victory came under protest, however, so the race was rescheduled for six days later; he won again, in 60.4 seconds. Kahanamoku also swam on the four-man 800-meter relay team with Pua Kealoha, Perry McGillivray, and Norman Ross. They won the event in 10 minutes and 4.4 seconds, setting yet another world record.

Following his return home from the 1920 Olympics, Kahanamoku was approached with a $50,000 offer to turn professional. He did not accept, however, because he was planning to participate in the 1924 Paris games, and his acceptance of the offer would have conflicted with the Olympic policy regarding the amateur standing of athletes. Kahanamoku made the 1924 team but did not win a gold medal. Johnny Weissmuller, another member of the American team, edged Kahanamoku in Indianapolis during the trials and again at the games in Paris. After his victory in the 100-meter event, Weissmuller demonstrated his respect for Kahanamoku when he commented, "I beat a better man than I'll ever be." Kahanamoku won the silver medal with a time of 61.4 seconds, just 2.4 seconds short of Weissmuller's new record.

Although he had been beaten by Weissmuller, Kahanamoku was not ready to quit. In 1932, at the Olympiad in Los Angeles, he participated once again. He failed to qualify for the swimming team, however, but competed as a member of the Los Angeles Athletic Club Water Polo team; they did not win. Thus ended a nearly impossible-to-equal Olympic swimming career.

When he was not participating in Olympic games and furthering his skills in water sports, Kahanamoku found a place in Hollywood following a path in acting similar to that of Buster Crabbe, another noted swimmer from Hawaii. Although he never became a star, he earned recognition as an accomplished character actor playing a variety of roles, among them a Hindu thief, a Sioux Indian chief, and even a native-born Hawaiian. His films included *Lord Jim* (1925) and *Wake of the Red Witch* (1948), in which he shared the screen with another "Duke," John Wayne.

In 1934, Kahanamoku came home to stay and entered the race for sheriff of Honolulu. The people of Honolulu elected him to this post for thirteen consecutive terms. While Kahanamoku was sheriff, the position took on a ceremonial focus, with his principal role becoming that of a promotional emissary for Hawaii. He left office in 1960 because the position of sheriff had been discontinued. In 1940, Kahanamoku married Nadine Alexander; the couple had no children.

Throughout his life as a four-time Olympic competitor, a surfer, an actor, and later the sheriff of Honolulu, Kahanamoku's warm personality, his courage, and his sense of fair play made him one of Hawaii's most beloved citizens. From the moment he left his native shores to become a swimming champion, he served as the islands' unofficial ambassador of goodwill. After his tenure as sheriff, that role took on a new meaning when he was appointed Hawaii's official "greeter," a post he held until his death in Honolulu. In 1965, Kahanamoku was inducted into the International Swimming Hall of Fame in Fort Lauderdale, Florida, along with Johnny Weissmuller and Buster Crabbe, and in 1969 a bust of him was placed in the International Surfing Hall of Fame in Huntington Beach, California. A statue on Kuhio Beach, Waikiki, also commemorates this famed Hawaiian.

A.M.Y.

MERIAN COLDWELL COOPER

[24 OCTOBER 1893–21 APRIL 1973]

*With the advent of aviation and motion pictures, it became possible to under-
take and record global adventure as never before. Cooper proved exceptionally
bold with both cameras and planes. Though trained as a Navy man, he served
as an aviator in three conflicts and was twice shot down behind enemy lines.
As a pioneering filmmaker, he followed nomadic tribesmen in Iran, documented
wild animals from Siam to Sudan, and turned his fascination with gorillas
into the story that became* King Kong. *He also became a movie executive with
a penchant for films about aviators and Western gunmen—while taking a break,
at the age of almost fifty, to return to the air in the Second World War.*

Merian Coldwell Cooper, filmmaker and adventurer, was born in
Jacksonville, Florida, the son of John C. Cooper, a lawyer, and
Mary Coldwell. He attended the U.S. Naval Academy, but resigned in his
last year. After a failed attempt to become an aviator early in World War I,
he worked for short periods on newspapers and then enlisted in the Georgia
National Guard, seeing service in Mexico.

When the United States entered the war, Cooper joined the U.S. Air
Service and saw action on the western front. In September 1918, he was
shot down behind enemy lines and finished the war in a German hospital. He later served with the American Relief Administration. In 1919,
Cooper and Major Cedric Fauntleroy formed the Kosciusko Squadron, a
group of American pilots who volunteered to fight the Bolshevik invasion
of Poland. Cooper was shot down in July 1920 and taken, under an assumed
name, to a Moscow prison. In April 1921 he escaped with two Polish officers to the Latvian border. At the squadron's demobilization, President
Pilsudski of Poland awarded Cooper the Cross of the Brave; a statue was
erected in his honor in Warsaw.

Taken in northern Siam, where he and Ernest B. Schoedsack filmed Chang: A Drama of the Wilderness *in 1926, this photograph shows Cooper with Bimbo, a white gibbon that provided comic relief in the movie.*

Returning to the United States, Cooper contributed articles to the *New York Times*. He also wrote a book about the Kosciusko Squadron which was published in Polish as *Faunt-le-Roy i jego Eskadra w Polsce* (*Fauntleroy and His Squadron in Poland,* 1922). Still restless, Cooper accepted a job as navigator and writer with Captain Edward A. Salisbury and, in September 1922, joined Salisbury's yacht in Singapore. With Salisbury he wrote a book about the voyage, *The Sea Gypsy* (1924).

Cooper and Ernest B. Schoedsack, a photographer on the Salisbury voyage, decided to organize their own filming expedition, and Cooper obtained funding from Marguerite Harrison, whom he had known in Poland. They traveled from Aleppo to Baghdad, stopping at an outpost of the Iraq Desert Patrol. Later they joined the nomadic Bakhtiari tribes of southern Iran and, during the spring of 1924, participated in their annual migration in search of fresh grass. Cooper wrote about the migration *Grass* (1925). After he and Schoedsack edited their film, Cooper accompanied it on lecture engagements. Paramount then released it to theaters as *Grass: A Nation's Battle for Life* (1925), one of the first important feature documentaries. *Grass* received excellent reviews, so Paramount financed another expedition.

In July 1925, Cooper and Schoedsack left for the Nan district of northern Siam (Thailand), returning in December 1926. It was the realization of Cooper's dream to spend a year in the jungle documenting wild animals. The filmmakers personalized the natives' struggle against the jungle by centering on one family and made full use of cinematic techniques. After observing, they wrote a story and re-created events for the camera. They even selected unrelated people to portray the family. This resulted in a kind of staged authenticity which they called "natural drama." The method produced a film of considerable impact. *Variety* called *Chang: A Drama of the Wilderness* (1927) "the best wild animal picture ever made."

When Paramount agreed to back another film, the team further developed their concept of natural drama by adapting A. E. W. Mason's novel, *The Four Feathers*. In spring 1927, they left for East Africa, then moved north to the Sudan, spending a year filming animal action and battle scenes. Back in Hollywood, they directed professional actors, then intercut those shots with the location footage. Later, though, the studio restructured the plot and added several new scenes. *The Four Feathers* (1929) retained its spectacle, but Cooper was disappointed by the changes.

In 1927 Cooper invested his earnings from *Chang* in aviation stocks, and he was elected to the boards of several airlines, including Pan American Airways, Western Air Express, and General Aviation. This kept him in New York from 1929 to 1931, and he became friends with financiers Cornelius Vanderbilt Whitney and John Hay Whitney, as well as naturalist W. Douglas Burden.

Cooper was interested in making a film about African gorillas, and also in filming the Komodo dragon lizards discovered in Indonesia by Douglas Burden. Through editing, he hoped to depict a confrontation between the two creatures. He also wanted to express his belief "that over-civilization destroys people," and he envisioned a dramatic juxtaposition of gorillas and airplanes.

When David O. Selznick became head of production at RKO Radio Pictures in fall 1931, he asked Cooper to evaluate the studio's projects. After viewing footage of animated dinosaur models created by Willis O'Brien, Cooper saw his chance. "I decided I'd make my gorilla picture . . . and make it right here." He outlined the story of *King Kong* (1933) to author Edgar Wallace, who started on a script, and in January 1932, he brought Schoedsack to RKO. Later, writer Ruth Rose (Schoedsack's wife) modeled two of the film's main characters on Cooper and her husband.

While developing *Kong,* Cooper produced a mystery (*The Phantom of Crestwood,* 1932), cowrote the story for an action film set in China (*Roar of the Dragon,* 1932), and had Schoedsack and Irving Pichel codirect the jungle adventure, *The Most Dangerous Game* (1932). For *Kong,* Cooper and Schoedsack shared directorial responsibility; they also played the aviators in the film's climax. In March 1933 *King Kong* played simultaneously at two New York theaters, the Radio City Music Hall and the Roxy, and was a tremendous hit.

Selznick resigned as RKO's vice president on 3 February 1933, and Cooper succeeded him, serving as executive producer on numerous features released between April 1933 and June 1934, including *Little Women* (1933) and *Flying Down to Rio* (1933). Cooper's program was varied, but several films reflect his interests and experiences. Airplanes were often featured, and he depicted such adventurous filmmakers as stuntmen (*Lucky Devils,* 1933) and newsreel cameramen (*Headline Shooter,* 1933). During his tenure as vice president, Cooper impressed others as energetic, sometimes blunt, and always honest.

After seeing a demonstration of Technicolor's new three-color system, Cooper wanted to film *Kong* and *Flying Down to Rio* in the process. When RKO resisted, he acted on his judgment by purchasing stock in the company, along with the Whitneys. In May 1933, he and John Hay Whitney formed Pioneer Pictures to produce films in Technicolor, but at first Cooper remained in the background. Also in May, he married actress Dorothy Jordan; they had three children.

For a time, Cooper enjoyed his executive position, but after suffering a heart attack in September 1933, he eased himself out of the studio's daily responsibilities by taking a leave of absence to combine recuperation with a delayed honeymoon. In May 1934 Cooper returned to Hollywood and resigned, but he remained at RKO to produce two films written by Ruth Rose—*She* (1935), from the novel by H. Rider Haggard, and *The Last Days of Pompeii* (1935), which Schoedsack directed. He then turned his attention to Pioneer, which had already made *Becky Sharp* (1935), the first feature in three-color Technicolor. For Pioneer he produced the color musical *Dancing Pirate* (1936). In 1935, the Whitneys and Cooper had invested in Selznick's new company, Selznick International, because the producer agreed to use Technicolor. Selznick International absorbed Pioneer in June 1936, and Cooper continued as vice president and producer. That fall, Cooper helped Selznick convince playwright Sidney Howard to adapt Margaret Mitchell's novel *Gone with the Wind.*

John Ford had contracted with the studio to direct two films; he selected a western story and wanted to cast John Wayne and Claire Trevor. Cooper agreed and, in summer 1937, described the idea to Selznick, who unexpectedly rejected the stars. Cooper angrily resigned and quickly signed with MGM, where he made *The Toy Wife* (1938). He also unofficially produced the western Selznick had rejected, *Stagecoach* (1939); he and Ford then formed the Argosy Corporation, which made Ford's *The Long Voyage Home* (1940).

In May 1941 Cooper reenlisted and, at one point, flew refugees out of Assam, India. He was chief of U.S. Army Air Corps intelligence and plans in China when, in 1942, he joined Claire Chennault's American Volunteer Group, known as the "Flying Tigers." He became Chennault's chief of staff when the A.V.G. was incorporated into the U.S. Air Corps as the China Air Task Force.

Cooper openly criticized what he and Chennault considered General Joseph W. Stilwell's neglect of China's strategic possibilities, so Stilwell ordered Cooper's return to the United States. In 1943 Cooper began serving with General George Kenney's Fifth Air Force in New Guinea, where he planned the attacks on Wewak and Hollandia that helped destroy Japanese air power in the area. In 1945 he was with Kenney and MacArthur on the battleship *Missouri* when Japan surrendered. Kenney recommended Cooper for promotion several times, but at the war's end he was still a colonel. In 1950, however, he became a brigadier general in the Air Force Reserve.

Cooper and Ford revived Argosy Pictures in spring 1946, with Cooper as president and Ford as chairman of the board. Cooper involved himself in every detail of the company, from casting to advertising. Mainly, though, he handled the finances and organization. *The Fugitive* (1947), Argosy's first film, was shot in Mexico, for RKO release. Argosy then made several westerns, which established the company's financial stability. *Fort Apache* (1948), *She Wore a Yellow Ribbon* (1949), and *Wagon Master* (1950) were released by RKO, and *Three Godfathers* (1948) by MGM. For Republic, Argosy made *Rio Grande* (1950) and *The Quiet Man* (1952); the latter won Academy Awards for direction and color photography. In the same year, Cooper received a special Oscar "for his many innovations and contributions to the art of motion pictures." *The Sun Shines Bright* (1953) was Argosy's last film.

In 1947, Cooper began his own project, *Mighty Joe Young* (1949). Like *Kong*, it featured a giant gorilla, but this one, Cooper said in 1949, "is not out to frighten audiences but to amuse them and to win sympathy and affection." The plot involved "the effects of civilization on animals transported from native habitats to such an incongruous jungle as a Hollywood night club." *Joe* reunited Cooper with several friends and veterans of *Kong*, including director Schoedsack. *Joe* contained impressive scenes, but it lacked the power of *Kong*. Based on Cooper's original story, it included some broad satire of the entertainment business and was his final personal film.

Fellow explorer and showman Lowell Thomas got Cooper involved with the first feature made in Cinerama, a process that used three cameras filming simultaneously; projected on three adjacent, angled screens, the images created a three-dimensional effect. Cooper and Robert Bendick edited and organized documentary footage already shot. Cooper also devised new sequences, including a tour across America filmed from the air. *This Is Cinerama* premiered in 1952. The Cinerama Corporation signed Cooper to a five-year contract as general manager in charge of production, and he announced plans to make four dramatic films. Louis B. Mayer replaced Lowell Thomas as chairman of the board, however, and declared that he had no commitments for productions. The resultant struggle between Mayer and Cooper, along with the company's financial problems, led to the departure of both men in 1954.

Cooper soon joined Cornelius Vanderbilt Whitney in the short-lived C. V. Whitney Productions, for which he produced John Ford's *The Searchers* (1956). In 1958, he formed Merian C. Cooper Enterprises and announced several projects, including a film about Chennault; however, his last film, produced with Thomas Conroy, was *The Best of Cinerama* (1963), an anthology of excerpts from the six previous travelogues.

Around 1968, under treatment for cancer, Cooper spent a year revisiting sites in Europe and elsewhere, then returned to California. His last public appearance was on 30 December 1971, to deliver a eulogy at the funeral of Max Steiner, who had composed the music for *King Kong*. Cooper died in San Diego, California.

P.M.J.

Recruited to train the Ethiopian air force (with their impressive fleet of three planes) three years before this photograph was taken, the "Black Eagle," as a New York journalist dubbed him, poses with his aircraft in 1933.

HUBERT F. JULIAN

[20 SEPTEMBER 1897–19 FEBRUARY 1983]

The decades between the World Wars were the heyday of racial segregation and the Ku Klux Klan in America—yet also a period during which black aviators barnstormed across the country. Julian, a flamboyant Trinidadian, patented a device for airplane safety, performed parachute jumps and other stunts, and attempted a solo flight across the Atlantic in a hydroplane that lifted off from the Harlem River. Julian was also an ardent black nationalist who joined the Ethiopian air force, and tried to confront Nazi racism by challenging Hermann Goering to an air duel over the English Channel.

Hubert F. Julian, aviator, was born Hubert Fauntleroy Julian in Port of Spain, Trinidad, the son of Henry Julian, a cocoa plantation manager, and Silvina "Lily" Hilaire Julian. He was educated at the Eastern Boys' School, an excellent private school in Port of Spain. In 1909 he saw his first airplane; minutes later, he witnessed its pilot's fatal crash. Nevertheless, Julian was instilled with a passion for both the exotic and the mechanical aspects of aviation. In 1912 his parents, who wanted their only child to be a doctor, sent him to England for further education. When World War I broke out, Julian went to Canada and attended high school in Montreal. Late in the war he took flying lessons with Canadian ace Billy Bishop. One of the earliest black aviators, he earned his Canadian pilot's license at the age of nineteen. In 1921, he was awarded Canadian and American patents for an airplane safety device he called a *parachuttagravepreresistra*. Although it was never produced commercially, the invention operated on principles that later propelled helicopters and deployed the parachute system that returned space capsules to earth. When activated by the pilot of a plane in distress, a parachutelike umbrella would blow open and lower the disabled plane to the ground by a system of rotating blades.

In July 1921, Julian settled in jazz-age Harlem, already cultivating the flamboyant elegance that would be his lifelong hallmark. He became active in Marcus Garvey's Universal Negro Improvement Association and an officer in its paramilitary unit. Under Garvey's influence, Julian became absorbed in African history, an interest that later led to an active role in the history of Ethiopia. He broke into the African-American aviation scene as a parachutist, appearing at an August 1922 air show on Long Island headlined by African-American aviator Bessie Coleman. Two highly publicized parachute jumps over Manhattan in 1923 inspired a New York journalist to dub him "the Black Eagle," a sobriquet which delighted Julian and which he retained for life.

Invitations to lecture and perform air stunts poured in. Although many of Julian's exploits were greeted with skepticism and charges of self-promotion, he maintained that his activities were all intended to demonstrate that African Americans were as capable of extraordinary achievement as anyone else. Early in 1924, he announced plans for a solo flight from New York to Liberia and Ethiopia. On 4 July 1924 his overhauled World War I–era hydroplane the *Ethiopia I* lifted off from the Harlem River. Within minutes a pontoon broke off. The plane plummeted 2,000 feet into Flushing Bay. A solo transatlantic crossing would not be achieved until Charles Lindbergh's successful flight in 1927.

Over the next five years, Julian barnstormed all over the United States. In 1927, he married Essie Marie Gittens, a childhood friend from Port of Spain. She remained Julian's "constant advisor and companion" until her death in 1975; one daughter survived her (*New York Amsterdam News*, 11 Jan. 1975, p. A3). Julian subsequently married Doreen Thompson, with whom he had a son.

In 1930, Julian was recruited by the prince regent of Ethiopia, Ras Tafari Makonnen, to train the nascent Ethiopian air force. Soon after his arrival in Ethiopia, Julian's aerobatic prowess so impressed the prince regent that he awarded him Ethiopian citizenship and an air force colonelcy. The Ethiopian cadets and their entire air power—two German-made monoplanes and a British Gypsy Moth recently given to the future emperor—were to perform at the prince regent's November 1930 coronation as Emperor Haile Selassie I. During an air show rehearsal, Julian took up the untried Gypsy Moth. The engine failed and the prized plane crashed. Whether or not the plane had been sabotaged, the Imperial Air Force had only two planes remaining; Julian was asked to leave the country.

On 30 July 1931 Julian received a U. S. Department of Commerce private pilot's license. On 6 December 1931 he took part in the Los Angeles air show, organized by African-American aviator William Powell, headlined "the Black Eagle and the Five Blackbirds." For the first time, six African-American pilots appeared together. Throughout the early 1930s, Julian flew in capacities as varied as barnstormer, rum runner, and private pilot for evangelist Father Divine. When the Italo-Ethiopian war became imminent in 1935, Julian returned to Ethiopia as a volunteer. He briefly commanded the air force, but a violent dispute with Chicago aviator John C. Robinson led to Robinson's appointment as air force commander in Julian's stead.

After the Italians overran Ethiopia in 1936, Julian publicly disavowed the Ethiopian cause—for which he was reviled in America. He traveled to Italy, ostensibly to offer his services to Benito Mussolini. He later wrote that his intent in fact was to assassinate Il Duce, but that his loyalties became known and their meeting never took place. During the summer of 1939, he was the war correspondent of the *New York Amsterdam News* in France. Back in New York, Julian announced that he would prove African Americans were as capable in the film industry as, he claimed, he had proved them in aviation. He assisted in producing two Oscar Micheaux films, *Lying Lips* (1939) and *The Notorious Elinor Lee* (1940).

In Europe the war was escalating. In 1940 Julian served briefly with a Finnish air regiment, then publicly challenged Reichsmarschall Hermann Goering to an air duel over the English Channel to defend the honor of the black race, which Adolf Hitler and Goering had defamed. The challenge was not accepted. Volunteering to join the Royal Canadian Air Force, Julian found he could no longer pass the flying test. In July 1942 he enlisted in the U.S. Army as an alien infantryman and became an American citizen on 28 September 1942. In May 1943 he was honorably discharged at the age of forty-five. After the war he parlayed his international contacts into global businesses, founding first a short-lived air freight charter, Black Eagle Airlines. In 1949 Black Eagle Enterprises, Ltd., was registered as a munitions dealer with the U.S. Department of State. Over the next two decades, Julian supplied arms and materiel to clients in developing nations and diplomatic crisis spots around the globe.

A resident of the Bronx, New York, since the 1950s, Julian died there in the Veterans Administration Hospital. Although for fifty years he carried the honorific "Colonel" from his Ethiopian days, he was buried in Calverton National Cemetery, Long Island, courtesy of his service as a private in the U.S. infantry.

C.M.F.

RICHARD
HALLIBURTON
[9 JANUARY 1900–?24 MARCH 1939]

Born nine days into the twentieth century, Halliburton personified a very modern breed of adventurer: nostalgic for bygone heroics, and determined to make his name with a self-conscious quest for extremes. Like his hero, Lord Byron, he swam the Hellespont; he climbed the Matterhorn and flew an open biplane to Timbuktu; he clutched cables to span the half-built Golden Gate Bridge. Halliburton also promoted his feats in schlocky travelogues and derby-clad stage shows, as well as gaining decadent renown for his Southern California mansion, "Hangover House." But Halliburton's self-destructive streak, and hunger for celebrity, forced him to keep upping the stakes, culminating in a theatrical finale he might have written himself.

Richard Halliburton, travel writer and adventurer, was born in Brownsville, Tennessee, the son of Nelle Nance, a music teacher, and Wesley Halliburton, a civil engineer and land developer. He was brought up in an affluent household in Memphis, Tennessee. Although his father wanted him to stay in Memphis, his mother wanted him to go away to school. Halliburton attended the Lawrenceville prep school, a stepping stone to nearby Princeton, which he entered in 1917. Novelist F. Scott Fitzgerald described the period at Princeton in *This Side of Paradise* as "lazy and good-looking and aristocratic." Halliburton, who had been an introspective boy, relished the camaraderie and festivities. He flouted university rules even as a freshman, refusing to don the beanie cap traditionally worn by first-year students. When he completed his schooling he was voted "Most Original Member of the Class."

In addition to his propensity for writing (he was editor of the Princeton *Pictorial*), Halliburton also showed enthusiasm for travel. Without informing his parents, he took a train to New Orleans during a summer break

In 1926, a year after he wrote "the pleasure of travel increases in direct proportion to the decrease of baggage" in The Royal Road to Romance, Halliburton *(right) paused in Chicago for a picture with weather forecaster Henry J. Cox.*

and became a seaman on a freighter bound for Europe. The next summer, he and three classmates took a pack trip in the Rocky Mountains. He sold his first travel article about this trip to *Field & Stream* (May 1921, pp. 18–20).

Immediately on graduating in 1921 Halliburton set off with a classmate for Europe. They established a pattern of feats and pranks he attempted to top throughout his career: he climbed the Matterhorn, was arrested for taking pictures of a militarily secure area of Gibraltar, and went bust at Monte Carlo gaming tables. Halliburton and his friend separated while they were still in Europe, and Halliburton subsequently traveled through India, China, and Japan, before returning home in the spring of 1923. The trip was the subject of his first book, *The Royal Road to Romance* (1925), which became a best-seller.

Halliburton's next book was *The Glorious Adventure* (1927), in which he tried to re-create (with various side trips) the path of Ulysses in the *Odyssey*. Lord Byron was one of Halliburton's heroes, and, like Byron, Halliburton swam the Hellespont (the Dardanelles). For *New Worlds to Conquer* (1929), he traveled throughout Latin America and became the only person ever to swim the full distance of the Panama Canal, including the locks. Both *The Glorious Adventure* and *New Worlds to Conquer* were best-sellers.

During the 1920s Americans were politically isolationist but fascinated by Halliburton's carefree style travels, even if they only enjoyed it second-hand in the *Ladies' Home Journal*. In addition to communicating through his writings, Halliburton commanded large audiences on speaking tours. With a bent for the theatrical, he appeared on stage carrying a derby hat and black silver-tipped cane and wearing spats, a double-breasted Chesterfield overcoat, pearl-grey suede gloves, and a flamboyant necktie. Despite his showmanship and popularity, he failed to interest Hollywood in making movies of his books but did appear in *India Speaks* (1933), a feature film that flopped.

By age twenty-six Halliburton was making $70,000 a year. As fast as he made money, however, he spent it, enjoying fine clothes and good living. During the depression he bought a Packard touring sedan and built Hangover House overlooking Laguna Beach, California. The house cost three times more than projected. Halliburton could be flamboyant and generous but also temperamental and self-centered. He wrote sentimentally about the women he met on his travels, but his longest relationship apparently was with Paul Mooney, who helped him write and lived with him at Hangover House.

Halliburton avoided writing about the unpleasantness of poverty, illness, deprivation, and strife. Reviewers described his books as sentimental and juvenile, but he responded in a Chicago news conference that "the American public is starved for romance." He wove his travel books into two volumes intended for a juvenile audience, *Richard Halliburton's Book of Marvels: The Occident* (1937) and *Richard Halliburton's Second Book of Marvels: The Orient* (1938).

In spite of his success, Halliburton was always concerned that he had not done more serious work. He was particularly interested in writing a biography of the British poet Rupert Brooke, who had died during World War I. He tried to get Brooke's mother to assist him, but she did not take Halliburton's work seriously and refused. His notes and research on Brooke later were used by Arthur Springer, who wrote a comprehensive Brooke biography.

In every adventure Halliburton felt pressured to outdo previous stunts. With pilot Moye W. Stephens, he flew a Stearman two-place open cockpit biplane around the world, landing in Timbuktu and other remote places where planes had not been seen before. The resulting book was called *The Flying Carpet* (1932). A public relations man convinced him to be the first person to walk across the Golden Gate Bridge, which Halliburton did, holding on to cables and girders, while the bridge was still under construction.

Halliburton's final adventure came in 1939. He left Hong Kong in a junk he planned to sail to the Golden Gate International Exposition in San Francisco. The vessel was unseaworthy and manned by a ragtag crew. Halliburton was plagued with money worries, but he set sail anyway. A little more than two weeks after leaving Hong Kong, the junk was caught in a typhoon, and radio contact was lost. Neither Halliburton nor his crew was seen again.

J.M.H./C.P.

A NOTE ON THE
AMERICAN NATIONAL
BIOGRAPHY

Tony Horwitz has served as a scout before, taking us hitchhiking through the Australian outback (1988), guiding us through Baghdad without a map (1991), introducing us to Confederates in the attic at various Civil War battle sites (1998), and piloting us through the blue latitudes sailed by Captain Cook (2002). As a writer for the *Wall Street Journal,* too, he has led us to Bosnia, the Middle East, Africa, and Northern Ireland. Readers have learned to respect his navigational skills and admire his keen eyesight.

In this book he plots a course through the vast, trackless reaches of the *American National Biography,* a 25-million-word collection of biographical essays on over 18,000 Americans, all of them dead. (An American is loosely defined as someone whose significant actions occurred during his or her residence in what is now the United States or whose life or career directly influenced the course of American history.) Published in 1999 and continuously updated by the American Council of Learned Societies and Oxford University Press, the *ANB* is the work of over 7,000 authors, hundreds of scholars who served as associate editors, and a veritable army of copyeditors.

Horwitz has undertaken an expedition into a small but fascinating patch of the *ANB,* a sorting of essays on the lives of fifty adventurers, travelers, and explorers. His expedition has produced many wondrous "discoveries," and we are grateful to him for sharing them with us. But I encourage readers to map their own trek through the *ANB.* Its twenty-five thick volumes dominate the shelves of most libraries, a towering Everest of the reference section.

Pundits proclaim ours as the "information age," and the *ANB,* consisting of hundreds of millions of bytes of data, is readily susceptible to virtual exploration. Readers who do not wish to contend with heavy books can sample the contents of the *ANB* online, available via subscription from Oxford University Press and also at most libraries. This allows new types of "key word" explorations. A full-text search of the word "Horwitz," for example, reveals that although the Three Stooges—Shemp, Moe, and Curly—used the stage name of "Howard," they were born, respectively, Samuel, Moses, and Jerome Horwitz. (We learn, too, that Larry Fine, the other "stooge," was born Louis Feinberg.)

Any foray into the *ANB* will yield some surprises and a few revelations. "All good adventures" lead down such "unforeseen byways," writes Horwitz (the scout, not the Stooge) in the introduction to this volume. The same holds for any exploration of the past. Even professional historians who plow the same fields year after year discover that the terrain never remains the same. They continuously spot something new or learn to view familiar sights from a different perspective.

The essays in this volume contain plenty of facts, but the *ANB* ultimately is not about bytes of data or factoids. Rather, these details are the informational skeletons of 18,000 people who constitute our nation's past. In looking for them, we discover more about ourselves.

Mark C. Carnes
General Editor, *ANB*
Ann Whitney Olin Professor of History
Barnard College, Columbia University

AUTHORS OF ARTICLES
from the *American National Biography*

E.T.S.   E. Thomson Shields *(Alvar Núñez Cabeza de Vaca)*

K.O.K.   Karen Ordahl Kupperman *(John Smith)*

J.H.W.   James Homer Williams *(David Pietersen de Vries)*

C.H.   Conrad Heidenreich *(Francesco Giuseppe Bressani)*

A.S.M.   Allida Shuman McKinley *(Hannah Duston)*

D.D.M.   Douglas D. Martin *(Sir Alexander Cuming)*

H.L.   Hedda Lautenschlager *(Ann Hennis Trotter Bailey)*

R.C.L.   Richard C. Lindberg *(Jean Baptiste Point du Sable)*

E.L.L.   Edward L. Lach, Jr. *(Samuel Mason)*

S.W.C.   Samuel Willard Crompton *(John Ledyard* and *Giacomo Constantino Beltrami)*

H.M.W.   Harry M. Ward *(Simon Kenton)*

H.S.   Haskell Springer *(George Crowninshield, Jr.* and *Joshua Slocum)*

J.M.M.   Jeanne M. Malloy *(Anne Newport Royall)*

J.L.   Jeff LaLande *(John Colter)*

A.T.K.   Ann T. Keene *(Marie Dorion)*

D.G.P.   Donna Grear Parker *(Frances Wright)*

B.W.D.   Brian W. Dippie *(George Catlin)*

L.R.G.   Larry R. Gerlach *(Samuel Patch)*

R.F.E.   Robert F. Erickson *(David Douglas)*

R.H.D.   Richard H. Dillon *(John August Sutter, Grizzly Adams, Agoston Haraszthy de Mokcsa,* and *Ishi)*

R.L.G.   Robert L. Gale *(James Bridger)*

D.C.F.   David C. Ford *(Jacob Netsvetov)*

G.G.   Geoffrey Gneuhs *(Eliza Hart Spalding)*

J.D.H.   J. D. Hunley *(John Wise)*

M.C.C.   Mark C. Carnes *(Albert Pike)*

P.H.   Pamela Herr *(John Charles Frémont)*
T.H.   Ted Heckathorn *(Elisha Kent Kane)*
J.D.C.   J. Donald Crowley *(Edward Zane Carroll Judson)*
J.A.S.   Joseph A. Stout, Jr. *(William Walker)*
E.D.L.   E. D. Lloyd-Kimbrel *(California Joe)*
R.P.C.   Rodney P. Carlisle *(John Morrissey)*
A.W.M.   Ann Whipple Marr *(Mary Ann Brown Patten)*
H.A.A.   H. Allen Anderson *(Buffalo Jones)*
M.L.F.   Marie-Luise Frings *(Agnes Elisabeth
              Winona Leclercq Joy Salm-Salm)*
J.L.P.   James L. Penick *(Railroad Bill)*
S.N.   Scot Ngozi-Brown *(David Fagen)*
L.H.   Lynn Hoogenboom *(Belle Livingstone)*
T.L.K.   Thomas L. Karnes *(Hiram Bingham)*
D.M.S.   David M. Schwartz *(Duncan Hines)*
G.S.F.   Greg S. Faller *(Annette Kellerman)*
C.F.J.   Cheryl Fradette Junk *(Louise Arner Boyd)*
A.M.Y.   Alan M. Yonan *(Duke Paoa Kahanamoku)*
P.M.J.   Paul M. Jensen *(Merian Coldwell Cooper)*
C.M.F.   Caroline M. Fannin *(Hubert F. Julian)*
J.M.H./C.P.   John Maxwell Hamilton/Carolyn Pione *(Richard
              Halliburton)*

SOURCES AND READINGS

FURTHER

Alvar Núñez Cabeza de Vaca
[c.1490–c.1559]
English translations of Núñez's *Naufragios* vary in quality, but the extensive notes in the version by Cyclone Covey, *Cabeza de Vaca's Adventures in the Unknown Interior of America* (1961), make it quite useful to historians and anthropologists, though the placement of notes within the text interferes with the work's literary quality. The standard English-language biography is still Morris Bishop, *The Odyssey of Cabeza de Vaca* (1933), while the most recent Spanish-language biography is Bibiano Torres Ramirez, *Alvar Núñez Cabeza de Vaca* (1990).

John Smith
[1580–1631]
John Smith's writings are collected in *The Complete Works of Captain John Smith*, ed. Philip L. Barbour (3 vols., 1986), which includes an extensive bibliography. *Captain John Smith: A Select Edition of His Writings*, ed. Karen Ordahl Kupperman (1988), is selected from the texts prepared by Barbour. The best modern biography is Philip L. Barbour, *The Three Worlds of Captain John Smith* (1964); the introduction to Barbour's edition of Smith's works presents information discovered since 1964. See also Alden Vaughan, *American Genesis: Captain John Smith and the Founding of Virginia* (1975). The literary aspects of Smith's work are the subject of Everett Emerson, *Captain John Smith* (1971). On Smith's reputation for truthfulness see Laura Polanyi Striker and Bradford Smith, "The Rehabilitation of Captain John Smith," *Journal of Southern History* 28 (1962): 474–481, and Bradford Smith, *Captain John Smith: His Life and Legend* (1953), with an appendix by Laura Polanyi Striker.

David Pietersen de Vries

[1593–1655?]

The principal source of information about de Vries is his memoir, *Korte Historiael, ende Journaels aenteyckeninge Van verscheyden Voyagiens in de vier deelen des Wereldts-Ronde, als Europa, Africa, Asia, ende Amerika gedaen* (1655), published in Alckmaer. The only reprint in Dutch, edited by H. T. Colenbrander (1911), includes the portrait of de Vries, two maps, and eighteen plates from the original. An English translation of the sections dealing with America was published as Henry C. Murphy, trans., *Voyages from Holland to America, A.D. 1632 to 1644* (1853), and then under the same title in the New-York Historical Society, *Collections*, 2d ser., 3, pt. 1 (1857): 3–136. A. J. F. van Laer revised parts of Murphy's translation in *Narratives of New Netherland, 1609–1664*, ed. J. Franklin Jameson (1909), and in *Narratives of Early Pennsylvania, West New Jersey, and Delaware, 1630–1707*, ed. Albert Cook Myers (1912). Charles McKew Parr, *The Voyages of David de Vries, Navigator and Adventurer* (1969), puts his life in context but reveals little new information outside of de Vries's own account. The location of Vriessendael is placed at Edgewater, rather than Tappan, New Jersey, in Reginald McMahon, "Vriessendael: A Note," *New Jersey History* 87 (1969): 173–180.

Francesco Giuseppe Bressani

[1612–1672]

Most of what is known about Bressani has to be deduced from his letters that he reprinted in his history of the Jesuit missions to New France, *Breve Relatione*. This book was republished by Reuben Gold Thwaites (ed.) as *The Jesuit Relations and Allied Documents* (1896–1901), a work that contains other references to Bressani. An original letter written by Bressani from Iroquois captivity in July 1644, containing a sketch of his mutilated hands, has been published in facsimile by Stelio Cro, "The Original Letter of Father Bressani Written from Fort Orange in 1644," *Canadian Journal of Italian Studies* 4, no. 1–2 (1980–1981): 26–67. Bressani's audience with the pope is related in Jeanne-Françoise Juchereau and Marie-Andrée

Duplessis, *Les Annales de l'Hôtel-Dieu de Québec, 1636–1716* (1939). References to Bressani's skills as an astronomer are in Peter Broughton, "Astronomy in Seventeenth-Century Canada," *Journal of the Royal Astronomical Society* 75, no. 4 (1981): 175–208.

Hannah Duston
[1657–1736]
Original accounts of Hannah Duston's Indian capture are in Cotton Mather, *Magnalia Christi Americana*, ed. Kenneth B. Murdock (1977), and Samuel Sewall, "Diary of Samuel Sewall," Massachusetts Historical Society, *Collections*, 5th ser., vol. 5 (1878). Additional information is in Robert B. Caverly, *Heroism of Hannah Duston* (1874), based on Caverly's research in the records of Boston and Haverhill, and Laurel Thatcher Ulrich, *Good Wives: Image and Reality in the Lives of Women in Northern New England* (1980). Another interpretation of Duston's place in American history is found in a book of woodcuts by Richard Bosman, *Captivity Narrative of Hannah Duston, Related by Cotton Mather, John Greenleaf Whittier, Nathaniel Hawthorne and Henry David Thoreau* (1987), with an introduction by Glenn Todd.

Sir Alexander Cuming
[c.1690/1692–1775]
Reports on the Cherokee delegation appeared in the London *Daily Courant, Daily Post*, and *Daily Journal*, June–Oct. 1730; see also Carolyn Foreman, *Indians Abroad* (1943). Robert L. Meriwether, *The Expansion of South Carolina, 1729–1765* (1940; repr. 1974), is helpful on South Carolina in 1729–1730. Cuming's journal appears in Samuel Cole Williams, ed., *Early Travels in the Tennessee Country, 1540–1800* (1928), pp. 112–143. For a twentieth-century discussion, see Verner Crane, *The Southern Frontier, 1670–1732* (1928; repr. 1956), pp. 276–280 and 294–302. Critical to understanding Cuming's efforts among the Cherokees are James Mooney, *Historical Sketch of the Cherokee* (repr. 1975) and *Myths of the Cherokee* (1900; repr. 1972); Henry T. Malone, *Cherokees of the Old South: A People*

in Transition (1956); David H. Corkran, *The Cherokee Frontier Conflict and Survival, 1740–62* (1962); and Theda Perdue, *Slavery and the Evolution of Cherokee Society, 1540–1866* (1979). For Cuming's reemergence in 1762, see Samuel Cole Williams, ed., *Lieut. Henry Timberlake's Memoirs, 1756–1765* (1927; repr. 1971).

Ann Hennis Trotter Bailey

[1742–1825]

No collection of Bailey papers exists, and little information is available about Bailey's life. A monologue by Frank Hill, "The True Life of Anne [*sic*] Bailey," was donated to the Gallia County Historical Society in 1979. Other works to consult are Elizabeth Ellet, *The Pioneer Women of the West* (1852; repr. 1973); William Oliver Stevens, *Famous Women of America* (1956); and Arnold Dolin, *Great American Heroines* (1960). In addition, Livia Nye Simpson-Poffenbarger edited and published a monograph entitled *Ann Bailey: Thrilling Adventures of the Heroine of the Kanawha Valley, Truth Stranger Than Fiction as Related by Writers Who Knew the Story* (1907). General histories of the battle of Point Pleasant include Lisa Wilson, *Life after Death: Widows in Pennsylvania, 1750–1850* (1992); Simpson-Poffenbarger, *The Battle of Point Pleasant: A Battle of the Revolution* (1909); and Reuben Gold Thwaites and Louise Phelps Kellogg, eds., *Documentary History of Dunsmore's War, 1774* (1989).

Jean Baptiste Point du Sable

[1745?–1818]

What little we know of Jean Baptiste Point du Sable is gleaned from surviving journal accounts, most notably the *Journal of a Voyage Made by Mr. Hugh Heward to the Illinois Country*. A copy of the original manuscript is in the reference library of the Chicago Historical Society. See also the manuscript collection of the Wisconsin State Historical Society for ledger records, diaries, and an extensive collection of data covering the early settlement of Illinois Territory. The earliest published account of du Sable's life is included in Juliette Kinzie's 1856 recollections of Chicago frontier life, *Wau Bun: The Early Days in the Northwest,* reissued by the Caxton Club in 1901.

Later volumes of history draw heavily from these incomplete papers and diaries. The most comprehensive research into du Sable's career and Chicago's "prehistory" was conducted by Dr. Milo M. Quaife. See his *Chicago and the Old Northwest, 1673–1835* (1913), *Checagou: From Indian Wigwam to Modern City* (1933), and "Property of Jean Baptiste Point Sable," *Mississippi Valley Historical Review* 15 (June 1928): 89–92.

Interesting bits of information that build on Quaife's research can be found in A. T. Andreas, *History of Chicago from the Earliest Period to the Present Time* (1884). See also J. Seymour Currey, *Chicago: Its History and Its Builders,* vol. 1 (1912); Bessie Louise Pierce, *A History of Chicago, 1673–1848,* vol. 1 (1937); and Charles B. Johnson, *Growth of Cook County,* vol. 1 (1961). These volumes have been out of print for a considerable time, but closed stack reference copies are available to researchers at the Chicago Public Library's Chicago collection and the Chicago Historical Society.

Of more contemporary vintage is Lawrence Cortesi, *Jean du Sable: Father of Chicago* (1972). A thumbnail sketch of du Sable can be found in June Skinner Sawyers, *Chicago Portraits: Biographies of 250 Famous Chicagoans* (1991).

Samuel Mason

[c.1750–1803]

Some of Samuel Mason's correspondence has survived and is held with the papers of Samuel Draper at the Wisconsin State Historical Society, Madison, and a manuscript in French of his trial at New Madrid is held by the Mississippi Department of Archives and History, Jackson. The best secondary source of the life and career of Samuel Mason remains Otto A. Rothert, *The Outlaws of Cave-in-Rock* (1924).

John Ledyard

[1751–1789]

Ledyard's papers are in the possession of the Ledyard family; the Baker Library at Dartmouth College; and the New-York Historical Society. The modern version of his book on the Pacific is *John Ledyard's Journal of Captain Cook's Last Voyage*, ed. James Kenneth Munford (1963), and his Russian adventure is chronicled in Stephen D. Watrous, ed., *John Ledyard's Journey through Russia and Siberia 1787–1788* (1966). See also Helen Augur, *Passage to Glory: John Ledyard's America* (1946); Henry Beston, *The Book of Gallant Vagabonds* (1925); and Jared Sparks, *The Life of John Ledyard* (1828). Journal articles include Donald Jackson, "Ledyard and Laperouse: A Contrast in Northwestern Exploration," *Western Historical Quarterly* 9, no. 4 (1978): 495–508, and Bertha S. Dodge, "John Ledyard: Controversial Corporal," *History Today* 23, no. 9 (1973): 648–655. Ledyard is mentioned briefly in Richard Hough, *Captain James Cook* (1994).

Simon Kenton

[1755–1836]

The Kenton papers, in the Lyman C. Draper Collections at the State Historical Society of Wisconsin, contain materials that Draper gathered for a biography of Kenton, including biographical sketches, depositions, notes by Kenton's comrades, and a few original documents, such as those relating to land surveys. Allan W. Eckert, *The Frontiersmen* (1967), is a thoroughly researched, lively narrative of Kenton's life, if at times with some poetic license; it interweaves Kenton's activities with those of his associates. Also a sound, dramatic narrative of lesser scale is Patricia Jahns, *The Violent Years: Simon Kenton and the Ohio-Kentucky Frontier* (1962). An older straightforward biography is Edna Kenton, *Simon Kenton: His Life and Period, 1755–1836* (1930). For Kenton's relationship with Daniel Boone, see John M. Faragher, *Daniel Boone: The Life and Legend of an American Pioneer* (1992). Sketches of Kenton include Lewis Collins, revised by Richard H. Collins, *Collins' Historical Sketches of Kentucky: History of Kentucky*, vol. 2 (1966), pp. 442–454; R. W. McFarland, "Simon Kenton,"

Ohio Archaeological and Historical Publications 13 (1904): 1–39; and John McDonald, *Biographical Sketches* (1838), pp. 197–267. A brief tribute to Kenton is in the *Western Christian Advocate*, 24 June 1836.

George Crowninshield, Jr.

[1766–1817]

Most of the Crowninshield family papers are in the Essex Institute and the Peabody Museum, both in Salem. A reconstruction of the interior of *Cleopatra's Barge* is also at the Peabody Museum. A rich source of information is Peter Smith, ed., *The Diary of William Bentley* (4 vols., 1962). James Duncan Phillips, *Salem and the Indies: The Story of the Great Commercial Era of the City* (1947), mentions Crowninshield a number of times. David L. Ferguson, *Cleopatra's Barge: The Crowninshield Story* (1976), is both deeply researched and entertaining to read.

Anne Newport Royall

[1769–1854]

The largest collection of Royall's papers, including the files of *Paul Pry* and the *Huntress*, is in the Library of Congress. The official records of her 1829 trial are in the National Archives, *U.S. v. Royall*, Records of the Circuit Court, District of Columbia. The best and most complete biography of Anne Royall is Bessie Rowland James, *Anne Royall's U.S.A.* (1972), but Alice S. Maxwell and Marion Dunlevy, *Virago!: The Story of Anne Newport Royall* (1985), should be consulted for an account of her trial. Although occasionally inaccurate, Sarah Harvey Porter, *The Life and Times of Anne Royall* (1909), and George S. Jackson, *Uncommon Scold* (1937), are still useful biographies. For an evaluation of Royall's contributions to journalism, see Madelon Golden Schilpp and Sharon M. Murphy, *Great Women of the Press* (1983), pp. 21–36.

John Colter
[c. 1775–1813]
Circumstantial evidence prompts historians to agree that Colter was probably literate; however, other than a December 1813 bill of sale for his estate,
no personal papers exist. For Colter's participation in the 1804–1806 Corps
of Discovery, see vols. 2 and 5 of *The Journals of the Lewis and Clark
Expedition*, ed. Gary Moulton (1986 and 1988). The three primary sources
(based on the authors' personal encounters with Colter) about Colter's
years in the Rockies are Henry M. Brackenridge, *Views of Louisiana* (1814);
John Bradbury, *Travels in the Interior of America* (1817); and Thomas James,
Three Years among the Indians (1846). Aubrey Haines's concise biographical sketch, in LeRoy Hafen, *The Mountain Men and the Fur Trade of the
Far West*, vol. 8 (1971), draws in part on the two classic, if somewhat
hagiographic, book-length works about Colter: Stallo Vinton, *John Colter,
Discoverer of Yellowstone Park* (1926), and Burton Harris, *John Colter: His
Years in the Rockies* (1952; repr. 1993). See also David Lavender's intro-
duction to the 1993 edition of Harris's book.

Giacomo Constantino Beltrami
[1779–1855]
Many of Beltrami's papers are housed at the Biblioteca Civica in Bergamo,
Italy. The primary source for Beltrami's travels in the United States not
already mentioned in the text is his *A Pilgrimage in Europe and America
Leading to the Discovery of the Sources of the Mississippi and Bloody River
. . .* (1828). See also Augusto Miceli, *Man with the Red Umbrella: Giacomo
Constantino Beltrami in America* (1974). Beltrami's story is discussed in
Roger Kennedy, *Rediscovering America* (1990); and Evan Jones, *Citadel in
the Wilderness: The Story of Fort Snelling and the Old Northwest Frontier*
(1966). For additional information, see Timothy Severin, "The Preposterous
Pathfinder," *American Heritage* (Dec. 1967): 57–63; and Michael Martin,
"Improbable Explorer: Giacomo Beltrami's Summer of Discovery," *Timeline*
7, no. 1 (1990): 32-43. The career of the countess of Albany is discussed in
Alex Charles Ewald, *The Life and Times of Prince Charles Stuart* (1883).

For a social study comparable to Beltrami's works about North America, see Theodore Dwight, Jr., *A Journal of a Tour in Italy in the Year 1821* (1824).

Marie Dorion
[c. 1790–1850]
Early accounts of Marie Dorion's life appear in Gabriel Franchère, *Relation d'un Voyage à la Côte du Nord-Ouest de l'Amérique Septentrionale* (1820; English trans., 1854, 1967); Ross Cox, *Adventures on the Columbia River* (1831; repr. 1957); and Alexander Ross, *Adventures of the First Settlers on the Oregon or Columbia River* (1849). Part of Washington Irving's *Astoria* is based on Franchère's and Cox's accounts. Biographical information is also found in J. Neilson Barry, "Madame Dorion of the Astorians," *Oregon Historical Quarterly* 30, no. 3 (Sept. 1929): 272–278, and T. C. Elliott, "The Grave of Mme. Dorion," *Oregon Historical Quarterly* 36, no. 1 (Mar. 1935): 102–104.

Frances Wright
[1795–1852]
Although there is no complete collection of Wright's papers, many of her letters are in the Robert Owen Papers at the University of Illinois; the library of the Working Men's Institute in New Harmony, Ind.; the Percy Bysshe Shelley Papers at Duke University; and the Lafayette papers at the University of Chicago. Rutgers University and Cornell University also house files of the *Free Enquirer*. Additional information on Wright is in the Theresa Wolfson Papers at Cornell's Martin P. Catherwood Library and in the Garnett letters at Harvard University's Houghton Library. For a sample of one of Wright's public lectures see *Address on the State of the Public Mind* (1829). A useful biography is Celia Morris Eckhardt, *Fanny Wright: Rebel in America* (1984). Older, but also useful, is A. J. G. Perkins and Theresa Wolfson, *Frances Wright: Free Enquirer* (1939). For a comparison of Wright with her contemporary Frances Trollope see Susan S. Kissel, *In Common Cause: The "Conservative" Frances Trollope and the "Radical" Frances Wright* (1993). For a feminist perspective of Wright, as well as other early female

reformers, see Elizabeth Ann Bartlett, *Liberty, Equality, Sorority* (1994). An obituary is in the *Cincinnati Daily Gazette*, 15 Dec. 1852.

George Catlin
[1796–1872]

The Catlin papers are scattered. The Smithsonian Institution holds an important collection that is readily accessible in the Archives of American Art microfilm series, rolls 2136–2137. The principal family collection is in the Bancroft Library, University of California, Berkeley, and has been published in Marjorie Catlin Roehm, *The Letters of George Catlin and His Family: A Chronicle of the American West* (1966). Some of his letters are in the Daniel Webster Papers at Morristown National Historical Park, Morristown, N.J. Beside his own books, the most useful works on Catlin are Thomas Donaldson's huge compilation *The George Catlin Indian Gallery in the U.S. National Museum (Smithsonian Institution) with Memoir and Statistics, Annual Report, Smithsonian Institution, 1885*, pt. 2 (1886); John C. Ewers, "George Catlin: Painter of Indians of the West," *Annual Report, Smithsonian Institution, 1955* (1955); Harold McCracken, *George Catlin and the Old Frontier* (1959); and William H. Truettner's masterly *The Natural Man Observed: A Study of Catlin's Indian Gallery* (1979). Brian W. Dippie, *Catlin and His Contemporaries: The Politics of Patronage* (1990), examines Catlin's unsuccessful quest for patronage and places the artist in a broad historical context. Helpful for understanding Catlin's artistic goals is Joan Carpenter Troccoli, *First Artist of the West: George Catlin Paintings and Watercolors* (1993). For a compilation of Catlin's paintings and writings from the 1850s, see Marvin C. Ross, *George Catlin: Episodes from Life among the Indians and Last Rambles* (1959). For an entire "album unique" in facsimile, see Peter Hassrick's edition of George Catlin, *Drawings of the North American Indian* (1984), and for a case study in Catlin's South American rambles, see Edgardo Carlos Krebs, "George Catlin and South America: A Look at His 'Lost' Years and His Paintings of Northeastern Argentina," *American Art Journal* 22, no. 4 (1990): 4–39.

Samuel Patch

[1799–1829]

The Rochester Public Library has a collection of newspaper and magazine clippings on Patch. For his family background, see Paul E. Johnson, "The Modernization of Mayo Greenleaf Patch: Land, Family, and Marginality in New England, 1766–1818," *New England Quarterly* 55 (Dec. 1982): 488–516, and Richard M. Dorson, "Sam Patch, Jumping Hero," *New York Folklore Quarterly* 1 (Aug. 1945): 133–151. For details on the Rochester jump, see Jenny M. Parker, *Rochester: A Story Historical* (1884), and contemporary reports in the *Rochester Daily Advertiser and Telegraph*. A brilliant analysis of the leap at Passaic and the phenomenon of falls-jumping is Johnson, "'Art' and the Language of Progress in Early-Industrial Paterson: Sam Patch at Clinton Bridge," *American Quarterly* 40 (Dec. 1988): 433–449. For the Patch plays, see Jonathan F. Kelly, *Dan Marble: A Biographical Sketch* (1851). William Getz, *Sam Patch: Ballad of a Jumping Man* (1986), is an utterly fanciful novel.

David Douglas

[1799–1834]

The letters and journals of Douglas are at the Royal Horticultural Society, London, and other materials are in the letters and manuscripts of W. J. Hooker at the Royal Botanic Gardens, Kew. There are two important sources for the story of the life of David Douglas. The first is William Jackson Hooker, "Brief Memoir of the Life of Mr. David Douglas, with Extracts from His Letters," in his *Companion to the Botanical Magazine*, vol. 2 (1836) (repr. *Hawaiian Spectator* 2 [1839]; *Oregon Historical Quarterly* 5 and 6 [1904, 1905]). The second is the Royal Horticultural Society's book, *Journal Kept by David Douglas during His Travels in North America 1823–1827* (1914). There is a lengthy critical discussion of both these sources in Susan Delano McKelvey, *Botanical Exploration of the Trans-Mississippi West, 1790–1850* (1955; rev. ed. 1991), chap. 14; chap. 18 is a continuation of the Douglas story.

Of the numerous secondary sources, excellent biographies are A. G. Harvey, *Douglas of the Fir* (1947), and W. Morwood, *Traveler in a Vanished*

Landscape (1974). Harvey's work is notable for its extensive bibliography, including depositories of manuscripts. For another list of books and articles about Douglas and his contemporaries, reference should be made to F. Stafleu, *Taxonomic Literature*, vol. 1 (1976), pp. 674–675.

John August Sutter

[1803–1880]

The best collection of Captain Sutter's papers is in the California State Library, Sacramento, but the University of California's Bancroft Library, in Berkeley, is another excellent source. The best biography of Sutter is Richard H. Dillon, *Fool's Gold* (1967; repr. as *Captain John Sutter: Sacramento Valley's Sainted Sinner*, 1981, 1987, 1991). Also useful are James P. Zollinger, *Sutter* (1939); Erwin Gudde, *Sutter's Own Story* (1936); and Oscar Lewis, *Sutter's Fort* (1966).

James Bridger

[1804–1881]

Biographies of Bridger include Grenville M. Dodge, *Biographical Sketch of Jim Bridger: Mountaineer, Trapper and Guide* (1905); J. Cecil Alter, *James Bridger* (1925; rev. ed., 1962); Stanley Vestal (Walter Stanley Campbell), *Jim Bridger: Mountain Man, a Biography* (1946); and Gene Caesar, *King of the Mountain Men: The Life of Jim Bridger* (1961). The following works place Bridger's actions in their historical context: J. Lee Humfreville, *Twenty Years among Our Savage Indians* (1897; later editions titled *Twenty Years among Our Hostile Indians*); Grace Raymond Hebard and E. A. Brininstool, *The Bozeman Trail* (1922); Bernard DeVoto, *The Year of Decision 1846* (1943); William H. Goetzmann, "The Mountain Man as Jacksonian Man" *American Quarterly* 15 (Fall 1963): 402–415; Dale Van Every, *The Final Challenge: The American Frontier 1804–1845* (1964); Fred R. Gowans and Eugene E. Campbell, *Fort Bridger: Island in the Wilderness* (1975); and Ted Morgan, *A Shovel of Stars: The Making of the American West, 1800 to the Present* (1995). Dee Brown, *Wondrous Times on the Frontier* (1991), repeats some of the whoppers told by Bridger.

Jacob Netsvetov
[1804–1864]
Netsvetov's journals have been published as *The Journals of Iakov Netsvetov*, trans. Lydia T. Black (2 vols., 1980 and 1984). For more on Netsvetov's mission and on Orthodox Christianity in Alaska, see Michael Oleksa, *Alaskan Missionary Spirituality* (1987); Oleksa, *Orthodox Alaska: A Theology of Mission* (1992); and Barbara S. Smith, *Orthodoxy and Native Americans: The Alaskan Mission* (1980).

Eliza Hart Spalding
[1807–1851]
The best sources of information are two works by Clifford M. Drury, *Henry Harmon Spalding* (1936) and *The First White Women over the Rockies* (3 vols., 1963–1966); volume one of the latter has much material on Eliza Spalding. See also Marvin M. Richardson, *The Whitman Mission* (1940), and Alvin M. Josephy, Jr., *The Nez Percé Indians and the Opening of the Northwest* (1965). Bernard DeVoto, *Across the Wide Missouri* (1947), and LeRoy R. Hafen and Anne W. Hafen, eds., *To the Rockies and Oregon* (1955), offer a broader glimpse of the migration west. References to her painting is in Susan Larsen-Martin and Louis Robert Martin, *Pioneers in Paradise: Folk and Outsider Artists of the West Coast* (1984), and in George C. Groce, *The New-York Historical Society's Dictionary of Artists in America, 1564–1860* (1957). See also Deborah Lynn Dawson, "Laboring in My Savior's Vineyard: The Mission of Eliza Hart Spalding" (Ph.D. diss., Bowling Green State Univ., 1988).

John Wise
[1808–1879]
On Wise's life and ballooning feats, see Pearl I. Young, "John Wise and His Balloon Ascensions in the Middle West," *Wingfoot Lighter-Than-Air Society Bulletin* (Oct. 1967): 2–6, and Tom D. Crouch, *The Eagle Aloft: Two Centuries of the Balloon in America* (1983). There is a biographical sketch in *Appleton's Cyclopedia of American Biography* (1900) that concentrates on his bal-

looning more than his life. For details of his longest flight, consult Wise's *Full Particulars of the Greatest Aerial Voyage on Record from St. Louis, Mo., to Adams, New York, in Nineteen Hours* (1859). Further information on Wise appears in two folders of newspaper clippings and biographical sketches at the National Air and Space Museum in Washington, D.C., including information on a flight on which he carried the first stamped letters in a balloon on 17 Aug. 1859.

Albert Pike

[1809–1891]

Pike's most important manuscripts, including his "Autobiography," are in the library of the Supreme Council of Scottish Rite Freemasonry in Washington, D.C. Pike published a volume of poems, *Nugae* (1854), but his more important poems appear in *Hymns to the Gods and Other Poems* (1872), which was privately printed. After his death his daughter also had printed three more poetry collections: *Gen. Albert Pike's Poems* (1900), *Hymns to the Gods and Other Poems* (1916), and *Lyrics and Love Songs* (1916). The only modern biography is Robert Lipscomb Duncan, *Reluctant General: The Life and Times of Albert Pike* (1961); an earlier biography by Fred W. Allsopp, *Albert Pike: A Biography* (1928), is uncritical. The most detailed information can be found in Walter Lee Brown, "Albert Pike, 1809–1891" (Ph.D. diss., Univ. of Texas, 1955). For Pike's life in Arkansas, see also John Hallum, *Biographical and Pictorial History of Arkansas* (1887). On the charges of devil worship, see Montague Summers, *The History of Witchcraft and Demonology* (1926).

Grizzly Adams

[1812–1860]

The only biography of Adams since T. H. Hittell's early and incomplete work, *The Adventures of James Capen Adams, Mountaineer and Grizzly Bear Hunter of California* (1860), is Richard H. Dillon's *The Legend of Grizzly Adams* (1966; repr. 1993).

Agoston Haraszthy de Mokcsa

[1812–1869]

Most of Haraszthy's papers are in the State Historical Society of Wisconsin. Others are in the Bancroft Library at the University of California, Berkeley, including the manuscript "The Haraszthy Family." Haraszthy is also mentioned in Wisconsin and California local histories and in most accounts of the California wine industry. Details of his life are in Brian McGinty, *Haraszthy at the Mint* (1975), and Theodore Schoenman, *Father of California Wine* (1979). The latter volume is especially important because it contains a reprint of Haraszthy's seminal document *Grape Culture, Wines and Wine-Making*. An obituary is in the *San Francisco Daily Alta California*, 27 Aug. 1869.

John Charles Frémont

[1813–1890]

Major collections of Frémont's papers are at the Bancroft Library, University of California, Berkeley; at the Huntington Library, San Marino, Calif.; at the James S. Copley Library, La Jolla, Calif.; in the Allan Nevins Papers at Columbia University; in the Jeremiah S. Black, Nathaniel Banks, and Francis Preston Blair Family Papers at the Library of Congress; and in the Billings Mansion Archives, Woodstock, Vt. The essential source for Frémont's career as a western explorer is Donald Jackson and Mary Lee Spence, eds., *The Expeditions of John Charles Frémont* (1970–1984), a multivolume compendium of documents, including the expedition reports. For Frémont's later career, particularly his 1856 presidential campaign, Civil War activities, and business ventures, Allan Nevins's classic biography, *Frémont: Pathmarker of the West* (1955), while too uncritical, remains the most comprehensive.

Elisha Kent Kane

[1820–1857]

Kane's original expedition journal is at the Stanford University Library, and part of the ship's log is at the Pennsylvania Historical Society. His account of his first polar trip was *The U.S. Grinnell Expedition in Search of Sir John Franklin* (1853). His book about his second expedition was *Arctic Explorations: The Second Grinnell Expedition in Search of Sir John Franklin, 1853, '54, '55* (1856). He also published articles in journals of the American Geographical Society, American Philosophical Society, and other institutions. The Smithsonian Institution published scientific results from his astronomical, magnetic, meteorological, and tidal observations. Other accounts of his second expedition include Isaac I. Hayes, *An Arctic Boat Journey in the Autumn of 1854* (1860); William C. Godfrey, *Narrative of the Last Grinnell Arctic Exploring Expedition in Search of Sir John Franklin, 1853–4–5, with a Biography of Dr. Elisha Kent Kane, from the Cradle to the Grave* (1857); and Oscar M. Villarejo, *Dr. Kane's Voyage to the Polar Lands* (1965). Biographies include William Elder, *Biography of Elisha Kent Kane* (1858); Samuel M. Smucker, *The Life of Dr. Elisha Kent Kane, and of Other Distinguished American Explorers* (1858); Jeannette Mirsky, *Elisha Kent Kane and the Seafaring Frontier* (1954); and George W. Corner, *Dr. Kane of the Arctic Seas* (1972). Margaret Fox wrote *The Love Life of Dr. Kane* (1866). Jay Walz and Audrey Walz wrote a well-researched novel about the Kane-Fox romance, *The Undiscovered Country* (1958).

Edward Zane Carroll Judson
[1823–1886]
A biography is F. E. Pond, *Life and Adventures of "Ned Buntline"* (1919). See also R. J. Walsh, *The Making of Buffalo Bill* (1928). An obituary is in the *New York Herald*, 18 July 1886.

William Walker
[1824–1860]
There is an important collection of material related to the Nicaraguan expedition, including more than 100 letters from Walker, in the papers of C. I. Fayssoux at the Latin American Library at Tulane University in New Orleans. The St. George Leakin Sioussat Collection at the American Philosophical Society Library in Philadelphia is also useful for informa-

tion on Walker's regime in Nicaragua. Official material relating to Walker's ventures is in the records of the State Department and Department of the Navy in the National Archives. See also William Scroggs, *Filibusters and Financiers: The Story of William Walker and His Associates* (1916); Joseph A. Stout, Jr., *The Liberators: Filibustering Expeditions into Mexico 1848–1862, and the Last Thrust of Manifest Destiny* (1973); Frederic Rosengarten, Jr., *Freebooters Must Die! The Life and Death of William Walker* (1976); Albert Z. Carr, *The World and William Walker* (1963). Central American sources include Enrique Guier, *William Walker* (1971), and Alejandro Hurtado Chamarro, *William Walker: Ideales y Propositos* (1965). An obituary is in the *New York Evening Post,* 21, 24, and 28 Sept. 1860.

California Joe

[1829–1876]

Some of California Joe's correspondence survives with the Milner family and some is collected in the Custer correspondence. Milner Family Papers, including the manuscript and letters relating to Joe's biography by his grandson Joe E. Milner, are in the archives of the Washington State University Library. Information is also contained in the Ricker papers at the Kansas State Historical Society. Photographs of California Joe, with his ever-present briar pipe, gun, and dog, are in the collection of the Kansas State Historical Society, as are contemporary newspaper articles. A full-length biography is Joe E. Milner and Earle R. Forrest, *California Joe: Noted Scout and Indian Fighter; With an Authentic Account of Custer's Last Fight* by Colonel William H. Bowen (1935; rev. ed., 1987); the 1987 foreword by Joseph G. Rosa is useful in correcting some of the hearsay and fiction that the subject's grandson let slip into the narrative. For contemporary accounts of California Joe, the most interesting is General George A. Custer, *My Life on the Plains* (1876; 1952, 1966 versions edited by Milo Milton Quaife). Julia B. McGillycuddy, *McGillycuddy Agent: A Biography of Dr. Valentine T. McGillycuddy* (1941), is useful because Dr. McGillycuddy knew California Joe at Fort Robinson. Almost wholly unreliable is J. W. Buel, *Heroes of the Plains* (1882), in which Moses Embree Milner/California Joe is confused with Truman Head, the "California Joe" of Colonel Hiram Berdan's Civil War sharpshooters; Buel also gets things wrong about Wild Bill Hickok and Buffalo Bill Cody. Among modern references, besides his foreword, see Rosa's *Wild Bill Hickok: The Man and His Myth* (1996); Arthur Woodward, "Historical Sidelights on California Joe," *The Westerners, Los Angeles Corral, Eighth Brand Book* (1959), pp. 208–209; and Edward S. Godfrey, "Some Reminiscences, Including the Washita Battle, November 27, 1868," *The Custer Reader*, ed. Paul Andrew Hutton (1992), pp. 159–179. See also Dee Brown, *The American West* (1994); Evan S. Connell, *Son of the Morning Star* (1984); Jay Monaghan, ed., *The Book of the American West* (1963); Paul Trachtman, *The Old West: The Gunfighters* (1974); and Keith Wheeler, *The Old West: The Scouts* (1978). Hollywood film renditions of the Wild Bill Hickok story often erroneously include California Joe as being present at the poker game during which Hickok was shot.

John Morrissey
[1831–1878]
Information on Morrissey is in Elliott J. Gorn, *The Manly Art, Bare-Knuckle Prize Fighting in America* (1986); Rex Lardner, *The Legendary Champions* (1972); Herbert Asbury, "John Morrissey and His Times," in *Sucker's Progress: An Informal History of Gambling in America from the Colonies to Canfield* (1938); and William E. Harding, *John Morrissey: His Life, Battles, and Wrangles* (1881).

Mary Ann Brown Patten
[1837–1861]
A. B. C. Whipple, *The Challenge* (1987), gives an excellent overview of the clipper ship era and fascinating details about Mary Ann Patten and her voyage around Cape Horn. Everett Hollister Northrop, *Florence Nightingale of the Ocean* (1959), prepared for the U.S. Merchant Marine Academy, incorporates primary accounts and newspaper articles about Patten. Other sources of interest include Ann Gifford and Basil Greenhill, comps., *Women under Sail* (1970), and Linda Grant De Pauw, *Seafaring Women* (1982).

Buffalo Jones

[1844–1919]

Most of Jones's surviving papers may be found in the files of the Yellowstone Park Headquarters and the Kansas State Historical Society in Topeka as well as in the collection of the Finney County Historical Society of Garden City, where his home is maintained as a museum. See also Ralph T. Kersey, *Buffalo Jones: A True Biography* (1958); Robert Easton and Mackenzie Brown, *Lord of Beasts: The Saga of Buffalo Jones* (1961); and *Encyclopedia of Frontier Biography*, vol. 2 (1990). Obituaries are in the *Topeka Capital* and the *New York Times*, both 2 Oct. 1919.

Joshua Slocum

[1844–1909?]

Letters and consular dispatches related to the *Aquidneck* events are in the National Archives; other letters are in various hands, including the Smithsonian Institution. Walter Teller, *The Voyages of Joshua Slocum* (1956), collects Slocum's writings and provides a detailed introduction to each, along with other information. The best biography of Slocum is Teller's *Joshua Slocum* (1971), which is the last of his several books on or including the captain. Slocum's son Victor wrote *Capt. Joshua Slocum: The Life and Voyages of America's Best Known Sailor* (1950). The literary connection between Slocum and Henry David Thoreau is the subject of Dennis Berthold, "Deeper Soundings: The Presence of *Walden* in Joshua Slocum's *Sailing Alone around the World*," in *Literature and Lore of the Sea*, ed. Patricia Ann Carlson (1986). Another treatment from a literary perspective is Bert Bender, "Joshua Slocum and the Reality of Solitude," *American Transcendental Quarterly* 6 (1992): 59–71.

Agnes Elisabeth Winona Leclercq Joy Salm–Salm

[1844–1912]

The private Salm-Salm Archives at Isselburg-Anholt do not provide access to the family correspondence to researchers interested in Agnes Salm-Salm, asserting that there is no material pertaining to her in their manuscript holdings. Thus her autobiography remains the main source for her life: *Zehn Jahre aus meinem Leben, 1862 bis 1872* (3 vols., 1875), published in English as *Ten Years of My Life* (London, 1876; Detroit, 1877). The events in Mexico are described by Felix Salm-Salm, *Queretaro* (2 vols., 1868), in English as *My Diary in Mexico in 1867* (2 vols., 1868), with an appendix by Agnes Salm-Salm. A scholarly work that includes photographs of Agnes and Felix Salm-Salm is Konrad Ratz, *Maximilian in Querétaro* (1991). For her family see James Richard Joy, *Thomas Joy and His Descendants* (1900). She plays a minor role in Franz Werfel's drama *Juarez und Maximilian* (1924) and features prominently in a number of novels and adventure stories, all based on her autobiography, among which the less sensational is Juliana von Stockhausen, *Wilder Lorbeer* (1964), with a new French edition titled *Agnes de Salm-Salm* (1982) that includes a reproduction of her portrait painted by Franz Xaver Winterhalter. Among the numerous newspapers in Europe and the United States that carried her obituary is the *Times* (London), 24 Dec. 1912.

Railroad Bill

[d. 1896]

A more or less complete listing of the literature on Railroad Bill is in A. J. Wright, comp., *Criminal Activity in the Deep South, 1700–1933* (1989). For a codification of the folk ballads, see Howard W. Odum, ed., "Folk-Song and Folk-Poetry as Found in the Secular Songs of the Southern Negroes," *Journal of American Folklore* 24 (1911): 289–293. The Brewton newspapers *Pine Belt News* and *Standard Gauge* are the best places to follow the story. For a fuller discussion of the identification question with citations, see James L. Penick, "Railroad Bill," *Gulf Coast Historical Review* 10 (1994): 85–92.

Ishi

[1862?–1916]

For the original story on Ishi see the *Oroville Register*, 29 Aug. 1911. There are two excellent books on Ishi and his people: Theodora Kroeber, *Ishi in Two Worlds* (1961), and Kroeber and Robert Heizer, *Ishi, the Last*

Yahi: A Documentary History (1979). The best semi-documentary movie is *Ishi, the Last Yahi*, directed by Jed Riffe and Pamela A. Roberts (1993). Obituaries are in the *Chico Record*, 28 Mar. 1916, and the *San Mateo Labor Index*, 30 Mar. 1916.

David Fagen

[1875–1901?]

Important sources at the National Archives include "Information Slip on David Fagen," RG 94, Adjutant General's Office File 431081; "[Filipino Nationalist] Infantry Captain's Commission in Favor of Mr. David Fagen," 6 Sept. 1900, RG 94, Adjutant General's Office File 431081; "Statement of Anastonio Bartollome," 6 Dec. 1901, RG 94, Adjutant General's Office File 431081; and Lieutenant R. C. Corliss, "1st Endorsement [of the Report of the Killing of David Fagen]," 6 Dec. 1901, RG 94, Adjutant General's Office File 431081. Williard Gatewood, *"Smoked Yankees": Letters from Negro Soldiers, 1898–1902* (1971), is an excellent compilation of letters written by African-American soldiers in the Philippines articulating their varied sentiments about the Filipino nationalists and racism in the U.S. Army. The most extensive overview of Fagen's experience in the Philippines is Michael Robinson and Frank Schubert, "David Fagen: An Afro-American Rebel in the Philippines, 1899–1901," *Pacific Historical Review* 44 (1975): 68–83. See also Scot Brown, "The Dilemma of the African American Soldier in the Philippine-American War, 1899–1902" (master's thesis, Cornell Univ., 1993). See the *New York Times*, 29 Oct. 1900, and the *Manila Times*, 30 Oct. 1900, for examples of U.S. Army clashes with Fagen that received media attention in the United States and the Philippines. For personal accounts of encounters with Fagen, see John Ganzhorn, *I've Killed Men: An Epic of Early Arizona* (1959), and Frederick Funston, *Memories of Two Wars* (1912).

Belle Livingstone
[1875?–1957]
Although they are to be approached with some skepticism, Livingstone's memoirs are the best sources on her life. Livingstone's Prohibition battles were covered thoroughly by all the New York City newspapers during 1930–1931. Useful obituaries appear in the *New York Times* and the *New York Herald Tribune,* both 8 Feb. 1957.

Hiram Bingham
[1875–1956]
Archival material is in the Bingham family papers, the Mitchell-Tiffany papers, and the Yale Peruvian Expedition papers located at the Yale University Library. Two of Hiram Bingham's sons published accounts of his life: Alfred M. Bingham, *Portrait of an Explorer: Hiram Bingham, Discoverer of Machu Picchu* (1989), and Woodbridge Bingham, *Hiram Bingham: A Personal History* (1989). A fine treatment of Hiram Bingham and several generations of his family is in Char Miller, *Fathers and Sons: The Bingham Family and the American Mission* (1982). For a brief biographical sketch, see Jerry E. Patterson, "Hiram Bingham, 1875–1956." *Hispanic American Historical Review* 37 (1957): 131–37. Specific aspects of his career are delineated in Thomas L. Karnes, "Hiram Bingham and His Obsolete Shibboleth," *Diplomatic History* 3, no. 1 (1979): 39–57; Victor Von Hagen, "Hiram Bingham and His Lost Cities," *Archaeology* 2, no. 1 (1949): 42–46; and Carmelo Astilla, "The Latin American Career of Hiram Bingham" (M.A. thesis, Louisiana State Univ., 1967).

Duncan Hines
[1880–1959]
For more on Hines, see Milton MacKaye, "Where Shall We Stop for Dinner?" and Duncan Hines and Frank J. Taylor, "How to Find a Decent Meal," *Saturday Evening Post,* 3 Dec. 1938 and 26 Apr. 1947; Marion Edwards, "They Live to Eat," *Better Homes & Gardens,* Mar. 1945, pp. 30–31; and David M. Schwartz, "He Cultivated Our Culinary Consciousness,"

Smithsonian, Nov. 1984, pp. 86–97. Obituaries are in the *New York Times* and the *Park City* (Ky.) *Daily News,* both 16 Mar. 1959.

Annette Kellerman

[1887–1975]
The most complete Hollywood biography of Annette Kellerman is DeWitt Bodeen and Larry Holland, "Neptune's Daughters," *Films in Review* 30 (Feb. 1979): 73–88. A full listing of her swimming accomplishments is in *The 1975 Yearbook of the International Swimming Hall of Fame,* ed. Buck Dawson. Other profiles and biographical sketches are in Caroline Caffin, *Vaudeville* (1914); Agnes Roger, *Women Are Here to Stay* (1949); Richard Lamparski, *Whatever Became of . . . ?* (1968); Philip Scheuer, "Annette Kellerman All for Esther Now," *Los Angeles Times,* 23 Mar. 1952; and Jack Pollard, *Swimming: Australian Style* (1963). Reviews of her first three films are in *Moving Picture World,* 6 Dec. 1909, and *Film Index,* 6 Dec. 1909, *Diving Venus; Variety,* 10 Apr. 1914, *Neptune's Daughter;* and *Variety,* 16 Nov. 1916, *A Daughter of the Gods.* Obituaries are in the *New York Times,* 6 Nov. 1975, and *Newsweek* and *Time,* both 17 Nov. 1975.

Louise Arner Boyd

[1887–1972]
The following house manuscript material on Louise Boyd: the American Geographical Society in New York; Henry J. Oosting's diary in the Special Collections Library, Duke University, Durham, N.C.; the Marin County Historical Society in San Rafael, Calif.; the Society of Woman Geographers file at the National Archives in Washington, D.C.; the National Archives' Civilian Personnel Records Office in St. Louis; the University of Colorado, Boulder; and the University of Wisconsin-Milwaukee Library. The scant biographical writings on Boyd include a chapter in Mignon Rittenhouse, *Seven Women Explorers* (1964); Margaret Edith Trussell, "Five Western Woman Pioneer Geographers," in *Yearbook of Pacific Coast Geographers* (1987); a meticulously researched essay in Elizabeth Fagg Olds, *Women of the Four Winds* (1985); and a memorial booklet, *Louise Boyd: Science and*

Society, Marin County Historical Society Magazine 14, no. 2 (Fall/Winter 1987–1988).

Duke Paoa Kahanamoku
[1890–1968]

The best biographical sources are Joe Brennan, *Duke Kahanamoku, Hawaii's Golden Man* (1974); Brennan, *Duke of Hawaii* (1968); Brennan, *The Father of Surfing: The Duke of Hawaii* (1968); Duke Kahanamoku, with Brennan, *Duke Kahanamoku's World of Surfing* (1968); and Sandra Kimberley Hall and Greg Ambrose, *Memories of Duke: The Legend Comes to Life* (1975). Robert W. Wheeler, *Jim Thorpe, World's Greatest Athlete* (1979), offers insight as to why Kahanamoku would not turn professional. Lord Killanin and John Rodda, eds., *The Olympic Games* (1976), pp. 210, 246, provides the record times achieved by Kahanamoku. Leevan Dasig, "The Bronze Duke of Waikiki" (unpublished paper, Univ. of Hawaii, 1992), and "Hawaii's Duke," *Paradise of the Pacific*, Sept. 1961, p. 12, provide overviews of his career. Charles Hogue, "A Day with Duke Kahanamoku," *Paradise of the Pacific*, Dec. 1950, pp. 16–17; Don Mayo, "Royal Hawaiian Champ of Champs: The Great Duke Kahanamoku" *Paradise of the Pacific*, June 1956, p. 27; "Mr. Ambassador," *Paradise of the Pacific*, May 1960, pp. 10–11; and Ann L. Moore, "The Living Waters of Oha," *Ka Wai Ola O Oha*, Aug. 1990, pp. 12–13, give magazine reviews of his life. Earl Albert Selle, *The Story of Duke Paoa Kahanamoku* (1959), written under the auspices of the Golden Man Foundation, is a commemorative tribute. *The Hawaiian Annual* (1913) records his early feats. "Duke's Own Story of Life," *Honolulu Star Bulletin*, 22 Jan. 1968, is an obituary. Cindy Luis, "Duke: A Century of Aloha," *Honolulu Star Bulletin*, 22 Aug. 1990, offers an adoring tribute. An extensive biography by Malcolm Gault-Williams is available at http://www.hawaiianswimboat.com/duke.html.

Merian Coldwell Cooper
[1893–1973]

Cooper's papers are in the Harold B. Lee Library, Brigham Young University, Provo, Utah. Rudy Behlmer summarized Cooper's life and career in *Films in Review,* Jan. 1966, pp. 17–35. Orville Goldner and George E. Turner detail his early adventures in *The Making of King Kong* (1975), and Ronald Haver covers his 1930s film work in *David O. Selznick's Hollywood* (1980).

Marguerite Harrison recounts the *Grass* expedition in *There's Always Tomorrow: The Story of a Checkered Life* (1935); A. J. Siggins recalls the filming of *The Four Feathers* in *Shooting with Rifle and Camera* (1931); and Fay Wray reminisces about *Kong* in *On the Other Hand: A Life Story* (1989). *Grass* and *Chang* are well documented in Kevin Brownlow's *The War, The West, and the Wilderness* (1979). George E. Turner profiles *The Most Dangerous Game* in *The Cinema of Adventure, Romance & Terror* (1989); *The Son of Kong* in *American Cinematographer,* Aug. 1992, pp. 67–71; and *She* in *American Cinematographer,* June 1995, pp. 103–108. Obituaries are in the *New York Times,* 22 Apr. 1973, and *Variety,* 25 Apr. 1973.

Hubert F. Julian
[1897–1983]

Contemporary accounts include a *New Yorker* profile by Morris Markey (11 July 1931, pp. 22–25, and 18 July 1931, pp. 20–23); passages in memoirs by two early aviators, Clarence Chamberlin, *Record Flights* (1928), pp. 232–246, and William A. Powell, *Black Wings* (1934), reprinted as *Black Aviator* (1994), pp. 22–28, 98–104; and journalist H. Allen Smith, *Low Man on a Totem Pole* (1941), pp. 72–81. Also included are newspaper articles, notably in the *New York Amsterdam News,* the *New York Times,* and the *Herald Tribune.* The only monographs are Julian's autobiography, *Black Eagle,* as told to John Bulloch (1964), and a biography by John Peer Nugent, *The Black Eagle* (1971). An informative although critical chapter in William R. Scott, *The Sons of Sheba's Race: African Americans and the Italo-Ethiopian War, 1935-1941* (1993), pp. 81–95, discusses Julian's involvement in Ethiopia. There is no known obituary. Six months after his death, the *New York Amsterdam News,* 1 Oct. 1983, noted that the lack of publicity was due to his second wife's dislike of his reputation as the "Black Eagle."

Richard Halliburton
[1900–1939]
Halliburton's first-person travelogues are not a completely accurate guide to his life. Although he seems to have undertaken all the adventures he ascribed to himself, he embellished them to heighten the drama and color. His papers are at the Firestone Library at Princeton University. Letters to his mother and father, which are part of that collection, appear in *Richard Halliburton: His Story of His Life's Adventure* (1940). His parents edited sections they thought were unpleasant or unflattering. Biographies of Halliburton are Jonathan Root, *The Magnificent Myth* (1965), and James Cortese, *Richard Halliburton's Royal Road* (1989). An informative profile is found in David M. Schwartz, "On the Royal Road to Adventures with 'Daring Dick,'" *Smithsonian*, Mar. 1989, pp. 159–178.

INDEX

PICTURE CREDITS

115. Lancaster County Historical Society, Lancaster, Pennsylvania
118. National Archives and Records Administration
124. Library of Congress
128. Wisconsin Historical Society/WHi-6276
134. Library of Congress
140. Courtesy of the National Library of Medicine
146. Library of Congress
150. Courtesy of the Bancroft Library, University of California, Berkeley/1984.56:238
158. Denver Public Library, Western History Department
164. Photograph courtesy of the George S. Bolster Collection of the Historical Society of Saratoga Springs
169. Library of Congress
172. Denver Public Library, Western History Department
178. Library of Congress
182. Courtesy of the Vermont Historical Society Library
187. Library of Congress
192. Courtesy of the Phoebe A. Hearst Museum of Anthropology and the Regents of the University of California. Photographed by Alfred J. Kroeber, PAHMA number 15-5742
196. U.S. Army Military History Institute
198. Collection of the New-York Historical Society/PR-052 Box 86 N.D.
204. Hiram Bingham Yale Peabody Museum, courtesy of the National Geographic Society
208. Courtesy of the Kentucky Library, Western Kentucky University
214. Library of Congress
218. Library of Congress
224. Library of Congress
230. L. Tom Perry Special Collections, the Meran C. Cooper Papers, Harold B. Lee Library, Brigham Young University, Provo, Utah/ Image number 453
236. Schomburg Center for Research in Black Culture
242. Chicago Historical Society/DN-0082038